Thinking About the Insanity Defense

Thinking About the Insanity Defense

◆

Answers to Frequently Asked Questions With Case Examples

Edited by Ellsworth Lapham Fersch

iUniverse, Inc.
New York Lincoln Shanghai

Thinking About the Insanity Defense
Answers to Frequently Asked Questions With Case Examples

Copyright © 2005 by Ellsworth Lapham Fersch

All rights reserved. No part of this book may be used or reproduced by any means, graphic, electronic, or mechanical, including photocopying, recording, taping or by any information storage retrieval system without the written permission of the publisher except in the case of brief quotations embodied in critical articles and reviews.

iUniverse books may be ordered through booksellers or by contacting:

iUniverse
2021 Pine Lake Road, Suite 100
Lincoln, NE 68512
www.iuniverse.com
1-800-Authors (1-800-288-4677)

ISBN: 0-595-34412-7

Printed in the United States of America

Contents

About the Book. xi
About the Contributors. xiii
Introduction xvii

Answers to Frequently Asked Questions

CHAPTER 1 History of the Insanity Defense 3
    What is the insanity defense?. 3
    Why is there an insanity defense? 3
    What historical changes have taken place in the insanity defense? 4
    How often is the insanity defense used?. 5
    How often is the insanity defense successful?. 5
    What determines whether the insanity defense will be successful? 5
    What are some well-known cases where the insanity defense has succeeded? 6
    What are some well-known cases where the insanity defense has failed? 6
    Which states do not have an insanity defense and why not? 7
    What happens in states where there is no insanity test? 7
    What is irresistible impulse? 7
    What is temporary insanity? 8
    What is mens rea? 8
    What is actus reus? 8
    What is an affirmative defense? 8
    Who should have the burden of proof of insanity? 8
    How is the insanity defense related to diminished capacity? 10
    What is competence to stand trial? 10

What is the relation between competence to stand trial and the insanity defense? ... 11
What does the American Psychological Association conclude concerning the insanity defense? ... 11
What does the American Psychiatric Association conclude concerning the insanity defense? ... 12
What does the American Medical Association conclude concerning the insanity defense? ... 12
What does the American Bar Association conclude concerning the insanity defense? ... 13

CHAPTER 2 Psychological Aspects of the Insanity Defense ... 14

Is insanity a psychological concept? ... 14
Is insanity the same as mental illness? ... 14
What is mental illness? ... 14
What types of mental illnesses does the American Psychiatric Association consider for an insanity defense? ... 15
Is insanity the same as psychosis? ... 15
What is the relation between psychopathology and psychosis? ... 16
How do the various diagnoses in the official Diagnostic and Statistical Manual of Mental Disorders fit with the insanity defense? ... 16
What characteristics of schizophrenia make it suitable or not for an insanity defense? ... 17
What characteristics of mood disorders and of anxiety disorders make them suitable or not for an insanity defense? ... 17
What characteristics of dissociative disorders make them suitable or not for an insanity defense? ... 18
What characteristics of sexual or somatoform disorders make them suitable or not for an insanity defense? ... 18
What characteristics of posttraumatic stress disorder make it suitable or not for an insanity defense? ... 19
What characteristics of retardation make it suitable or not for an insanity defense? ... 19
If an individual is not insane, what mental disorders might make that individual less than fully responsible for acts? ... 20
Can one prove that someone is sane? ... 20
How is brain science used in insanity defense cases? ... 21
How are psychoanalytic theories used in insanity defense cases? ... 21

What is malingering?...22
How can malingering be assessed?.....................................22
How often do defendants malinger?....................................23
Why have psychological explanations for behavior dominated in the legal system as opposed to economic or racial or cultural or other explanations?..........23
How can the legal assumption of free will and full criminal responsibility be compatible with the psychological assumption of determinism and lessened or no criminal responsibility?..............................24
Does the insanity defense contribute to the stigmatization of the mentally ill?...25
Are religious fundamentalists mentally ill?..........................25
Should religious fundamentalists have an insanity defense available?............26
Are terrorists mentally ill?...27
Should terrorists have an insanity defense available?........................28
How is brainwashing related to insanity?.............................28

CHAPTER 3 Effects of Different Standards of Determining Insanity.......................................29

What are the primary tests of insanity?..............................29
What is the M'Naghten test?..29
What is the Durham test?...30
What is the American Law Institute test?.............................30
What is the guilty but mentally ill verdict?.........................31

CHAPTER 4 Arguments for Retention, Abolition, and Revision of the Insanity Defense...................33

What are the arguments for retaining the insanity defense?...................33
What are the arguments for abolishing the insanity defense?..................34
What are the arguments for reforming the insanity defense?...................35

CHAPTER 5 Media and Other Responses to the Insanity Defense..36

Why does the public react to someone's causing terrible harm by saying the perpetrator must have been crazy?...................................36
Given how seldom it is used, how and why has the insanity defense occupied such a prominent position in the interaction between psychology and the law?..36

What do jurors think of the insanity defense? 37
What does the public think of the insanity defense? 38
How serious are most of the charges in insanity defense cases? 39
Why does the public have the idea that the charges are usually very serious? 39
Who are the most significant expert witnesses on the insanity defense and what are their views? 40
What is the argument for the view of the myth of mental illness? 41
What is meant by the abuse excuse? 42
What predictions are made concerning the future of the insanity defense? 43
How has the insanity defense been portrayed in film? 44
How has the insanity defense been portrayed in fiction? 45
How has the insanity defense been portrayed in non-fiction? 46

CHAPTER 6   Controversies Surrounding Pre- and Post-Conviction Commitment 47

What happens to individuals found not guilty by reason of insanity? 47
What shifts have taken place in the placement of individuals found not guilty by reason of insanity? 48
Should a person found not guilty by reason of insanity be automatically committed to a mental hospital? 49
Why would someone found not guilty by reason of insanity be evaluated as if he were simply a civilly committed individual? 50
If the best predictor of future behavior is past behavior, why would not a person found not guilty of a very serious act due to insanity be committed for a long time as a precaution? 50
What should the consequence be for an individual who has been advised to take antipsychotic medication, who has taken it and then discontinued it, and subsequently commits a serious act? 52
Should a person who was sane at the time of the crime and sentenced to death but who becomes insane be executed while insane? 53
Should a lawyer be able to prevent forcing a psychotic client to take medication in order to preserve, for the jury, the state of mind in which that person committed acts for which he is charged? 53

CHAPTER 7   Roles of Psychologists and Lawyers in Defining, Implementing, and Questioning the Insanity Defense 55

What is the reasoning behind allowing psychoforensic expert witnesses to testify?..55
What are the reasons for not allowing psychoforensic experts to testify?..........56
How can the problems with psychoforensic expert witnesses be addressed?.......56
Are some experts known as pro-prosecution experts and others known as pro-defense experts?..57
Do experts ever defy expectations?..58
Why does the public assume that the court-appointed psychoforensic expert will be the most unbiased and accurate?..58
Should forensic psychologists and psychiatrists testify as to insanity or only as to mental illness?..59
To what extent should a psychoforensic expert be a detective?...................60
Can psychologists and psychiatrists tell accurately who is malingering or faking?..61
How successful are psychologists and psychiatrists in predicting future dangerousness?..62
What strategic and what tactical moves do prosecutors use in insanity defense cases?..63
What strategic and what tactical moves do defense counsel use in insanity defense cases?..64
How important is the lawyer's advocacy to the success of the insanity defense?..65
On what do prosecutors and defense counsel agree concerning the insanity defense?..65
On what do psychologists and psychiatrists agree concerning the insanity defense?..66
How important is the judge's attitude toward the insanity defense?.............66
How important are jurors' attitudes toward the insanity defense?..............66

Case Examples

Chapter 8   Collective Cases....................................71
Ralph Tortorici...71
Richard Herrin...96
Dan and Ron Lafferty..111

Chapter 9   Case Studies 126
    Kenneth Bianchi 126
    Ted Bundy. 134
    Jeffrey Dahmer 145
    John duPont 153
    John Wayne Gacy 160
    Andrew Goldstein 165
    William Bergen Greene 175
    Patty Hearst. 183
    John Hinckley, Jr. 189
    Michael A. Jones 197
    Ted Kaczynski 204
    Hedda Nussbaum 209
    Andrea Yates 224

Bibliography 241

About the Book

This volume grew out of my Harvard seminar on *The Insanity Defense* in which the contributors participated by discussing these topics and cases and by writing these materials. They had previously taken my lecture course on *Psychology and Law*. Profiles of all appear in *About the Contributors*.

This volume is modeled on one on a different subject that answered ninety-seven frequently asked questions in seven chapters. This book does the same. Because the answer to each question is self-contained and because readers may choose to explore the book in various ways, some materials are repeated where necessary to answer each question. For simplicity, the masculine pronoun has been used throughout when both males and females may be involved. On some occasions, a plural accompanies a singular to make the same point.

In addition to the questions and answers, this volume includes a number of case examples. As the contributors to this book began to examine their own case studies, they worked together on a number of *Collective Cases*. At the first meeting of the seminar, they viewed the 2002 Frontline documentary *A Crime of Insanity*, and then each generated two questions concerning the case of Ralph Tortorici and answered them. Everyone next read Willard Gaylin's *The Killing of Bonnie Garland* about the case of Richard Herrin and Jon Krakauer's *Under the Banner of Heaven* about the case of Dan and Ron Lafferty, and collectively generated responses to a set of comprehensive factual questions concerning those cases as well as parts of the John Hinckley, Jr. case. Each contributor then explored a case illuminating an important aspect of the insanity defense and wrote an individual study about it. These *Case Studies* are arranged alphabetically.

Although this volume includes an extensive bibliography, it does not refer specifically to each listing within the text itself. Intended for the general reader and not for the researcher or for the scholar, this volume assists that reader in thinking about the insanity defense by presenting competing approaches to law and mental health. At the same time, it provides a complete list of references for those who may wish to examine further some aspect of the topic. All involved with this volume urge those who read it to explore at length the contributions of authors Gaylin and Krakauer and of the documentarians of Frontline, as well as of many of the other sources, for their interpretations and particular styles. It is the hope of everyone who contributed to *Thinking About the Insanity Defense* that this volume will encourage all readers to pursue cases and concepts in the exciting world where psychology and law interact.

About the Contributors

Vijay Bal studies Psychology with an emphasis on law and interpersonal psychology at Harvard University. He is active in the Small Claims Advisory Service, and in the film departments of *The Harvard Crimson* and *The Harvard Independent*. For this book, he wrote the Hedda Nussbaum case, and contributed to the Collective Cases and to the sections on Psychological Aspects and on the Roles of Lawyers and Psychologists.

Alexander J. Blenkinsopp is concentrating in Social Studies at Harvard University, where he has worked as a research assistant for Frankfurter Professor of Law Alan Dershowitz and where he is completing a thesis on the treatment of those found not guilty by reason of insanity. He was Executive Editor for *The Harvard Crimson*. For this book, he wrote the Michael Jones case, and contributed to the Collective Cases and to the sections on Media Responses and on the Roles of Psychologists and Lawyers. He served as Associate Editor for the entire book.

Sayles Braga studies Economics at Harvard University with an informal secondary focus on psychology in its relation to law. For this book, he wrote the John duPont case, and contributed to the Collective Cases and to the sections on History and on the Effects of Different Standards.

Michael E. Clear is concentrating in Psychology at Harvard University, where he has done extensive work as a research assistant in the Harvard Social Psychology Laboratory and where his adviser is Professor Daniel Wegner. He is completing a thesis on moral decision making. For this book, he wrote the John Wayne Gacy case, and contributed to the Collective Cases. He helped coordinate all the Frequently Asked Questions sections and assisted in the final formatting and compiling of the book.

Diara Dankert studies Psychology with an emphasis on law and society at Harvard University and is active in the Small Claims Advisory Service and the Bureau of Study Counsel. She has participated as a tutor in the Franklin After-School Enrichment and Mission Hill After-School Program. For this book, she wrote the

Andrew Goldstein case, and contributed to the Collective Cases and to the sections on Psychological Aspects and on the Roles of Lawyers and Psychologists.

Ellsworth Lapham Fersch has taught at Harvard University, in the Medical and Extension Schools and in the College, during the three decades since receiving his J.D. in law and his Ph.D. in clinical psychology there. He has been a visiting faculty member at various colleges and universities, including Boston University, Yale University, and the University of Massachusetts. A licensed clinical psychologist and member of the Massachusetts bar, he served as the long-time director of the Massachusetts Court Clinic and practiced clinical and forensic psychology. He has written about topics at the intersection of psychology and law. As General Editor of this volume, he guided its preparation in his seminar on The Insanity Defense, contributed material, and wrote the Introduction.

Jessica Gonzalez concentrates in Psychology with a foreign language citation in Spanish and Chinese at Harvard University. Her principal area of psychological interest is the development of racial biases in minority children. For this book, she wrote the John Hinckley case, and contributed to the Collective Cases and to the sections on Psychological Aspects and on Arguments Concerning the Defense.

Megan Gubbins studies Psychology at Harvard University where she has been a research assistant in the Harvard Psychophysiology Laboratory of Professor Wendy Berry Mendes. For this book, she wrote the Andrea Yates case, and contributed to the Collective Cases and to the sections on History and on the Effects of Different Standards.

Jennifer Hadiaris studies Psychology at Harvard University. For this book, she wrote the Patty Hearst case, and contributed to the Collective Cases and to the sections on Media Responses and on Commitment Controversies.

Ford Harrington concentrates in History, with a principal area of emphasis on international relations, and with a foreign language citation in Spanish at Harvard University, where he also plays Varsity Lacrosse. For this book, he wrote the Ted Kaczynski case, and contributed to the Collective Cases and to the section on History.

Nahye Hwang concentrates in Psychology at Harvard University with an emphasis on legal studies. She is a member of the Harvard Legal Committee and has had significant interaction with convicts in Massachusetts and South African prisons, and experience in civil rights, housing, and domestic violence law. For this book, she wrote the Ted Bundy case, and contributed to the Collective Cases and to the section on Controversies Surrounding Commitment.

Katherine Kleindienst studies Psychology, with an emphasis on its applications to law, at Harvard University. She has served as a research assistant in Professor Daniel Schacter's memory laboratory and has been active in the Suffolk Prison Tutoring program. For this book, she wrote the Jeffrey Dahmer case, and contributed to the Collective Cases and to the sections on the Arguments Concerning the Defense and on the Roles of Psychologists and Lawyers.

Christopher Sully concentrates in Psychology with a foreign language citation in Spanish at Harvard University. He has been a member of the Harvard Mock Trial Team and a recruiter for the Harvard Undergraduate Minority Recruitment Program. For this book, he wrote the Kenneth Bianchi case, and contributed to the Collective Cases and to the sections on Psychological Aspects and on Arguments Concerning the Defense.

Kimberly Terca studies Psychology at Harvard University with a particular interest in exploring the role of psychology in the studies of law and politics. For this book, she wrote the William Bergen Greene case, and contributed to the Collective Cases and to the sections on Psychological Aspects and on Media Responses.

Introduction

This brief volume answers a need I have experienced for some time in teaching courses on psychology and law to diverse students, and in answering questions from them, the general public, and those who work in court and clinical settings. That need arises from the fact that the insanity defense constitutes one of the most talked about and controversial interactions between psychology and the law. An excellent example of the way in which our legal system has emphasized psychology, the insanity defense has provided the focus for heated discussions among psychologists and psychiatrists, lawyers and judges, and the general public, and has raised questions which lie at the root of our political views of society, our moral and religious notions of good and evil, our medical and psychological conclusions about healing and sickness, our philosophical ideas about free will and determinism, and our linguistic concerns about language and semantics.

The insanity defense spurred a storm of controversy over twenty years ago when John Hinckley, Jr., who attempted to assassinate President Reagan, was found not guilty by reason of insanity. Recent attempts by Hinckley and his parents to free him from strict clinical supervision, as well as other prominent cases in which the insanity defense has been invoked, have continued to raise important issues in the relationship between criminal law, and clinical psychology and psychiatry. In fact, the insanity defense, though rarely invoked, is, especially in high profile cases, the most prominent and controversial interaction between the mental health and the legal systems.

As is generally known, the criminal law attempts to hold people accountable for their actions. The insanity defense, on the contrary, attempts to excuse some individuals from responsibility for their actions on the theory that their mental illness prevented them from choosing the lawful act, knowing what they were doing, or understanding that their action was wrong. Insanity defense cases have caused a stir at least partly because of the nature of the controversy embedded in the defense. A former president of the American Psychiatric Association concluded that the insanity defense poses an insoluble problem because it occurs at the point where two incompatible, contradictory theories cross: the modern determinist theory of causation which underlies psychology, neuroscience, and related disciplines, and the continuing free will theory of morality which underlies the criminal law.

In other words, however individual cases are resolved, the controversy remains because two great theories about human nature and human action are involved: the criminal justice theory that individuals of their own free will choose to act as they do and ought to be punished for wrongful acts; and the psychological and modern scientific theory that individuals' actions are determined by their personality, genes, environment, and other factors largely beyond their control and ought rather to be understood and helped.

While the contradiction may be insoluble, the suggestions concerning the insanity defense range across a broad spectrum. Those who follow the approach of the American Psychiatric Association, the American Psychological Association, and the American Bar Association argue that it should be retained, accepting the deterministic view and attempting to find for those acquitted the psychological help evidently needed. They agree that the moral basis of the law requires the special defense of insanity. Yet, among those who argue for its retention, some want it available to a wide range of mentally ill defendants. Others propose limiting it to the most seriously disturbed individuals. Still others suggest adding to it a possible finding of guilty but insane or guilty but mentally ill. Further along the spectrum some argue that the finding of guilty but mentally ill should supplant the insanity defense itself. And finally some agree with the American Medical Association and argue in favor of abolishing the special defense of insanity, unifying the criminal justice and mental health responses to antisocial or illegal acts by holding individuals responsible for their behaviors subject to the limits imposed by the legal requirement of mens rea, or guilty mind.

Whichever approach one follows, other factors complicate the relation between psychological diagnosis and moral decision making. Among the most important are the varying views of the participating psychologists and psychiatrists, and the differing laws of each state and of the federal system, which set forth the test of insanity to be used. However those psychoforensic professionals approach the defense, whether they are retained by the prosecution or the defense or the court itself, and whatever conflicting conclusions their expert testimony may bring forth, the central issue of the relation between the legal and mental health approaches to and explanations of human behavior remains.

Although a great deal has been written about the insanity defense, this volume fills a special need. It answers in a concise and easily available format the most frequently asked questions about the insanity defense; it provides a variety of illustrative case examples of its use; it encourages further exploration of the subject through a comprehensive bibliography; and it focuses, in the editor's view, on the importance of thinking about the insanity defense.

Answers to Frequently Asked Questions

1
History of the Insanity Defense

What is the insanity defense?

The insanity defense is one of a number of defenses available to individuals who have committed an act which the law has declared criminal. An individual who commits such an act may be found not criminally responsible for the act with a successful plea of insanity. The individual is, in other words, determined to be not guilty by reason of insanity. Because insanity is a legal and not a psychological term, the defense is often misunderstood by the public at large and by juries who must grapple with it. A more clearly understood defense which, when successful, may excuse an individual from criminal responsibility is self-defense. When that plea is successful, the individual is simply found not guilty, though by adding the phrase by reason of self-defense would be an appropriate way to understand the finding. Because of the connotations of insanity and of mental illness and because of the history of attempts to deal with those mentally disordered individuals who come to the attention of the police and the courts, the insanity defense has been the center of controversy within the legal and mental health professions and with the public at large.

Why is there an insanity defense?

Supporters of the insanity defense argue that it exists as an attempt to impose a moral check on a system largely designed to assume mental stability while weighing facts and evidence. They contend that it humanizes the criminal justice system and makes it moral. Opponents of the insanity defense argue that it unduly emphasizes an inexact science, excuses individuals who acted purposefully, and denies some their human dignity by labeling them as insane rather than dealing directly with their contentions and arguments.

What historical changes have taken place in the insanity defense?

The question of insanity in the context of court cases was present in England as early as 1581. Before the case of Daniel M'Naghten, English courts had asked whether a defendant had greater ability to distinguish good from evil than would a wild beast or whether the defendant had acted on an irresistible impulse. In 1843 Daniel M'Naghten attempted to shoot Robert Peel, the British prime minister, but shot and killed his secretary instead. M'Naghten's defense team contended he was insane because of his paranoid ideation, and the judge directed a verdict of non-responsibility. Subsequently, because of outrage at the acquittal, a panel of judges responded to House of Lords' questions, and set forth the test which came to be known as the M'Naghten rule. That rule stated that an individual might be found not guilty by reason of insanity if he proved he was laboring, because of a disease of the mind, under such a defect of reason that he did not know the nature and quality of his act or if he did know it that he did not know his act was wrong. The rule was sometimes referred to simply as the right-wrong test. The irresistible impulse test was later dropped in English courts. In 1859 Daniel Sickles was the first person in the United States to employ an insanity defense, walking free after killing his wife's lover while in an uncontrollable rage. Since then, the law was virtually unchanged until the mid-twentieth century, though not guilty by reason of insanity was not used often.

In the 1950s, the insanity defense was altered in the Durham case to include more scientific evidence and less moral reasoning. In 1962, the American Law Institute began allowing medical evidence in the insanity defense cases, using ideas such as substantial capacity to soften the M'Naghten test. States such as Connecticut instituted tougher release systems, where even if a defendant were proven insane, they would have a tougher time being released from their mental facility. As the 1970s approached, more was done to protect those who pled insanity, a movement which came to an end following the Hinckley case of 1982. Irate federal and state governments immediately cracked down on all aspects of the insanity defense, changing the approach from forcing the prosecution to prove the defendant sane to having the defense prove their client insane. In 1984, Congress passed twenty-six pieces of legislation to abolish or modify the insanity defense. Guilty but mentally ill was added as option in as many as twenty states by the year 2000. As of 1998, twenty-five states and Washington, D.C. still used a form of the M'Naghten test, while twenty-two used a form of the American

Law Institute test. The remaining states used an alternate or abolished the insanity defense altogether.

How often is the insanity defense used?

Every review of the insanity defense has shown that it is rarely used throughout the United States. Studies have concluded that the insanity defense is used in less than one percent of criminal trials and is successful only about a quarter of the time it is used. The reason that the public may believe this defense is used more frequently is due to the large amount of media attention given to high-profile insanity defense cases involving violent acts.

How often is the insanity defense successful?

The insanity defense is generally unsuccessful. A 1991 eight-state study performed by the National Institute of Mental Health showed the insanity defense was used in less than one percent of all cases, and when it was used only twenty-six percent of those pleas succeeded. A 2001 study revealed that over a ten year period only sixteen of ten thousand indicted used the insanity plea, and success almost always came in the form of a plea bargain with the prosecutors.

What determines whether the insanity defense will be successful?

The insanity defense is not often successful. Studies have shown that in trials involving the insanity defense, a verdict of not guilty by reason of insanity is only obtained about a quarter of the time. One study found that in about three-quarters of those cases resulting in a verdict of not guilty by reason of insanity, the prosecution and defense agreed about the appropriateness of the insanity plea before the trial began. Therefore, prosecutorial consent is probably the most influential factor determining the success of an insanity defense. Additional factors that determine success are the particular definition of insanity used in the state in which the defendant is tried, the effectiveness of psychological testimony, and the skills and competence of the defense attorney.

What are some well-known cases where the insanity defense has succeeded?

One trial in which the insanity defense helped the defense team was the 1976 case of Officer Robert Tornsey. Tornsey shot and killed a young boy in New York City on Thanksgiving night without provocation, and claimed his emotional distress for working on a holiday was the reason for the killing. Pleading not guilty by reason of insanity, Tornsey was acquitted of his charges and spent much of his rehabilitation time at home with his family. In 1981, John Hinckley, Jr. shot at President Ronald Reagan, injuring the president, his press secretary, and two law enforcement agents. Hinckley successfully pled not guilty by reason of insanity and was sent to St. Elizabeths Hospital, a federal mental institution, for rehabilitation, causing outrage that led to alterations or abolition of many insanity laws throughout the country.

What are some well-known cases where the insanity defense has failed?

In 1943, the Esposito brothers, William and Anthony, murdered a postal worker in New York City, then in the ensuing chase killed a police officer as he pleaded for his life. They went to trial with a determination to use the insanity defense, acting like wild beasts in the courtroom and causing a disorder. The jury refused their antics and found them guilty in a one-minute deliberation, among the fastest in United States history. The brothers were executed at Sing Sing. In 1979, Dan White, a firefighter who had resigned his city councilor position and then sought unsuccessfully to regain it, killed the mayor and an openly homosexual city councilor in San Francisco. While White was not found insane, he was found to have diminished capacity because of his ingestion of junk food and was convicted of manslaughter rather than the murder which his plans and actions in the killings seemed to suggest. San Francisco and the nation were shocked at his successful abuse of a psychological excuse. In his murder trial, Jeffrey Dahmer's plea of not guilty by reason of insanity failed despite his hideous acts. In 1995, the insanity defense failed after wealthy philanthropist John duPont murdered an Olympic wrestler living on his property. The defense pleaded not guilty by reason of insanity, but the millionaire was still found guilty of third degree murder.

Which states do not have an insanity defense and why not?

Five states, Utah, Idaho, Montana, Nevada, and Kansas, do not allow a formal insanity defense. The very existence of the insanity defense is a highly controversial topic. Some who argue against it feel that it serves as a loophole in the criminal justice system, allowing guilty defendants to get off free. This feeling was heightened following the highly publicized Hinckley trial in 1982, in which John W. Hinckley, Jr. was found not guilty by reason of insanity after attempting to assassinate President Reagan. The success of the insanity defense in that case led many states, as well as the federal government, to enact reforms that tightened the standards for an insanity verdict. Utah, Idaho, Montana, Kansas, and Nevada went one step further, omitting the option of a special plea of insanity.

What happens in states where there is no insanity test?

In the minority of states that have abolished the insanity defense, Utah, Idaho, Montana, Kansas, and Nevada, evidence of the defendant's mental state may be presented to the court as a mitigating factor. In these states, the issue of mens rea, or requisite guilty mind, is assessed. The defense may attempt to negate mens rea, by showing that the defendant did not know the nature or quality of his illegal act, and therefore the crime was not committed with the necessary guilty mind needed for a specific conviction. If the defense is able to negate mens rea, charges in the case can be reduced. The defendant would still be found guilty of a lesser charge and sentenced to prison, rather than being sent to a mental hospital for treatment.

What is irresistible impulse?

Some jurisdictions have added an irresistible impulse test to standards for determining insanity. If someone is able to understand that his behavior is wrong, but still lacks the capacity to stop himself from committing the act, then that person may be said to have acted on an irresistible impulse. Critics argue that it is generally impossible to differentiate between an impulse which is acted on as a matter of choice and one which has been impossible to resist. Irresistible impulse as a test has been added to the M'Naghten rule in some states, and is often referred to as a police officer at the elbow rule. In other words, one should ask whether an individual would find an impulse so irresistible that he would still act if a police officer were standing beside him.

What is temporary insanity?

Temporary insanity means one was briefly insane at the time he committed a crime, and was therefore incapable of knowing the nature of his or her criminal act. This test has nothing to do with the criminal's state at the time of the trial.

What is mens rea?

Mens rea means guilty mind. In other words, one has mens rea when he commits a crime intending to do something wrong. This idea follows the provision that people should only be punished when they have acted in a way that makes them morally blameworthy.

What is actus reus?

Actus reus refers to the wrongful act which is an element of a criminal statute.

What is an affirmative defense?

An affirmative defense is one in which the defendant provides evidence that removes civil or criminal responsibility, regardless of whether the defendant has been proven to have actually committed the charges. Self-defense is a prominent example of an affirmative defense. In most jurisdictions insanity is an example of an affirmative defense.

Who should have the burden of proof of insanity?

Two years after John Hinckley, Jr. was found not guilty by reason of insanity for the attempted assassination of President Reagan in 1982, Congress passed the Insanity Defense Reform Act, which made it more difficult for defendants in federal criminal cases to employ a successful insanity defense. One of the most important aspects of the reform was that it shifted the burden of proof from the prosecution to the defense in trials involving an insanity defense. Before the change, the prosecution had to prove beyond a reasonable doubt that the defendant was sane when he committed the offense; after the change, the defense had to prove by clear and convincing evidence that the defendant was insane at the time of the offense. Virtually every state has adopted the same burden allocation in insanity defense cases as the federal government.

The American Psychiatric Association has declined to articulate a stance on who should bear the burden of proof in insanity cases, calling it a legal question that legislatures should answer. Arguments, of course, can be advanced for both sides.

Some, and clearly defense attorneys are among them, have contended that the prosecution should bear the burden of proof because it has long been a hallmark of our criminal justice system that a person is innocent until proven guilty. And in proving guilt, their argument has said, the prosecution ought to have to prove every element of its case, from the committing of a prohibited act to the state of mind of the accused, which must be shown to be free from insanity. With the burden shifted to the defense, this would no longer be the case. Further, with the burden shifted, they argue that it would be possible for the prosecution not to have to address the question of the defendant's state of mind or to call even a single witness concerning the issue of mens rea, or guilty mind. And with a vigorous prosecution, the defense would have an even more difficult task.

On the other side of the debate, some, especially prosecutors and other law enforcement personnel, have contended that it would be excessively difficult, to the point of near impossibility, for the prosecution to bear the burden of proof and win the case. They have argued that proving someone sane is an almost impossible task. Prosecutors have pointed out that the Diagnostic and Statistical Manual of Mental Disorders, the American Psychiatric Association's official list, focuses exclusively on mental illness and does not contain any entry for mental health. The prosecution would have to refute almost every mental and emotional dysfunction that might be a cause of insanity, and would also have to prove sanity at the time the crime was committed, even though substantiating evidence might be remarkably difficult to come by. Further, they have argued, the lack of any definition for mental health or emotional well-being has oriented the official psychiatric text toward so many symptoms that anyone committing a particularly atrocious might be found to have some. To the extent that the official manual suggests that everyone is somewhat mentally disordered, the fact that a defendant has committed a proscribed act, often a serious one, makes proving sanity even more difficult. Finally, because a serious, or heinous, antisocial act has often been considered by the public at large, from whom juries are drawn, as a clear indication of what may be termed crazy behavior, and therefore of mental illness, placing the burden of proving sanity on the prosecution may defeat their case from the outset.

How is the insanity defense related to diminished capacity?

The diminished capacity defense, as does the insanity defense, examines the mental state of the defendant at the time of the antisocial act which has been charged as a crime. It is similar to the insanity defense in that it involves evidence related to mental illness, but differs in that it does not require the defendant to be unaware of the difference between right and wrong. It differs in that a successful insanity defense means the defendant has been found not guilty while a successful diminished capacity defense means that the defendant has been found guilty, but of a lesser offense. The legal doctrine concerning diminished capacity applies to defendants who lack the necessary mens rea, or guilty mind, to commit a more serious crime with the knowing purpose and intent required for it. While both the insanity defense and the diminished capacity defense focus on the cognitive question of whether the defendant knew his or her behavior was wrong, and on the motivational question of whether they were able to control that behavior, they differ in the role that mental disease or defect played in the antisocial act. Diminished capacity negates the mens rea required for the more serious crime, but does not prove insanity. A successful diminished capacity defense results in a conviction for a lesser offense, but not in acquittal. The rationale for the diminished capacity defense is that the crime for which the offender is convicted should accord with his mental state.

What is competence to stand trial?

Competence to stand trial requires the defendant's cognitive and affective ability to aid meaningfully in his court case. It is a completely separate inquiry from the question of insanity, which refers to the defendant's mental state at the time of the act which brought him to court. The question of competence arises at all stages of the proceedings, from arrest, to preparation of the case, to sentencing, even to execution when that is the sentence. In order to be found competent to stand trial, the defendant must demonstrate that he understands the charges and the proceedings, can communicate knowingly with their attorney, and can make legally rational decisions. The premise behind competence to stand trial is that people should not be placed on trial if they do not understand their own and others' roles at the trial, or the purpose of the proceedings. Whether the standard is a difficult one to meet or is much more readily met is arguable. As an argument that the standard is incredibly low, the prosecutor in the Ralph Tortorici case, for example, said that the standard is so low that a defendant's ability to distinguish a judge from a grapefruit meets the standard.

What is the relation between competence to stand trial and the insanity defense?

The relation between competence to stand trial and the insanity defense may or may not be a close one. Where insanity is raised as a defense, the question of competence to stand trial often accompanies it, and where the question of competence to stand trial arises, the issue of insanity at the time of the offense often accompanies it. If a defendant is found incompetent to stand trial, the trial halts until the defendant is restored to competency. In some instances, the defendant is never found competent. In some less serious cases, the charges might be dismissed; in more serious cases, hospitalization of the defendant as incompetent may serve much the same purpose as would hospitalization as not guilty by reason of insanity. In fact, it has often been suggested that in states which have abolished the insanity defense, such alternative institutionalization of mentally ill defendants has taken the place of insanity acquittals.

What does the American Psychological Association conclude concerning the insanity defense?

The American Psychological Association is primarily interested in providing empirical research to serve as a basis for informed public decisions, assisting the judge and jury in making legal, scientific and moral determinations, and ensuring appropriate treatment for mentally impaired offenders. The American Psychological Association supports the insanity defense and believes that all mentally impaired defendants, regardless of guilt or innocence, deserve sufficient treatment following the verdict, especially if they pose a threat to themselves or others. The organization is greatly concerned over the issue of releasing dangerous individuals to society after inadequate treatment and would like to provide further research in order to prevent such occurrences.

The American Psychological Association acknowledges but is not yet willing to accept or reject the proposal to eliminate the volitional elements of the American Law Institute test of insanity, which take into account the defendant's ability to conform his or her behavior to the requirements of the law. The organization believes that more research needs to be examined and more new studies to be conducted on behavioral control before it can take an informed position on this proposal. Based on current psychoforensic analysis and available research on the issue, it does not support the guilty but mentally ill defense as a replacement for or a supplement to the not guilty by reason of insanity verdict. And it believes that the issue of burden of proof is a legal, not psychological one, and therefore takes no stance on whether the defense or prosecution should bear the burden of proof in cases involving the insanity defense.

What does the American Psychiatric Association conclude concerning the insanity defense?

The American Psychiatric Association, like the American Psychological Association, believes in the retention of the insanity defense, and does not endorse the guilty but mentally ill plea or the irresistible impulse test. In its Statement on the Insanity Defense the American Psychiatric Association refused to take a position on the burden of proof issue, but did advocate that only serious mental illness form the basis for a defense of insanity. Further it advocated the elimination, for heuristic reasons, of such mental illnesses as antisocial personality disorder, and it approved preventing psychiatric testimony on the ultimate issue of sanity or insanity.

What does the American Medical Association conclude concerning the insanity defense?

The American Medical Association advocates the elimination of the special defense of insanity. It supports the decision of a minority of states, Utah, Idaho, Nevada, Kansas, Montana, to abolish the insanity plea and to replace it by providing for any acquittal under the mens rea statute. The American Medical Association believes that mentally impaired defendants who are acquitted should be released into society only after a sufficient judicial and medical determination that the defendant poses no risk to the public. The organization supports the concept that mental illness can be used as a mitigating factor and can help determine where a defendant will carry out his or her sentence. Further, it concludes that the period of hospitalization should not exceed the maximum jail term possible for the crime for which the defendant was charged.

What does the American Bar Association conclude concerning the insanity defense?

The American Bar Association, in response to the Hinckley trial, advocated a tightened insanity defense. Nonetheless, within two years, the American Bar Association had also approved Standard 7-6.2, which allowed defendants to avoid the tightened insanity defense by making admissible expert testimony and other evidence that may or may not show that the defendant, at the time of the criminal act, had the required mental state for the charged offense.

2
Psychological Aspects of the Insanity Defense

Is insanity a psychological concept?

No. Insanity is a legal concept, not a psychological diagnosis. In fact, there are no psychological criteria to determine insanity. Insanity is a purely legal concept used to determine the degree to which a defendant is responsible for his actions.

Is insanity the same as mental illness?

No. Insanity is a legal concept, while mental illness is a psychiatric and psychological concept. Consequently, a person could be minimally or even seriously mentally ill but not found to be insane, and thus could be held partially or even fully criminally responsible for his acts. A manslaughter verdict, in place of a murder conviction, and a verdict of guilty but mentally ill are examples of these discrepancies. Additionally, it is possible for a person who is not mentally ill to be deemed insane by a jury. For example, if a person ingests a drug involuntarily and this severely impairs his judgment and actions he may be found to be insane despite no history of mental illness.

What is mental illness?

There is no universally accepted federal or state definition of mental illness. In fact, researchers examining clinical literature have discovered two major classification systems. The first system, called by some broad-based, has used the American Psychiatric Association's Diagnostic and Statistical Manual of Mental Disorders. That manual features a multiaxial classification system and states that mental disorders are characterized by a behavioral or psychological syndrome associated with disability or suffering. Those who evaluate and testify as experts in court and other settings rely almost exclusively on the Diagnostic and Statistical Manual of Mental Disorders, and often differentiate between serious and less serious mental illnesses. The second system classifies mental illnesses as brain disorders and organizes them by their biochemical markers, their heritability, and their lesions. This biologically-based view of mental illness is considerably less used in legal settings.

What types of mental illnesses does the American Psychiatric Association consider for an insanity defense?

Officially, the American Psychiatric Association has endorsed defining someone as legally insane if because of mental disease or mental retardation he was not able to understand the wrongfulness of his conduct at the time of the offense. Consequently, the American Psychiatric Association stated that only severely abnormal mental conditions, like schizophrenia, fit properly within the insanity defense. And they excluded disorders resulting from the voluntary ingestion of alcohol or other psychoactive substances. Further, the Association did not support the irresistible impulse test for insanity.

Is insanity the same as psychosis?

No, it is important to differentiate psychosis from insanity. Psychosis is a psychiatric concept and insanity is a legal concept. Psychosis is essentially defined as a state of mind during which one's perception of reality is distorted. Psychosis is sometimes accompanied by hallucinations, personality changes, disorganized thinking, and delusional beliefs. As with mental illness, someone who was found legally insane may have been experiencing psychosis; however psychosis does not mandate legal insanity and being found insane does not necessarily mean that psychosis was present.

What is the relation between psychopathology and psychosis?

Psychopathology is basically a synonym for mental disease. It indicates the presence of disturbed, abnormal, or pathological conditions either mentally or behaviorally. As a result, psychosis is a form of psychopathology.

How do the various diagnoses in the official Diagnostic and Statistical Manual of Mental Disorders fit with the insanity defense?

Many of the diagnoses in the Diagnostic and Statistical Manual of Mental Disorders could theoretically be used as the basis for an insanity defense. This fact underscores one of the major issues with the insanity defense: How serious a mental disorder must be to persuade the legal system that an individual with that mental disorder should be excused from criminal responsibility; where, in other words, the line should be drawn between mental disorders which may qualify as legitimate causes of insanity, and those which either merely seek to reduce an individual's culpability or which do not impact the degree of culpability at all.

As an initial dividing line, those disorders which are the most serious, schizophrenia and bipolar disorder, are generally thought to be good candidates for a plea of insanity. Most legal and mental health experts agree that either schizophrenia with its potential for hallucinations and delusions and consequent loss of touch with reality, or manic-depressive illness, renamed bipolar disorder, with its potential for psychotic features, may potentially fit the requirements for a plea of insanity. Similarly, multiple personality disorder, renamed dissociative identity disorder, is, according to those who agree that it exists and is independent of therapist-induced origins, serious enough to be a good candidate as well.

Less generally acceptable for pleas of insanity are such disorders as attention deficit hyperactivity disorder, obsessive compulsive disorder, and posttraumatic stress disorder.

Least acceptable for pleas of insanity, in fact rejected by the American Psychiatric Association, are the disorders of antisocial personality disorder, characterizing individuals formerly labeled as psychopaths or sociopaths, and of conduct disorder, for those younger than the eighteen required for antisocial personality disorder. Individuals, in other words, whose behavior is characterized by repeated criminality cannot argue that their criminality ought to be excused because it is itself a mental disorder.

Finally, although substance use, abuse, or dependence and related disorders are often associated with crime, they are rarely used as the basis for the insanity defense: nearly all of the people who have committed a crime while under the influence of a substance ingested the substance voluntarily. Those who ingested a substance unknowingly or against their will, on the other hand, might employ an insanity defense.

What characteristics of schizophrenia make it suitable or not for an insanity defense?

One of the mental disorders most used in insanity defense cases is schizophrenia. This disorder, together with related disorders, such as delusional disorder and brief psychotic disorder, provide good foundations for an insanity defense because their effect is to potentially alter severely a person's sense of reality, which in turn may affect his ability to differentiate right from wrong, or to understand his motivations or the consequences of his actions. Additionally, an individual with most of these disorders has a history of the disorder which makes a plea of insanity more credible. Though brief psychotic disorder falls under this category, its lack of a history might not prevent it from being used to argue for temporary insanity.

What characteristics of mood disorders and of anxiety disorders make them suitable or not for an insanity defense?

Mood disorders, such as major depressive disorder and bipolar disorder, and anxiety disorders, such as panic disorder, agoraphobia, obsessive compulsive disorder, and posttraumatic stress disorder, are generally used rarely in insanity defenses, with a few notable exceptions. Those exceptions occur when the individual experiences a psychotic level of the disorder, as for instance, a person in the manic phase of bipolar illness who may argue insanity.

Though posttraumatic stress disorder could be used as insanity defense, it is more often cited as a precursor to a brief psychotic disorder, which is then used to argue insanity. Also, in a few cases, obsessive compulsive disorder has been used as the basis for an insanity defense. Typically, this has happened in states in which irresistible impulse is part of the test for insanity.

What characteristics of dissociative disorders make them suitable or not for an insanity defense?

Dissociative disorders have often been used in insanity cases and are among the most controversial disorders used by attorneys to argue for lack of, or reduced, criminal responsibility. Their main use concerns the individual with multiple personalities, some of which were unaware of and thus unable to control other personalities. The defense has argued that those law-abiding personalities were not legally and should not be morally responsible for the actions of the other personalities. The major problem with the use of these disorders in insanity pleas has been that dissociative identity disorder itself is a very controversial diagnosis. While some experts believe it exists and the Diagnostic and Statistical Manual of Mental Disorders does include it, others argue that it does not exist, or that defendants fake it by making up the symptoms, or they are led to their multiple selves through hypnosis or through overly eager therapists or evaluators. Furthermore, some argue that it is extremely difficult to differentiate between someone with a real dissociative identity disorder and someone trying to mimic it in order to receive no or a lesser sentence. This controversy is exacerbated by the fact that some defendants in very high-profile cases, such as Kenneth Bianchi, the Hillside Strangler, have used dissociative identity disorder as the basis of an insanity defense and have later been shown to be faking the disorder.

What characteristics of sexual or somatoform disorders make them suitable or not for an insanity defense?

Sexual disorders have occasionally been used as the basis for an insanity defense, but have rarely been successful. Usually juries and judges have not accepted exhibitionism, frotteurism, and voyeurism as excuses for exposure, groping, or peeping, respectively. Similarly, impulse control disorders have rarely been successfully used as the basis for an insanity defense. For example, kleptomania and pyromania have rarely been seen as anything other than excuses for stealing or arson.

Somatoform disorders, as somaticization disorder and conversion disorder, factitious disorders, eating disorders, sleep disorders, and adjustment disorders have very rarely been used in insanity defense cases. Sleepwalking has been an interesting exception in a few cases where it has been the foundation for the use of the insanity defense.

What characteristics of posttraumatic stress disorder make it suitable or not for an insanity defense?

Posttraumatic stress disorder was officially introduced in the third edition of the Diagnostic and Statistical Manual of Mental Disorders. Posttraumatic stress disorder occurs after a person has been exposed to a traumatic stimulus, either once, as in a car accident, or repeatedly, as in recurring physical, sexual, or emotional abuse. The most common symptoms of posttraumatic stress syndrome include reexperiencing of the traumatic event, avoidance of stimuli associated with the trauma, extreme fear and anxiety or numbness when exposed to stimuli associated to the trauma, and the presence of hypervigilance or hyperarousal symptoms.

Posttraumatic stress disorder has had an interesting relationship with the insanity defense. Though it has occasionally been thought of in cases involving temporary insanity, as for example when an abused woman is said to have snapped and killed her abusive husband, the more common use has been when the crime was one of inaction. For example, as in the case of Hedda Nussbaum, when a woman has been severely abused by her partner, she may have suffered from posttraumatic stress syndrome. As a result, it could be argued, when he beat their children she might have been unable to respond because of her own trauma. In cases such as that, posttraumatic stress syndrome could be the basis for an insanity defense as one could argue that the defendant was not responsible for the abuse of her children since she was unable to intercede on their behalf because of posttraumatic stress syndrome.

What characteristics of retardation make it suitable or not for an insanity defense?

Mental retardation has been fairly controversial when used as the basis for the insanity defense. Much, of course, has depended on the level of retardation. The U.S. Supreme Court, for example, decided on an IQ level below which an individual may not be executed. With the insanity defense, however, there is no direct correlation between lower IQ levels, presence of psychiatric mental disorder, and ability to form the guilty mind required for a criminal offense. Some advocates, focusing on the therapeutic aspects of the interaction between the legal and mental health systems, have argued that those suffering from mental retardation ought either to be excused completely from criminal responsibility or at least partially because their retardation in itself suggests diminished capacity to understand lawful behavior and act accordingly. Others have argued that though they may have diminished capacity, most mentally retarded people can tell the difference between right and wrong and can conform their behavior to the requirements of law.

If an individual is not insane, what mental disorders might make that individual less than fully responsible for acts?

While generally only the more serious mental illnesses form the basis for a plea of insanity, a great many more mental disorders form the basis for an argument for diminished responsibility. In fact, the entire Diagnostic and Statistical Manual of Mental Disorders enables some attorneys to use whatever diagnostic labels they can to decrease their client's jeopardy. All the diagnoses previously discussed may make the individual less than fully responsible for his acts. Beyond those, a few other examples will suffice. Sleepwalking, for example, might not make one insane, but could make one less responsible, since one is less in control of his actions if genuinely sleepwalking. Dependence on or addiction to substances, Munchausen syndrome by proxy, paranoid personality disorder, intermittent explosive disorder, depression, and delirium are among other diagnoses which might be used.

Can one prove that someone is sane?

It is extremely difficult to prove that someone is not insane, in effect that he is sane, because there is no one undisputed psychological or legal definition of normalcy, or sanity, or any definitive criteria to evaluate the same. Even if there were, it would still be difficult to prove conclusively the sanity of an individual, because few, if any, individuals would completely conform to such a definition of sanity.

It would be extremely difficult to establish a point at which an individual's deviation from this ideal norm constituted insanity.

In the case of John Hinckley, Jr., who attempted to assassinate President Reagan, the burden of proof that he was not insane rested on the prosecution. In other words, the prosecution was charged with proving that Hinckley was sane at the time of his crime. When Hinckley was found not guilty by reason of insanity, many critics argued that the prosecution was the bearer of an impossible task. How could they prove that an individual was sane, beyond a reasonable doubt or even by clear and convincing evidence or even by a preponderance of the evidence, especially when his reasons for attempting to kill the president appeared to many to be what the public termed crazy? As a result, after the Hinckley case, the federal government and many states changed their legislation to shift the burden of proof to the defense. The defense became, in those jurisdictions in which it did not already have the burden, responsible for proving insanity.

How is brain science used in insanity defense cases?

Brain science is often used to bolster and validate the diagnosis of a mental disorder. For example, in the case of John Hinckley, Jr., biological irregularities in his brain were used in his trial to assist his insanity defense. Dr. David Bear presented to the court the results of a CAT-scan of Hinckley's brain that revealed widened sulci, the folds and ridges of the brain, which were allegedly consistent with schizophrenia. He also said that Hinckley's brain was smaller than normal. Hinckley's trial established important precedents for the use of brain science in insanity defense cases. Whereas a CAT-scan had reportedly never before been admitted as evidence, the judge eventually admitted it in Hinckley's case.

And, though the time may be somewhat far off, it has been argued that in the future mental illness might be diagnosed not through careful behavioral observations but by highly detailed brain scans.

How are psychoanalytic theories used in insanity defense cases?

Psychoanalytically-oriented theories are the most frequently used defense explanations for acts which bring individuals into court. Because it is almost always possible to look back into a defendant's past for examples of family dysfunction or emotional disturbance or problematic behavior or some form of mental illness, these theories rely on that past for indications of insanity or at the least of mitigating factors. These theories are the most prominent ones used to bolster and validate the diagnosis of a mental disorder. For example, in the case of Richard Herrin, who was accused of murdering his girlfriend, psychoanalytic theories concerning Herrin's early life and his relationship with his mother and his girlfriend were used to provide a rationale for his adult adjustment problem, which, in turn, contributed to the diagnosis of transient situational reaction that the defense psychological experts used.

What is malingering?

Malingering is pretending to have a mental disorder for a certain purpose, such as to avoid legal sanctions or to gain monetary advantage. Malingering can also occur when one actually has a mental disorder but exaggerates the severity of the condition.

How can malingering be assessed?

One way to detect malingering is to compare the symptoms exhibited by the individual to those of the condition in question. Someone, however, may malinger well enough to exhibit the same symptoms as someone who is not malingering. This can make it more difficult to detect malingering. In such cases, malingering can be revealed by uncovering the possible motivation for the generation of symptoms. For example, serial killer Kenneth Bianchi initially duped several psychological experts into believing that he suffered from multiple personality disorder. Yet he was found to create more alternate personalities under hypnosis when a psychologist explained to him in the wake state that doing so could help his case. In another example, a defendant may answer incorrectly on an ability test in order to seem less mentally competent. This can be revealed if the defendant answers incorrectly at a higher rate on the easier questions than on the more difficult questions, on which the defendant might not know the correct or incorrect answers. And certainly the comparison between present symptoms and past records and behavior can point to discrepancies.

Many specific tests exist to evaluate malingering, including: the Minnesota Multiphasic Personality Inventory-2, the Validity Indicator Profile, the Minnesota Multiphasic Personality Inventory-Adolescent, and the Test of Memory Malingering. Tests of malingering, however, are not perfectly accurate at its detection.

How often do defendants malinger?

Research estimates that one in four or five defendants exhibits a moderate degree of malingering. This drives many psychologists to receive training to detect malingering. Some argue that the training is effective; others argue that even those who receive the training can be easily or somewhat easily misled unless they are willing to become detectives in search of ancillary materials concerning the individual they are evaluating.

Why have psychological explanations for behavior dominated in the legal system as opposed to economic or racial or cultural or other explanations?

As a field of study, psychology has attempted to understand human behavior. As the field has evolved and as the public's faith in psychological science has grown, society has become increasingly willing to explain most behavior in psychological terms. The criminal justice system has especially opened up to the field. Psychology and psychological experts are now used to evaluate many aspects of the criminal process. In fact, there has been a reciprocal escalation. The legal system has asked psychology and psychologists to do more. Psychology and psychologists have claimed they can do more and have been willing participants within the legal system. The legal system has then asked more and the science of psychology and its practitioners have complied. This psychoforensic escalation has by far outstripped other sciences or explanations or fields.

Wherever one turns in the criminal justice system, psychoforensic professionals participate. Thus criminal profilers analyze crime scenes to develop a psychological description of the suspect. Forensic psychologists and psychiatrists evaluate a defendant's competency to stand trial, and evaluate defendants and testify regarding the insanity defense. Psychoforensic specialists participate in sentencing and correctional and institutional release issues and in myriad other issues as well, and that is only within the criminal justice system. These specialists also participate in the civil justice system in such probate matters as awarding custody of children or determining the need for guardianship, to name but a few examples.

Because the criminal justice system often requires judges and juries to look inside the mind of a criminal, such as when assessing criminal intent, it is natural that psychology, the study of the mind, would gain importance in the courts. As such risk factors for criminal behavior as low socioeconomic status, ethnic or racial minority status, and housing conditions have emerged, psychology has often been used to explain these factors as well. The reciprocal escalation between the legal and mental health systems has reduced the impact of new theories.

How can the legal assumption of free will and full criminal responsibility be compatible with the psychological assumption of determinism and lessened or no criminal responsibility?

Much time has been spent debating the insanity defense in terms of criminal responsibility. The question has been raised whether someone with a severe mental illness, in a legal condition of insanity, should be held less responsible for their actions than someone else or not held responsible at all. This question and the law itself presume that most of us are responsible for our actions. The law is based on free will, an assumption of one's freedom and capacity to choose to act or not to act. Determinism, on the other hand, is a scientific theory that presumes that every action is explainable by analyzing the state of the universe before the action and integrating all natural and scientific laws. Consequently, in a deterministic view, every action is in essence a reaction. This set of reactions, according to deterministic theory, is understandable and ought to excuse individuals from what would otherwise flow from their freely willed choice.

The law has largely maintained the theory of free will in the face of much of society's deterministic thrust. The insanity defense has been used to carve out a reserved space for the deterministic theory within a system oriented toward free will. In fact those who argue for the insanity defense see it as a way of maintaining the morality of a system which otherwise would force everyone to accept responsibility for what many consider to be acts beyond their control. The insanity defense proponents see it as allowing the criminal justice system to operate largely on a theory of free will. And they recognize that determinism could not exclusively work in our legal system because then no one would be guilty. The therapeutic state, with its focus on treatment, would dominate. The insanity defense appears to allow determinism and free will to coexist. Many philosophers, psychologists, and lawyers, however, suggest that the insanity defense wraps in scientific garb what is essentially a philosophical argument about the nature of action and of free will. It creates for some and appears to create for others a bridge between the extremes of determinism and free will.

Does the insanity defense contribute to the stigmatization of the mentally ill?

Many critics say that the insanity defense can contribute to the stigmatization of the mentally ill when the public perceives that defendants are malingering or are using the insanity defense to avoid responsibility that they should accept. On the other hand, supporters of the defense say that when the public believes that a defendant is truly so mentally ill as not to be criminally responsible then it does not contribute to that stigmatization. Some critics, however, argue that the mere presence of the insanity defense, which is used rarely, together with its significant media exposure in some widely-publicized extreme cases, lead the public at large to conclude that the mentally ill are much more dangerous than they in fact are. Those critics suggest that by supporting the insanity defense, the American Psychiatric Association and the American Psychological Association, both of which advocate for the insanity defense and argue against stigmatizing the mentally ill, are themselves lending powerful voice to that very stigmatization.

Are religious fundamentalists mentally ill?

Religious beliefs are not included in the American Psychiatric Association's lists of diagnostic criteria for mental disorders, but opinions on the relationship between religion and mental illness vary widely among experts.

At one extreme, Sigmund Freud considered belief in religion to be a symptom of mental illness. Thus, in Freud's opinion, he would have considered all of the ninety-one percent of Americans who subscribed to a religion in 2002 as suffering from mental disorders. It would be unreasonable, of course, to have ninety-one percent of defendants plead not guilty by reason of insanity. Freud himself did not believe that religion as mental illness ought to diminish criminal responsibility. Rather, he believed it was the moral belief system of a religious follower that was ill, while the decision-making part of the brain, which decides whether to follow through on religious beliefs, remained illness-free. As an example, a person who believed that homosexuality was a sin would still be able to decide whether to murder a gay man or to leave him alone. Having a religious belief system, then, would not be automatic grounds for insanity. Yet, one could imagine a scenario in which the person's decision-making processes were sufficiently impaired as to prevent him from making rational decisions about acting on religious beliefs. In such an instance, an insanity defense would be viable, given that the defendant appeared to have no control over his actions. However, the defendant's insanity would stem not from the religious belief itself, but rather from his under-developed control mechanisms. John Salvi, who killed two employees at abortion clinics, unsuccessfully pled not guilty by reason of insanity. His attorney argued that Salvi's religious belief against abortion did not cause him to kill, but rather that his schizophrenia did. Found guilty and sentenced to prison, Salvi was subsequently discovered dead in his prison cell. Authorities said he had committed suicide.

While Freud considered religious belief to be a psychological illness, some researchers have reached the opposite conclusion, that religiosity appeared to decrease the likelihood of mental illness. A large study discovered that non-religious people were more likely to seek psychiatric treatment than religious people, with increased involvement in the religion correlating with decreased rates of psychiatric treatment. The researchers hypothesized that this difference could be a result of the mental health promoting aspects of religion, such as its social support structure and its emphasis on marriage and the avoidance of drugs and alcohol. All of these factors have been known to promote mental health, and it may be these secondary causes, rather than religion itself, that produced the apparent decrease in mental illness among religious followers. Because the researchers examined only whether the subjects were receiving psychiatric treatment and not whether they actually suffered from mental disorders, another possible explanation for the results could be that religious people simply may have sought professional treatment less frequently but did not necessarily suffer from less mental illness. Instead of consulting a psychiatrist, religious followers may have sought the help of a religious leader, whereas non-religious people had only psychological professionals to turn to for help. Further research would be needed to understand the exact relationship between religiosity and mental health, but, whatever the underlying cause, increased religious observation appeared to be associated with decreased psychiatric care.

Should religious fundamentalists have an insanity defense available?

Since the standards for an insanity defense apply equally to religious defendants as to their non-religious counterparts, religious fundamentalists should have an insanity defense available to them, but not one that is any different from that available to the rest of the population. The line between insanity on one side, and adherence to a religion in general or to its fundamental version on the other, might be a difficult one to draw at times. That does not preclude a religious fundamentalist also being insane, however.

Zealous religiosity can share some traits with psychotic thinking, as for instance a belief in something unseen or a seemingly irrational obedience to a religious law which requires disobedience to society's laws. But to adjudge a belief in one's ability to talk to God, for example, as intrinsically insane is to pass judgment on many people's sanity.

The question of insanity in religious followers became most apparent when the religion was either uncommon or particularly bizarre. Ron and Dan Lafferty, for instance, as one of the collective cases examines, subscribed to their own strange brand of Mormon fundamentalism, and their religion effectively consumed their lives. Because they believed that God had instructed them to do so, they murdered an innocent woman and her baby daughter. The Laffertys' strange take on a religion which was founded in America but had not gained wide adherents certainly raised questions about their sanity at trial, but their insanity defense was rejected by the jury, which found both men guilty. The bottom line was that the standards for the insanity defense applied equally to religious defendants as to their non-religious counterparts, with little regard for how strange that religion might seem or how much one's beliefs might vary from the core beliefs of the religion. Religious belief, even extreme or deviant religious belief, in itself did not automatically qualify someone as insane, but a religious person could, of course, suffer from a mental disorder that rendered him insane. Odd religious practices may prove to be a symptom of underlying mental illness, but it is the mental illness and not the religion itself that renders a defendant insane.

Are terrorists mentally ill?

When an atrocious crime is committed, society has a tendency to question immediately the mental health of the perpetrator. The public asks itself what person in his right mind could do such a thing and often labels both the act and the person as crazy. That initial reaction becomes even more pronounced when the crime concerned was a result of terrorism and especially when it included self-destruction of the perpetrator as well. The forces that led groups and individuals to commit mass murder of innocent citizens, especially as suicide bombers willing to donate their lives in order to kill others, were beyond the comprehension of most citizens. Compounding the difficult to understand nature of terrorism was the fact that many terrorist acts are committed in the name of religion. As these terrorist acts have spread around the world, more have called them evil, and previous efforts to deal with them solely through the criminal law have given way to efforts to understand and deal with them in a more military fashion.

However they might be viewed, it is not the nature of these acts of terrorism that qualifies a defendant as insane, but rather, his state of mind at the time of the act. There must be a serious mental disease or defect to qualify as the insanity that prevented responsibility for the crime. The horrendous quality of a terrorist attack, even the suicidality, may well indicate underlying mental illness, but it is the illness and not the act itself that would possibly render the terrorist insane. While some argue that indoctrination into the belief system that turns one into a suicide bomber is a form of brainwashing which ought to excuse the perpetrator, others argue that such a belief system is better understood as evil rather than as a symptom of mental illness.

Should terrorists have an insanity defense available?

In the courts many argue that a terrorist defendant is no different from any other defendant, and, therefore, both must have all of the same defenses available, including the insanity defense, and both must be subjected to the same standard of insanity. Regardless of how reprehensible the terrorist act was, the nature of the crime does not either qualify the defendant as insane or disqualify him. Instead, the defendant must prove that he was sufficiently mentally ill as to not be responsible for the crime, whether that crime was terror related or not. Others argue that a terrorist defendant is different and society must fashion different ways of dealing with terrorists.

How is brainwashing related to insanity?

Brainwashing can and has been used as an insanity defense. For example, in the case of the Washington, D.C. area snipers, seventeen year old John Lee Malvo alleged that he had been brainwashed by forty-two year old John Muhammad. And Patty Hearst, as is shown in one of the case studies, alleged, unsuccessfully, that she had participated in criminal acts as a result of brainwashing by the Symbionese Liberation Army.

3

Effects of Different Standards of Determining Insanity

What are the primary tests of insanity?

The primary tests of insanity are the M'Naghten rule, the Durham rule, and the American Law Institute rule. Each state and the federal government can use any one of the three it chooses, or it can choose none, or it can add irresistible impulse as a test, or it can choose the somewhat related test of guilty but mentally ill.

What is the M'Naghten test?

The M'Naghten rule provided one of the earliest definitions of insanity and was derived from English case law in 1843. The M'Naghten rule was created in response to the public fury over the trial outcome of Daniel M'Naghten, who shot and killed the secretary to England's Prime Minister. Daniel M'Naghten suffered from paranoid delusions, believing that the prime minister was part of a conspiracy against him. He shot the secretary, mistaking him for the prime minister. Nine medical examiners testified that he suffered from mental illness and was insane. M'Naghten was acquitted by reason of insanity and spent the rest of his life in the Bedlam institution for the mentally ill.

Not only was the public outraged by the successful use of the insanity defense in this high-profile trial, but Queen Victoria was also apprehensive about the verdict, given that she had been the target of a few assassination attempts. The House of Lords issued the M'Naghten ruling, which called for stricter standards for defining insanity. Under the M'Naghten rule, the defense must clearly prove that the defendant was suffering from such a defect of reason from disease of the mind that he either did not understand the nature and quality of the act he committed, did not in other words know what he was doing, or did not know that it was wrong.

For over a century this narrow definition of insanity was adopted and used in both English and American courts of law. Today, about one-third of the states use some variation of the M'Naghten rule. Modifications to the standards of insanity were eventually made in numerous states due to the criticisms that accompanied the M'Naghten rule. Those mental health professionals who opposed the M'Naghten rule argued that it was too restrictive in its focus on the cognitive distinction between right and wrong. They thought that the focus of a suitable test ought to be on affective or emotional factors as well, and that volitional ability to control one's acts ought also to be a consideration.

What is the Durham test?

The Durham rule, first used in 1954, and named after a case, was based on the question of whether or not the defendant's behavior was the product of mental disease or defect. If it were such a product, then the defendant was not criminally responsible for his otherwise unlawful actions. The Durham rule thus emphasized the role of psychology and psychiatry and relied heavily on expert witnesses who would, the judge who decided the case concluded, be able to tie mental illness directly to the act. It was expansive and allowed more instances of mental disease or defect to impact the determination of criminal nonresponsibility. Because its promise was not fulfilled it fell into disuse.

What is the American Law Institute test?

The American Law Institute rule, promulgated by the Model Penal Code in 1962, found favor in the Brawner case in 1972. It tried to combine the cognitive component of the M'Naghten test with the focus on mental disease or defect in the Durham test. It was broader than the M'Naghten test, but narrower than the Durham test. In other words, when followed, it appeared to permit more defendants to be found not guilty by reason of insanity than did the M'Naghten test and fewer than did the Durham test.

The American Law Institute test stated that a defendant was not criminally responsible if, at the time of his act, he lacked, as a result of mental disease or defect, either substantial capacity to appreciate the wrongfulness of his conduct or to conform his conduct to the requirements of the law. The part of the test about appreciation contained the cognitive or knowledge component of the test.

The part of the test about conforming contained the volitional component of the test. The part of the test about mental disease or defect contained the psychological component of the test. And the part of the test about substantial capacity defined the degree of impairment necessary.

What is the guilty but mentally ill verdict?

Since 1976, approximately twenty-five percent of the states have passed reforms incorporating guilty but mentally ill as a possible verdict in trials involving the insanity defense. The uses and consequences of a guilty but mentally ill verdict have varied from state to state. Typically, guilty but mentally ill has been added to the possible verdicts of not guilty, guilty as charged, guilty of a lesser offense because of diminished capacity, and not guilty by reason of insanity. Occasionally it has replaced not guilty by reason of insanity. Under this verdict, an offender found guilty but mentally ill would be sentenced to the same amount of time as a simple guilty verdict would require, but would begin serving his term in a mental institution instead of jail. The mentally ill offender would receive appropriate treatment before being transferred to prison in order to serve the remainder of his sentence.

The guilty but mentally ill verdict arose out of an attempt to avoid certain criticisms associated with the not guilty by reason of insanity verdict. Jurors and the public had trouble grappling with the issue that a defendant could be found not guilty by reason of insanity but still have committed the crime, meaning the act itself, in essence making him guilty. They had difficulty distinguishing the issue of factual guilt, that is having committed the act, from the issue of legal guilt, which could result in a finding of not guilty by reason of insanity. The guilty but mentally ill option was proposed as a compromise between factual guilt on the one hand and legal guilt on the other.

Critics of the option have argued that it does not make conceptual sense because mental illness of the degree that would be specified in the verdict should lead to a finding of not guilty by reason of insanity. They have said that the option simply gives jurors an easy way out of making a difficult decision by allowing them to agree to both possibilities, mental illness and guilt. They have also argued that adding a phrase to a guilty verdict in order to direct the corrections department where to place the convicted mentally ill offender makes as much sense as adding a phrase that a defendant is guilty but physically ill as a way of suggesting to the corrections system where that defendant should initially be placed. Critics also have stated that the guilty but mentally ill option confuses jurors even more than regular insanity instructions because jurors are then faced with making the distinction between regular mental illness and mental illness that results in insanity. Finally such groups as the American Psychiatric Association have contended that the guilty but mentally ill option eliminates the jury's legal function of making decisions regarding responsibility for criminal acts.

Proponents of guilty but mentally ill verdicts have denied the contentions of the critics. They have suggested that its addition would lessen the number of not guilty by reason of insanity verdicts, which they have supported, and would allow for better treatment of offenders suffering from mental illness, which they have said everyone, proponents and critics alike, have favored. Studies have produced mixed conclusions as to whether or not the inclusion of a guilty but mentally ill verdict has actually decreased the number of defendants acquitted due to insanity. In addition, overcrowding in mental hospitals has eliminated the option of hospitalization from many defendants found guilty but mentally ill with the majority going directly to prison without treatment or after very brief periods of treatment.

4

Arguments for Retention, Abolition, and Revision of the Insanity Defense

What are the arguments for retaining the insanity defense?

The primary arguments for retaining the insanity defense are moral arguments. They are based on the view that the criminal justice system in America has its ethical foundations in the belief that human beings have the capacity for rationality, have free will, can be deterred by the threat of punishment, and ought to be punished or rewarded for their behavior. Proponents of the insanity defense argue that if mental illness damages or destroys these basic human capacities in some individuals, those individuals should not be held responsible for their actions in the same way as those who are not impaired should be. In addition to professional organizations like the American Psychiatric Association and the American Psychological Association, supporters of the insanity defense include such groups as the National Alliance for the Mentally Ill who are advocates for the protecting the rights of the mentally ill.

The American Psychiatric Association argues for the retention of the insanity defense in order to preserve the moral integrity of criminal law. They base their assertion on the premise that the punishment of criminals should derive from moral culpability and that defendants who do not have the capacity to rationally control their actions do not have free will. As such, those defendants do not choose to commit crimes and should not be punished like other criminals.

In addition to the moral argument, the American Psychiatric Association argues that retaining the insanity defense is important on medical grounds. They believe that many defendants who are found or potentially could be found not guilty by reason of insanity are better served by receiving psychiatric treatment than by being punished and imprisoned. And they point out that, statistically, individuals found not guilty by reason of insanity spend more time locked in a mental hospital than they would have spent behind bars if found guilty.

Dr. Willard Gaylin has declared that the retention of the insanity defense is an absolute necessity in any humanistic society. He claimed that a person who was truly not knowledgeable or truly not responsible for his actions should not be punished. The outcome of the act itself was not enough to justify punishment. Gaylin has gone so far as to argue that even if the insanity defense were abolished, it would somehow be reintroduced into the system in different language. Yet even Gaylin has differed from some others in what he has thought the scope of the insanity defense should be. He has said it should be reserved for those who are truly insane, and he has defined that in a more limited way, as by the M'Naghten test, than have some others, as Dr. Judith Otnow Lewis, who have defined it much more broadly, even to the extent of suggesting that it ought to be available to all violent offenders. Gaylin has been particularly strong in his condemnation of those who would abolish the insanity defense to replace it with a guilty but mentally ill verdict. He has argued that this verdict would constitute a contradiction of terms in our system. According to Gaylin, if a person is determined to be insane, he is by definition not legally culpable, and therefore cannot simultaneously be found guilty as well. Thus, Gaylin has found the idea of guilty but insane morally objectionable, legally unsound, and politically dangerous.

Thus, the main advocates for the retention of the insanity defense tend to focus their arguments on the moral issues of criminal responsibility and on the need of the mentally ill for treatment and rehabilitation.

What are the arguments for abolishing the insanity defense?

Critics have argued that the insanity defense gives too prominent a place to the inexact findings of psychiatry and psychology and allows them to intrude on the important task of guiding all citizens into what behavior is lawful and what is not. They contend that in so doing the insanity defense depends inordinately on expert psychiatric and psychological testimony which is often contradictory and, critics contend, for sale to high bidders. Further, critics have said that insanity acquittees have then been handled as if they were civilly committed to an institution and therefore kept for too short a time before being released to society. Some abolitionists have argued that the insanity defense allows these criminals to get away with their crimes and to return too quickly to the community where they pose a serious threat.

What are the arguments for reforming the insanity defense?

Because of widespread public disfavor with the insanity defense, especially after the acquittal of John Hinckley, Jr., who attempted to assassinate President Reagan, many in politics, in society, and in psychology and law called for reform of the defense.

Three of the most prominent suggested reforms were the introduction of the guilty but mentally ill verdict, the clarification of diminished capacity, and the effort to limit the use of the insanity defense, as through the Insanity Defense Reform Act of 1984.

The guilty but mentally ill verdict was praised as an alternative to not guilty by reason of insanity or as a substitute for it. It would allow a jury to place responsibility on a defendant for his actions, yet establish provisions for a defendant to receive care for his mental illness. While acknowledging the weakness of this verdict in that it ultimately placed discretion for mental care in the hands of the correctional and mental facilities, its supporters said that it at least signaled to these facilities that the defendant required mental health care.

Diminished capacity allowed a defendant to receive a lower sentence on a lesser charge by recognizing that a mental disorder contributed to his criminal activity, while not fully exculpating the defendant. An example of this was the case of Richard Herrin who was accused of murdering his girlfriend. His transient situational reaction led to his conviction on the lesser charge of manslaughter, rather than on the more serious charge of murder. While some of course applauded this verdict, others roundly condemned it. Diminished capacity, as a reform, has generated a mixed reaction.

Some reforms aimed to limit the use of the insanity defense in order to prevent its abuse. For example, the Insanity Defense Reform Act of 1984 enacted three limits on the insanity defense. First, it abolished the volitional aspect of the American Law Institute, or Brawner, rule. Second, it prevented experts from testifying as to the ultimate issue of insanity. Third, it shifted the burden of proof to defendants to prove their insanity.

5

Media and Other Responses to the Insanity Defense

Why does the public react to someone's causing terrible harm by saying the perpetrator must have been crazy?

Many people do not feel that they are capable of committing crimes that are especially senseless or heinous. Crime scene pictures make many people queasy, detailed accounts of violence frequently elicit feelings of unease, and the notion of ignoring the enormous legal deterrents to serious crime confuse many people. Thus, compared to these people's standards, someone who causes terrible harm must have lacked rationality, emotions, or humanity. This deficiency leads the public to call these people crazy. The public generally does not have the legal conception of insanity in mind when it bandies about the word crazy. It is referring more broadly to its collective inability to understand how someone brought himself to commit a particularly harmful act.

Given how seldom it is used, how and why has the insanity defense occupied such a prominent position in the interaction between psychology and the law?

Although the insanity defense is not often used, there is a common misconception in American society that people frequently plead not guilty by reason of insanity in felony cases. One study on the use of the insanity defense in eight states between 1976 and 1985 showed that the public estimated that the insanity defense was used an average of thirty-seven percent of the time. The study found that, in fact, during those years, the insanity plea was only utilized in nine-tenths of one percent of cases in those eight states. Based on their incorrect assessment of how large a role the insanity defense plays in the legal system, it is understandable why Americans attribute to it so much attention and prominence in the interaction between psychology and the law.

The misconceptions held by Americans may also be linked to how often they are exposed to insanity trials. The insanity defense remains an extremely controversial issue in the legal system, and for that reason, any large case involving the insanity plea is widely covered by popular media. Based on the airtime and print space that insanity trials receive as compared to non-insanity trials, it is understandable why people believe that the insanity defense is utilized in a large percentage of criminal cases.

The controversy surrounding the insanity defense also aids in the public attributing more prominence to its role within the legal system than it would otherwise warrant, based on its infrequent use. In addition to the legal definitions of insanity, the insanity defense is based on psychological definitions, found in abnormal psychology, which are related to insanity. Psychology is a young science, compared to biology and physics and the other hard sciences, and for that reason, people are more skeptical or unsure about how to find truth in psychology. Though DNA results are rarely questioned, even when they are interpreted by expert witnesses, many people question anyone's ability to determine another person's mental state especially at a time in the past. Psychology within the courtroom seems to be more subjective than the physical sciences, which are deemed more objective in the eyes of most Americans. As a controversial issue, the insanity defense has always and will continue to maintain a central position in the relationship between psychology and the law.

What do jurors think of the insanity defense?

Jurors in general take their roles very seriously and try to follow impartially the judge's instructions in the law, including instructions on the insanity defense. In the case of John Hinckley, Jr., who shot President Reagan in order to impress the actress Jodie Foster, the jury was instructed that the prosecution had the burden of proving that Hinckley was sane. Of course, it is very difficult to prove that anyone is sane, particularly someone like Hinckley. Given the instructions that the jury received, it would have been difficult for them to reach any other verdict than the one they reached, not guilty by reason of insanity. The public in general, however, strongly disagreed with the verdict. One report found that seventy-three percent of interviewees believed they would have convicted Hinckley had they been on the jury. Fully eighty-seven percent of respondents considered the insanity defense to be a loophole for guilty defendants to escape punishment. While those interviewed were likely to be especially upset about the insanity defense because of the recency of the Hinckley case, it is likely that most of them were also distrustful of the defense even before the Hinckley verdict. Thus, it is probable that most of the Hinckley jurors initially came to the trial with a negative opinion of the insanity defense. The fact that they were able to put their lay opinions aside and return an acquittal is a testament to the fact that jurors strive to be unbiased, fair administrators of the law. Yet, it is still important to remember that jurors are regular people who likely come to trial with unfavorable impressions of the insanity defense, and they may not always be willing or able to put aside their personal feelings when determining a verdict.

What does the public think of the insanity defense?

The vast majority of Americans do not have favorable opinions on the insanity defense. In the aftermath the John Hinckley, Jr. case, one study found that eighty-seven percent of those polled considered the defense to be a loophole for criminals. Nearly forty percent reported that they had no confidence in the testimony of psychiatric experts, and only eighteen percent believed that psychiatrists were capable of determining insanity in most instances.

The public's negative opinion on the insanity defense may be due to the lack of knowledge the most people have on the defense. When asked to define insanity, only twenty-nine percent of those asked could provide a correct or partially correct answer. Fully forty-four percent believed that someone found not guilty by reason of insanity would spend less than a year in custody, while a mere twenty-one percent believed that a not guilty by reason of insanity defendant would spend more than five years in custody. In truth, the average not guilty by reason of insanity defendant spends more time in a treatment facility than he would have spent in prison had he been found guilty. Furthermore, most people seriously overestimate the prevalence of insanity pleas in the court system, as well as the success rates of those pleas. One study found that although the public believed that the insanity defense was used in thirty-seven percent of cases, it was actually used in only nine-tenths of one percent of cases.

Given the unfavorable opinions and misinformation of the general public, it is little wonder that most people are opposed to the insanity defense. Some states, in fact, abolished the insanity defense altogether after the Hinckley verdict, and other states made their insanity standards more strict. While much of the public outcry over the insanity defense has abated, people have remained skeptical of the defense. If another controversial not guilty by reason of insanity verdict equivalent to the Hinckley case were to be announced in the future, perhaps the public's rage over the insanity defense would be sufficient to abolish the plea more widely.

How serious are most of the charges in insanity defense cases?

For the most part, cases which employed an insanity defense involved very serious felony charges. The stakes were high. Whether the resultant long periods of possible institutionalization were spent in a prison or in a mental hospital made a difference. For misdemeanor cases the stakes did not appear so high as the periods of institutionalization were much shorter. Yet this changed in 1982. In that year the U.S. Supreme Court ruled in the *Jones* case that it was constitutionally permissible to detain a not guilty by reason of insanity acquittee for longer than that person's hypothetical maximum prison sentence. In that particular case, a man arrested for attempted shoplifting, a misdemeanor with a maximum prison sentence of one year, was found not guilty by reason of insanity, and then detained in a mental hospital for nearly three decades. In the wake of the *Jones* decision, many commentators said that it is a strategic misstep to use an insanity defense for anything but the most serious cases that would involve long prison terms. In an attempt to revive the viability of the insanity defense for minor crimes, several states have imposed caps on the lengths of institutionalization for those who have been found not guilty by reason of insanity for misdemeanors.

Why does the public have the idea that the charges are usually very serious?

The public is under the impression that the charges are usually very serious for two reasons. The first is that in many states, the charges usually are very serious. The second is that cases involving especially heinous offenses generally get more media attention. Thus, when the defendant in a heinous offense employs the insanity defense, most people find out about it. These same people seldom hear about the insanity defense being used for minor crimes.

Who are the most significant expert witnesses on the insanity defense and what are their views?

One of the most notable participants in insanity defense cases has been Park Elliot Dietz, a psychiatrist. He has been widely recognized for his conservative views on the death penalty and has been a witness for the prosecution in a number of high-profile cases including Andrea Yates, Jeffrey Dahmer, and John Hinckley, Jr. More than anything, Dr. Dietz has promoted strict adherence to the law within the particular state in which he was testifying. He has acknowledged that in some instances laws can work against people and actually promote the prosecution of a sick person. For instance, in his testimony in the Andrea Yates trial, Dr. Dietz stated that he did feel that Yates was operating under a delusional thought system, but these delusions included fear of God and fear of the wrath of society and punishment for her actions. Thus, Dr. Dietz argued, despite the fact that Yates was in fact delusional, those delusions included a method of determining right from wrong, and therefore, according to Texas law, Yates should be found guilty. He also testified that she had viewed an episode of *Law and Order* in which a mother drowned her children and that that gave her the idea to kill her own. Later it was shown that the episode had never aired. Two years later the Texas appellate court reversed Yates' conviction because of Dietz's untrue statements. Dietz has oftentimes been criticized as a hired gun, a person who will testify for anything in return for his high rates, and he has also been criticized for representing his opinion as fact in court, and for being unduly harsh on the mentally ill.

Another important participant in insanity defenses has been Phillip Resnick. Most recently, Dr. Resnick became well-known for his views in the Andrea Yates case, which opposed those of Dr. Dietz. He testified for the defense in the Yates case, though he has not commonly been considered an expert tending towards either the prosecution or the defense. Dr. Resnick testified for the prosecution in the case of Jeffrey Dahmer, stating that Dahmer understood that what he was doing was wrong. Dr. Resnick has specialized in cases of infanticide, and has held the view that a parent's feelings of guilt do not necessarily negate their ability to plead insanity. He has stated that many depressed people feel extremely guilty about a number of things, but their guilt is within their delusional thought system, and therefore can be considered part of insanity. For instance, he noted that Andrea Yates was expecting and even desired punishment for killing her children yet he said that she felt this way because she thought that God felt that she should be punished for being a bad mother, which was partially what had led her to kill her children in the first place. Therefore, although she showed some understanding of the guilt associated with her act, Resnick argued that this guilt was part of her delusions and therefore, she could be considered criminally insane. For this opinion and others, Resnick was widely regarded as much more lenient on the criminally insane than Dr. Dietz.

Dorothy Otnow Lewis has been another frequently cited participant in the insanity defense. She has conducted research about violence and has offered her expert opinion in a number of cases involving death-row inmates. Some of her research has dealt with the issue of why only a small fraction of insane people are violent. Dr. Lewis has come to the conclusion that two factors can lead to a mentally unstable person becoming violent. They are the combination of a history of early ongoing abuse coupled with some kind of brain dysfunction and psychotic symptoms, particularly paranoia. She has found that the more serious the neurological and psychotic symptomatology, if the individual has been abused, the more violent the individual seems to be. As a result of her research, Lewis has said that it is important for psychiatry to inform lawyers and the judicial system about the effects of psychiatric, neurological, and experiential factors, and about the fact that these factors have a profound influence on individual choice and a person's level of control. She has often been a witness for the defense in high-profile cases, including the serial killer Arthur Shawcross. She claimed that the combination of mental illness and abuse can be enough to impair people's memories or make them dissociative, and therefore they could not have understood what they were doing at the time of the crime. Her arguments oftentimes boil down to a person's ability to understand their actions at the time of the crime, which negates their ability to have understood that what they were doing was right or wrong.

What is the argument for the view of the myth of mental illness?

In 1960, Thomas Szasz first introduced the idea of the myth of mental illness. In an article with that title, Szasz, a psychiatrist and professor, described how the recent trends in psychology had been to link mental illness with some sort of defect within the brain, an effort to point to a biological basis for all mental disorders. Szasz attributed this trend to the discovery of syphilis of the brain and its subsequent effect on behavior, and to the influence of toxins on the brain and on behavior. As a result of these discoveries, he argued, people began to look for biological reasons for abnormal psychology, or mental illnesses.

Szasz continued by arguing that mental illnesses were considered the same as all other diseases, diseases of the body. The only difference between these two types of illnesses, mental and bodily, was that mental illnesses manifested themselves as mental symptoms that then affect behavior, while body illnesses manifest themselves as symptoms associated with a body part. Szasz, however, saw this logic as completely wrong. He said that it was illogical to attribute changes in behavior or thinking to a physical problem within the central nervous system. He believed that a lesion on the brain could cause a defect in a person's visual field, but it could not cause an overarching change in that person's entire outlook on the world by causing delusional thoughts. Simply put, Szasz argued that mental symptoms, such as the false belief systems attributed to schizophrenia, could not be linked with a physical impairment in the central nervous system.

Furthermore, Szasz argued that mental symptoms were not at all the same as physical symptoms. Mental symptoms were only diagnosed when a person's thoughts or beliefs were different from those of the observer or society. For instance, if someone claimed to be Henry VIII, this would only be considered a mental symptom, or disordered, if the observer judged that the person was not actually Henry VIII. Therefore, determining whether or not a belief or behavior was a mental symptom involved some type of judgment about whether that symptom aligned with the general beliefs or behaviors of society. This, he said, was the main difference between mental and physical illness. While physical symptoms were tied to an anatomical or genetic basis that could be observed, mental symptoms were simply tied to a judgment in comparisons with norms. Therefore, Szasz argued, mental illness was simply a metaphor for abnormal behavior in society. Mentally ill individuals were merely those whose behaviors had been deemed bad in relation to other people around them. Thus, Szasz found that mental illness was only a myth, and that the classification of misbehavior as illness dangerously provided justification for the state and society to control behavior under the guise of providing medical treatment.

What is meant by the abuse excuse?

The term abuse excuse can refer to two different phenomena. In the first, it refers to the tactic used by criminal defendants in which they explain their violent actions as retaliation for or defense against abuse. Typically, the victims in these cases are the individuals who had supposedly perpetrated or were going to perpetrate the abuse. The abuse excuse has been used to describe the defenses launched by the Menendez brothers who killed their parents and claimed that they did so after years of abuse, and by Lorena Bobbitt who cut off her husband's penis and argued in court that he had abused her.

In its other use, as a term coined by Harvard Law Professor Alan Dershowitz, it refers to the myriad excuses which have been offered by defendants either to show that they are not guilty by reason of insanity or as mitigating factors to reduce their charged crime to a lesser one. They may include the actual abuse noted above as well as such matters as racial taunting, poor neighborhood, illiteracy, inadequate education, ineffective parenting, a hostile society, and so on.

What predictions are made concerning the future of the insanity defense?

There are several schools of thought regarding what should be done about the insanity defense. One reform that has spread across one-quarter of the states is the creation of a verdict of guilty but mentally ill. The motivation behind this change was that it would supposedly decrease the number insanity acquittals. The actual results, however, have been mixed, and this verdict option has had the disadvantage of making insanity only more complicated for jurors to understand and evaluate. Because of these problems, it seems unlikely that the option of guilty but mentally ill will continue to be a strongly advocated reform of the insanity defense.

The most extreme proposed reform has been the abolition of the defense altogether. The main arguments for abolition have been that juries are unable to reach an unbiased decision on insanity, that the defense has encouraged psychological experts to present their opinions as scientific fact, and that because society views most criminals to be crazy anyway, it does not make sense to label some defendants as legally insane. The general public also would prefer to do away with the insanity defense.

Much of the insanity defense reformation was enacted in the immediate aftermath of the John Hinckley, Jr. case, which caused a massive public outcry over the insanity defense. After these reforms were passed and the rage over the Hinckley verdict gradually subsided, the public again lost interest in the insanity plea. Although the public disapproves of the defense, its general ambivalence about the matter probably indicates that no drastic reforms will take place in the near future. If, however, another Hinckley-level hysteria were to erupt over an insanity acquittal in the future, if, for example, Osama bin Laden were found not guilty by reason of insanity, it is likely that the insanity defense would be seriously reformed or even abolished.

How has the insanity defense been portrayed in film?

One of the most common portrayals of the insanity defense in popular film is of the defendant who uses an insanity plea to try to get out of a harsh punishment, oftentimes for murder. This portrayal has led to the popular belief in society that people who gain a verdict of not guilty by reason of insanity are literally getting away with murder, and that the defense itself is a fraud or a tool for criminals. Additionally, in a theatrical twist, the audience is sometimes made to feel sympathetic towards the defendant because the plot has been formulated to justify their crime somehow. This situation nevertheless perpetuates the devaluation of the insanity defense in society because the audience understands that the defendant, although morally justified in his or her criminal actions, is not actually insane.

While not about the insanity defense itself, perhaps one of the most famous movies which showed this sympathy for the criminal was *One Flew over the Cuckoo's Nest*, with Jack Nicholson. Nicholson played a criminal who faked mental illness in order to be transferred from prison to a mental institution where he hoped to receive better treatment and to be released in a shorter amount of time. Once in the institution, he realized that there was no limit to how long he might be kept in custody, even if that term were longer than the prison term he would have served in prison. And because the film generated sympathy for him, his antisocial behavior became heroic in a way and the head nurse became the villain who in her own way helped bring about his death.

Another common portrayal is of the defendant who assumes a kind of heroic status by faking mental illness and thereby being found not guilty by reason of insanity. In 1996's *Primal Fear*, Edward Norton won a Golden Globe award for his portrayal of a defendant who won an insanity acquittal by faking multiple personality disorder so convincingly that even his lawyer believed his act. Norton's character killed a priest who brutally abused him and other young members of the church community. Therefore, while the audience sympathized with Norton's character and came away with the feeling that his act of murder was justified, the film still left them with the impression that insanity is an easy condition to fake. Another movie that invoked sympathy for the defendant was 1996's *A Time to Kill*. In this film, a southern defendant was found innocent of murdering two Ku Klux Klan members who raped his young daughter. The jury believed the defendant was operating under diminished capacity caused by the strain of seeing his daughter suffer. Based on these films, and many other popular movies, the audience is often left feeling that diminished capacity and the insanity defense are only reasonable in cases where murder or any other crime was justifiable, which leads people to mistakenly associate justifiable crime with crimes caused by insanity.

Films most commonly portray the controversial cases involving the insanity defense, those in which a criminal tries to fake or those in which the insanity defense is a tool for juries to release defendants who committed justifiable crimes. Films that follow these themes only help to perpetuate the idea that criminals who are found not guilty by reason of insanity are in effect getting away with murder, which makes jurors and society alike much more skeptical of insanity pleas in general.

How has the insanity defense been portrayed in fiction?

As one might expect, portrayals of the insanity defense in fiction tend to be highly dramatized, with little relation to the typical use of the defense in real life. Naturally, authors choose extreme examples of insanity because they make for a more interesting story, but the unrealistic representations seen in fiction may be partly responsible for the public's misconception of insanity defense cases.

Shane Stevens's bestselling novel *By Reason of Insanity* depicted a twenty-five year old man who escaped from a mental asylum and immediately commenced a serial killing spree. The story was written from the murderer's point of view, so the reader knew his disturbed, psychopathic thoughts and experienced each grisly, detailed murder first-hand.

G.H. Ephron's *Delusion: A Mystery* followed psychiatric expert Peter Zaks, who often testified in court and evaluated defendants. Zaks was assigned to examine a man accused of stabbing his own wife and suspected of being mentally ill with paranoia. The man was temporarily placed in a psychiatric facility, the same facility where the man who murdered Zaks' wife currently resided. Zaks soon found himself the object of a mysterious stalker and was left to unravel the mystery. Clearly, the strange coincidences and consequences that followed in this novel were beyond the realm of possibility in typical insanity defense cases.

The public ought to realize that examples of insane defendants in fiction are simply that, fiction. However, repeated exposure to extreme examples of the insanity defense leads people to assume that those are the typical cases. Most likely, this is an explanation for why most people believe that the majority of murder trials feature insanity pleas.

How has the insanity defense been portrayed in non-fiction?

Non-fiction has produced a wide variety of portrayals of the insanity defense. About the only common sentiment is that the insanity defense, as it stands now, is far from perfect. As a consequence, some writers back the abolition of the insanity defense, while others advocate tweaking it in order to meet their conceptions of justice. Much non-fiction reflects the sentiments of the broader population. Just as there was wide outrage with the insanity defense after the John Hinckley, Jr. acquittal, much non-fiction expresses similar displeasure with the insanity defense. Many case studies of those who used the insanity defense are attempts to get inside the mind of individuals who committed acts that the average reader would find disturbing.

6

Controversies Surrounding Pre- and Post-Conviction Commitment

What happens to individuals found not guilty by reason of insanity?

Depending on the state, there are two routes that an individual acquitted for insanity might take. In some states, the individual may be automatically committed to a mental institution. After treatment, the judge would later decide whether it was safe enough to release the individual to his community. One study showed that the average period of confinement in a mental institution for defendants found not guilty by reason of insanity in New York was three years, and was increasing. The period of confinement was also shown to lengthen with the degree of seriousness of the crime.

In other states, the individual may be released to his community after a brief hospital stay, while continuing to receive monitoring by mental health professionals and outpatient care. This option is termed conditional release and is the mental health equivalent to parole. Under the conditional release system, a four-state study showed that sixty percent of five-hundred twenty-nine insanity defendants were conditionally released within five years of being institutionalized. The median length of confinement for released violent offenders was approximately three and a half years, and one and a third years for minor offenders.

A common belief of the public is that individuals found not guilty by reason of insanity are quickly released, as in the case of Lorena Bobbitt, who was released after only several weeks in a mental institution. At times, however, insanity defendants have been confined more frequently, and for longer periods of time, than non-insanity defendants who have committed similar crimes. For example,

Michael Jones was acquitted under a plea of not guilty by reason of insanity for shoplifting but was institutionalized for decades longer than the maximum possible prison sentence for the offense. One explanation for this phenomenon is that under the commitment system, the standards by which the judge decides whether the individual should be released are civil and may be stricter than those for a prison inmate. Though an individual can remain committed to a mental institution only so long as he or she is considered mentally ill and dangerous, the circumstances which brought an individual to the attention of the police in a misdemeanor case may replay themselves sufficiently to insure longer term commitment to a mental hospital.

What shifts have taken place in the placement of individuals found not guilty by reason of insanity?

Before mental health laws were revised, individuals found not guilty by reason of insanity were often given what amounted to life sentences in hospitals specially designated for the criminally insane. Because of this result, only the most serious charges saw a plea of not guilty by reason of insanity. While the finding of insanity might satisfy the moral view of its advocates, the conditions in the special hospitals were often as bad as or worse than those in prisons to which guilty individuals were sent. With the revision of civil commitment laws and with the conceptualizing of the insanity acquittee as the equivalent of a civil committee, changes took place in the placement of individuals found not guilty by reason of insanity and in their potential length of confinement.

Two primary options replaced lengthy inevitable commitments. One remained automatic commitment to a mental institution after an evaluation following a verdict of not guilty by reason of insanity, with periodic reviews as to whether the committed individual remained dangerous by reason of mental illness. The other involved conditional release of the individual into society with requirements for continuing care for the mental illness. While there were few complaints from the public over the harsh earlier consequences for insanity acquittees, many more complaints surfaced with these changes in the system.

One objection has been that criminals have faked mental illness while pleading not guilty by reason of insanity to avoid serving their sentence in prison. Then, once they have been committed to a mental institution, they have feigned recovery, and have been released. Although this complaint may be valid, the public has overestimated the actual number of instances where this strategy has been successful.

Another source of complaint have been studies that show that recidivism rates of those committed to mental institutions through the insanity plea are similar to those of average criminals placed in prison. For instance, a study showed that half of all insanity defendants committed to the Oklahoma state forensic hospital in a five-year period were hospitalized or arrested again within two years of being released from mental facilities. Studies comparing the status of insanity acquittees who were legally discharged and those who escaped also show conflicting results about whether hospitalization benefited the individuals themselves.

One of the suggested reforms has been to have those acquitted by reason of insanity remain in institutions until they showed no symptoms of mental illness. A criticism of it has been that while it may indeed increase the safety of society, it would jeopardize the rights of the wider institutionalized population because of a few violent individuals. Another suggested reform has been to give those found not guilty by reason of insanity a combination of prison and hospital time. As is clear, this type of sentence has been associated with the verdict of guilty but mentally ill, and has placed the defendant first in a mental hospital, and then in a prison to serve the remainder of his sentence.

Should a person found not guilty by reason of insanity be automatically committed to a mental hospital?

Presumably, the individual is found not guilty by reason of insanity because he was insane at the time of his offense. Thus, the expected reaction would be that these individuals belong in mental hospitals, at least initially, especially if the individual is a danger to himself or herself. After all, it seems inhumane to confine the mentally ill in a hostile prison environment that is not equipped to tend to their needs adequately. Yet there may be some lapse between the offense and the verdict and the individual may have recovered in that time. Based on this possibility, some argue that automatic commitment is not warranted.

While it seems clear that most insanity defendants should first be treated in a mental hospital, their status should be regularly reviewed in order to prevent either premature release or excess confinement. Current practice seems to show that laws indeed require monitoring by judges and mental health professionals.

Why would someone found not guilty by reason of insanity be evaluated as if he were simply a civilly committed individual?

Both the defendant who is found not guilty by reason of mental illness of a violent act and the individual who is found to be dangerous by reason of mental illness share two factors: Each has been judged to be mentally ill and each has been found to be dangerous. As a consequence, both should be evaluated for commitment to a mental hospital in a similar fashion. Yet, the fact that the defendant in the criminal proceeding has actually committed a dangerous act ought, some argue, to make his bid for freedom less easily accepted. But for his mental illness he would be guilty as charged and however serious the offense was, the fact of his having done it means that he is different from the individual who has not faced a criminal proceeding but who is deprived of freedom nonetheless. Many critics of the insanity defense have feared that individuals who are found not guilty by reason of insanity will be quickly treated and then released back into society, as civilly committed individuals often are. Short hospital stays have become the norm for philosophical, psychological, and economic reasons. The fact that insanity defendants are indeterminately committed ought, these critics have said, to mean that they will not be so readily released. Advocates of the system, however, say that many studies have shown that because of their civil commitment status, most individuals who are acquitted by reason of insanity spend equal or longer periods of time in mental institutions than defendants found guilty of similar crimes and sent to prison.

For civil commitment generally, proof must be given through clear and convincing evidence that a person is both mentally ill and dangerous. After a trial and a verdict of not guilty by reason of insanity, both of these prerequisites appear to have been met for the defendant. Therefore, advocates of the present system have said, the trial has proven that the person committed a criminal act and thus may pose a threat to society or themselves, and in addition, a jury has deemed the person mentally ill. Consequently, they conclude, an insanity acquittal in itself meets the standards of civil commitment.

If the best predictor of future behavior is past behavior, why would not a person found not guilty of

a very serious act due to insanity be committed for a long time as a precaution?

In the case of a person found not guilty by reason of insanity, many states follow a procedure of automatically committing that person to a mental institution. That person can then only be released when a judge is convinced that he can be released safely. Therefore, the procedure places a focus on the evaluation and progress of a defendant who has become a patient. A person's future progress cannot be determined at the time of his commitment, and as a result, it would be impossible to sentence a person to a certain length of commitment, because this would assume that the judge could predetermine the minimum length of time the patient would need to get better.

Furthermore, the insanity defense operates on the assumption that people were not aware of their actions at the time of their crime, or that mental illness prevented them from understanding that their actions were wrong. This assumes that their past behavior was influenced by a mental illness. When a defendant who is found not guilty by reason of insanity is committed to a mental institution, the purpose is to treat them for their mental illness. If patients are not released until they are satisfactorily treated for that illness, then their behavior would no longer be under the influence of that illness. As a consequence, after release, their future behavior should not actually resemble past criminal behavior because the cause of that behavior, the mental illness, has ideally been eliminated or mitigated.

Under this system of treatment, it cannot then be assumed that past behavior would be a predictor of future behavior, and the notion that there should be minimum lengths of commitment falls within punitive ideals, not rehabilitative ideals, which are fundamental to procedures of commitment and treatment of those found not guilty by reason of insanity.

As critics note, the system is not flawless, however, and in order to protect against the possibility of releasing back into society a person who is not fully treated and dangerous, some states have instituted a procedure known as conditional release. In this procedure, people found not guilty by reason of insanity are placed in confinement until a judge or mental health professional deems their illness adequately treated. Mental health professionals continue to monitor the released patients for a period of time in order to ensure their safety to the community and to themselves.

What should the consequence be for an individual who has been advised to take antipsychotic medication, who has taken it and then discontinued it, and subsequently commits a serious act?

Adherence to antipsychotic medication and other medications for mental illnesses is very difficult to ensure. Many of the medications have side effects that patients may consider worse than the symptoms of their illness. Therefore, it is common that mentally ill people who commit crimes had been prescribed medication for their illness, but were not taking it at the time of their crime. Many people question an individual's personal responsibility for choosing not to adhere to their prescription, and thus their responsibility for the subsequent crime. They ask whether deliberate discontinuation of medication ought to preclude invocation of the insanity defense much as deliberate ingestion of alcohol or other substances would preclude use of that defense.

In the case of Andrea Yates, she had been placed on medications multiple times and had been put in mental facilities months before she murdered her children. She discontinued her medications, and was found guilty of murder. It remains unclear to what degree the verdict hinged on her choice to discontinue medication. In fact, many psychiatric experts and jurors supported their finding of her guilty by pointing to the fact that Yates had an understanding that what she was doing was wrong, not that she should have been held responsible for ending her medication.

If a person is placed on medication, particularly antipsychotic medication, it is highly likely that they required some sort of aid in choosing to receive treatment and in gaining a prescription. Oftentimes aid included physicians, mental health practitioners, and family members. If a patient needed help gaining treatment based on their mental illness, then it is understandable say defense attorneys and advocates for the mentally ill that they would also need help adhering to the treatment, and therefore should not be held responsible solely because they stop medication which would ameliorate their mental illness.

In the case of Andrea Yates, her husband had brought her to mental health practitioners and she had at least two doctors who prescribed her powerful antidepressants. When she discontinued her medication, and subsequently murdered her children, many people wondered why her husband had not sought out more treatment for her or requested that she receive more medications, which had seemed to help her in the past. Also, many people questioned why her doctor had released her so quickly from the mental health institution in prior months when she and her husband had voluntarily admitted her, and why one of her doctors had himself been unclear about her medication.

Attorneys and advocates conclude that people who are ill enough to be placed on medication, particularly antipsychotic medication, cannot be held solely responsible for their own adherence. In addition, when determining criminal responsibility, jurors have not officially considered adherence to medication, though some have argued they should. Responsibility is instead determined by a person's mental state and awareness at the time of the crime, on or off medication.

Should a person who was sane at the time of the crime and sentenced to death but who becomes insane be executed while insane?

A variety of arguments have been offered regarding this question. Most of them revolve around the reasoning behind capital punishment. Many proponents of capital punishment claim that it is an effort both at deterrence for others and at just desserts for the criminal. A sentence of death, they argue, sets a precedent for similar crimes, which theoretically should prevent their repeated occurrence while at the same time meting out suitable punishment in the case. With such a perspective, the answer to the question is an obvious one. The convict's mental state should have little to no bearing on the decision to execute. The state is setting an example by executing the criminal.

On the other hand, opponents argue that the purpose of capital punishment is to seek retribution from an individual who has violated a societal code. If the individual is mentality incapacitated to the extent that he or she does not understand the punishment, it is scarcely a punishment at all. In such a case, they argue, capital punishment does not meet its designed end and ought not to be imposed until the individual has regained his sanity.

Should a lawyer be able to prevent forcing a psychotic client to take medication in order to

preserve, for the jury, the state of mind in which that person committed acts for which he is charged?

Whatever their position on this question, most would agree that the justice system has an interest in proceeding with a case, in having a defendant able to assist his attorney, and in having an attorney vigorously representing his client.

All would agree that a lawyer has the responsibility of acting in his client's best interest. If a defendant's lawyer believes that the defendant will be better served by avoiding a conviction than being treated for psychosis, then some would argue that it is the lawyer's right to make that decision. They argue that if a judge believes that such behavior would not be in the defendant's best interests, the judge should not simply make the client take medication. Instead, the judge should find that the lawyer is not acting in the client's best interest and dismiss the lawyer from the case entirely.

Others would argue, however, that a defendant must be deemed mentally fit to stand trial, for the defendant must be able to assist his lawyer fully in the case. Thus, the defendant must know what is in his or her own best interest, and if the defendant is psychotic how is he to know this. This argument would hold that instead of forcing the client to not take medication, the lawyer should file for a reexamination of his client on the grounds that he does not deem the client to be competent enough to understand what is in his best interest.

Finally, some would argue for a middle ground that would force the defendant to take enough medicine to become less psychotic at which time he could then make the rational decision as to whether to continue taking medication and remaining free from psychosis or stopping the medication and becoming psychotic again.

7

Roles of Psychologists and Lawyers in Defining, Implementing, and Questioning the Insanity Defense

What is the reasoning behind allowing psychoforensic expert witnesses to testify?

In court cases, adequately qualified expert witnesses can testify if their topic is beyond the scope of general knowledge for a layperson, if their evidence is reliable and accepted by the scientific community, and if their testimony is more likely to be important than prejudicial. Expert witnesses provide the only instance where inferences and opinions are deemed admissible as evidence in a court of law. Because psychologists and psychiatrists fit these criteria, their testimony is commonly admitted as evidence for trials in which the defendant has offered an insanity plea.

In the case of an insanity plea, psychoforensic experts are necessary to provide the jurors with a clear and detailed description of what mental disorders provide the basis for a verdict of not guilty by reason of insanity. Such testimony allows jurors to make informed decisions regarding how a certain alleged crime should or should not be punished. Without psychological experts, advocates argue, many defendants who truly were insane would likely receive no consideration in a court of law. Psychological experts, they say, allow for a full consideration of mens rea, rather than a more simple conception of crime.

What are the reasons for not allowing psychoforensic experts to testify?

Critics argue that the prevalence of psychological experts in criminal cases today serves only to overwhelm jurors. When both sides offer similarly qualified experts who present opposing evidence and conclusions, this may provide more confusion than clarity. Further, critics maintain that significant financial rewards mean that anyone can find a psychoforensic expert to testify to anything. In a scathing critique of their participation and testimony, one critic has termed these experts whores of the court.

Other critics have contended that the comparative youth of psychology as a field of study means that psychological experts testify according to theories that are too new and untested and controversial to be valuable in a court of law. Further they say that because psychology is not an exact science, psychological experts can often offer only probabilities and likelihood. In a forum in which conclusions have to be drawn beyond a reasonable doubt, such inexactitude is not entirely useful.

Finally, research psychologists may be prevented from testifying in a particular case because they have not examined the defendant in question. In seeking to present only the results of their research, they have at times been excluded from testifying. Judges may conclude that their findings do not add to what the jury already knows or to what cross-examination by attorneys can bring out.

How can the problems with psychoforensic expert witnesses be addressed?

One way suggested to improve on the credibility of psychological expert witnesses, aside from continuously collecting new data in the field, is to create a central forensic psychology service that offers advice to the courts in an objective format. This would rid the current practice of accusations of biased interpretations that inevitably follow payment to an expert. As an alternative, some have suggested that lawyers could be trained in psychology. In this way, jurors would not be presented with supposed objective analysis. The testimony would be slanted, but that would be no secret.

Are some experts known as pro-prosecution experts and others known as pro-defense experts?

Most psychological experts are hired either by the defense to support the case that the defendant should be found not guilty by reason of insanity, or by the prosecution to testify that the defendant should be legally accountable for the crime of which he is accused. Generally, in an insanity defense trial, experts for both the defense and the prosecution present information about mental illness and their own diagnoses of the defendant.

Much controversy has resulted from using psychological experts in court who have been hired by one side or the other, for these witnesses do not seem to be neutral or unbiased. Since they are hired by one side, many believe that the expert will slant the information to help the side that hands him a paycheck. The criticism has some basis in the fact that quite often psychological experts from the defense and from the prosecution have competing diagnoses of the defendant, and that quite often the same experts always appear for the defense or for the prosecution.

Most agree that experts who provide testimony biased toward their side may have a large impact on the outcome of the trial. Since the jury presumably does not know much about mental illness, they are likely to be both skeptical and heavily influenced by what they hear. If they perceive the experts to be biased, jurors may completely disregard any psychological information even if it is relevant. At the same time, they may not realize whether an expert is bringing in irrelevant or false information, and they may also be heavily influenced by this. Experts have at times stretched clinical definitions to fit the defense or the prosecution argument. The fact that psychological experts generally cannot agree about the defendant reflects the idea that the psychological profession itself can never really come to a consensus. The lack of hard, definite science tends to devalue the profession as well as the testimony of the experts.

Furthermore, it is not always the defendant and his actions that cause the contradictory opinions. Sometimes the experts themselves have strong views about criminal justice and mental health and responsibility for their own personal or philosophical or clinical reasons, and this can affect their testimony and outlook on a case. Some psychiatric experts are known to be pro-prosecution as has been Dr. Park Elliott Dietz, while some experts are known as pro-defense as has been Dr. Dorothy Otnow Lewis. Further, experts might identify only with those from an economic and social background similar to their own, or fail to acknowledge fully the problems of defendants who come from very different backgrounds.

Experts may be quietly or unknowingly biased towards poorer individuals or those of a different ethnicity. Since experts are paid witnesses some defendants may not be able to hire them, and they may lose the only persons who could testify about their mental illness.

Do experts ever defy expectations?

Psychological experts are hired by either the defense or the prosecution to testify. When trying to locate a psychological expert, defense lawyers generally try to find someone who will support their argument in favor of the defendant. Similarly, the prosecutors generally attempt to locate an expert who will take an opposing viewpoint and be persuasive.

Despite being hired by a particular counsel, experts will occasionally surprise the court by testifying against what the lawyer who hired him is arguing. A prosecution expert may believe that the defendant is not responsible for his actions at the time of the crime, and his testimony may support the defense's case instead of the prosecution's. On the other hand, a defense expert may feel that after having examined the defendant, he believes that the defendant showed no signs of mental illness or loss of impulse control. Instead of supporting the defense, he may testify that there is little evidence to show that the defendant should be found not guilty by reason of insanity.

And sometimes, because a lawyer is arguing two contradictory theories about a case, an expert witness who will assist in one of the arguments may not in the other. In the case of Richard Herrin who viciously killed a woman he had been dating, the prosecution hired a well-known psychiatrist to help defeat the insanity defense, which he did. But the psychiatrist also testified that Herrin suffered from a psychotic mental disorder which aided the defense's claim that he should only be found guilty of manslaughter not of murder. In that sense, the expert defied the prosecutor's expectations by only helping with half the arguments the prosecutor made.

Why does the public assume that the court-appointed psychoforensic expert will be the most unbiased and accurate?

The public in general is not well-informed about mental illness or the insanity defense and rarely is sympathetic toward defendants who invoke the defense.

Many see the insanity defense as an attempt to escape punishment for their criminal behavior. Psychological experts are hired by both sides to try to explain the terms of not guilty by reason of insanity from their perspectives and how the defendant does or does not meet these conditions. Other experts are hired by the court itself. Since psychological experts often disagree about the defendant, and because they are generally paid by the side they support, the public has become even more skeptical of psychologists and expert testimony. The public often views these experts as paid to provide biased conclusions that will help their side.

This leaves only the court-appointed independent psychological expert who, though paid, appears to be neutral and to be interested in objectively assessing the defendant and the situation. Naturally the public assumes such an expert will be the most unbiased and accurate. As a consequence of this it is always instructive to be reminded that such independence may not assure accurate evaluation and testimony. In the Frontline documentary Mind of a Murderer the court-appointed psychiatrist concluded that the defendant Kenneth Bianchi suffered from multiple personality disorder and therefore was neither competent to stand trial nor criminally responsible, and so reported to the court. Near the end of the documentary he had left private practice and begun working in a prison. Sitting on a rock outside the prison he declared that he was surprised to learn that defendants in criminal settings, as in prison, often lie to psychiatrists and that he now found it impossible to tell who was telling the truth and who was lying. Meanwhile the judge in the case concluded that the psychiatrist hired by the prosecution was most accurate in evaluating the defendant and in testifying because of the methods he had used to understand the mental state of the defendant. While it might appear that court-appointed experts have the advantage of greater freedom to conclude independently, this documentary reminded everyone that the nature and quality of the evaluation might count for more than the source of the funds paid to the expert.

Should forensic psychologists and psychiatrists testify as to insanity or only as to mental illness?

Both the American Psychiatric Association and the American Psychological Association conclude that forensic psychiatrists and psychologists should only testify as to mental illness, and not as to ultimate opinions about insanity or responsibility, or whether or not a defendant fits various legal tests for insanity. The primary objection to psychologists and psychiatrists testifying in such manners is that they are primary psychological experts, not legal experts. Thus, they should testify only in their realm of expertise, the defendant's mental state, and not be forced to make leaps of logic into the realm of the law. In addition, many critics believe that only jurors, not expert witnesses, should be answering the question about a defendant's criminal responsibility for an act.

Therefore, since mental illness and insanity are not equivalent, as they are concepts from the medical and psychological field and the legal field respectively, it makes sense to leave the mental illness testimony to the psychological and psychiatric experts and the insanity testimony to the legal experts. Further, when expert witnesses for the defense and prosecution only testify on psychological grounds about mental illness, their reports are much more likely to agree, or at least be compatible.

In 1984, the U.S. Congress enacted the Insanity Defense Reform Act. As part of its provisions, it prohibited expert witnesses from giving ultimate opinions or inferences about the insanity of the defendant at the time of the crime.

To what extent should a psychoforensic expert be a detective?

The job of the psychological expert is to evaluate the defendant and attempt to make an accurate diagnosis of his mental illness. In order to do this effectively, the expert must try to delve into both the defendant's past and present life. He must postdict what type of mental state the defendant could have been in at the time of the crime and whether or not the defendant knew what he was doing or could control himself. To do this, some legal and mental health professionals argue that he needs more material than the responses of the defendant to interviews and various psychological tests. They say that psychoforensic experts must act like detectives to gain ancillary materials, to check the accuracy of statements, and to explore fully the mental state and behavior of the person they are evaluating. In Mind of a Murderer for example, the judge accepted the conclusions of a psychiatrist hired by the prosecution because of his methods: He read all the police reports, he sought out individuals who had had contact with the defendant, he examined other bits of evidence, he set traps for the defendant to attempt to discover whether he was being truthful or not, and, most significantly, he approached his task with the awareness that the defendant had a motivation to lie and might do so successfully unless found out. The other experts had thought their detective work involved only interviewing the defendant, examining the results of some psychological tests, and comparing that defendant clinically with other individuals they had seen. They did not see the need for all the ancillary information. This, the judge concluded, was their mistake. He found the more complete detective work by the psychiatrist hired by the prosecution to be more persuasive.

Can psychologists and psychiatrists tell accurately who is malingering or faking?

This question addresses one of the public's main concerns about the insanity defense. People worry that defendants will malinger, intentionally producing false or grossly exaggerated physical or psychological symptoms in order to escape conviction for a crime. They are concerned that psychologists and psychiatrists will be deceived by patients who are faking mental illness.

This seems to be a valid concern, as detecting malingering is not an exact science, and there are many challenges a professional faces in detecting falsehood, even with patients who have self-referred and are not facing court action. With those self-referred patients, psychologists and psychiatrists have a much harder time detecting malingering compared with other kinds of medical specialists because they rely much more on the accurate self-report of internal mental states of their patients. They are also often hesitant to make a diagnosis of malingering as it represents a direct accusation that the person being examined is a liar. They are hesitant to make such an accusation because they realize that they are not human lie-detectors and such an accusation may damage or destroy their relationship with the patient. Clinicians want to help and treat patients, not create adversaries. In addition, malingering can be hard to detect because a person undergoing evaluation may have a legitimate mental illness but may still malinger. In a court setting these problems are compounded, for there a patient with a mental disorder might try to fake a more serious disorder in order to increase his probability of being found not guilty by reason of insanity. In such settings it can be very difficult to tease out which symptoms are real and which are not.

Studies have confirmed that the issue of detecting malingering should be a concern. Currently, no studies have been able to demonstrate that psychologists and psychiatrists can consistently and accurately detect malingering based solely on an unstructured clinical interview. In fact, psychiatrists' ability to detect lies in strangers is only slightly better than chance, and clinician's confidence in their ability to detect faking is completely unrelated to their actual ability.

In addition, individual case studies attest to the potential difficulty in determining whether a defendant is malingering. One of the most notable cases was the suspected Hillside Strangler, Kenneth Bianchi, who raped and killed young women in California and then in Washington state. Bianchi managed to convince several psychiatric experts that he had multiple personality disorder and that his uncontrollable alternate personality was responsible for the rapes and murders. However, an expert witness hired by the prosecution was able to convince the judge that Bianchi was faking hypnosis and multiple personality disorder. That expert, a professor of psychiatry at the University of Pennsylvania, had done extensive research on faking hypnosis, and as an expert in the field, he expressed serious doubts about the claims of most psychological or psychiatric professionals that they could detect fakery without extensive experience.

However, even though it appears that detecting malingering is a difficult task which most clinicians seem not qualified to do well, there are some steps that can be taken to increase the chances of successful detection. Among them, psychologists and psychiatrists should limit their use of leading questions or symptom checklists which can help even the uninformed malinger and qualify for a diagnosis by merely affirming the clinician's suspicions. Instead, they should use open-ended questions or if a person is suspected of possible malingering, leading questions designed to mislead the patient. As an example, a clinician might ask a leading question that emphasized a different illness or a symptom that a patient should not have. Evaluators should also be familiar with some of the more standard errors that people make when trying to fake a mental illness including these: Malingerers often are more eager to call attention to their illnesses, try to take control of their interview through bizarre or intimidating behavior, and sometimes accuse clinicians of thinking that they are faking. In the end, the two most important aids for evaluators trying to detect malingering are a detailed knowledge of the symptoms of various diseases and a detailed knowledge of all circumstances concerning the defendant. Successful detection often depends on the psychologist or psychiatrist having a greater knowledge of the disease and its symptoms than the person who is trying to fake it, and more information about the individual than he expects him to have.

How successful are psychologists and psychiatrists in predicting future dangerousness?

Studies indicate that psychologists have generally performed very badly in predicting future dangerousness based on subjective clinical evaluations. Some research showed accuracy levels of prediction in the range of twenty to thirty-five percent for forensic specialists. One study compared the abilities of forensic psychiatrists with the abilities of high-school teachers in determining the likelihood of future offenses. Members of each group were given file information about offenders who had been released three years earlier and asked to rate the likeliness of offenses after release. Psychiatrists were unable to demonstrate any superiority in predictive abilities and tended to disagree more about their predictions as a group. In addition, research found that forensic specialists often over-predicted the likelihood of future violence.

One of the biggest problems facing psychoforensic experts was the lack of standard and reliable tests or tools to help predict future dangerousness. Because violence is statistically very uncommon in society, it is difficult to predict violence in individuals in the general population. However, in the late 1990s, two types of assessment devices were developed to predict future dangerousness amongst people in more violent subsets of the population, such as those who are incarcerated or in maximum-security hospitals.

The first kind of device was a structured checklist, which was designed to assess relevant factors that had been shown to correlate with recidivism in empirical studies or that were extremely intuitively significant. However, these structural devices have been criticized because some of their factors are subjective and do not present probabilistic estimates of recidivism.

The second kind of device used statistical or actuarial techniques. These devices have been praised for being consistently easy to score and for being validated by empirical evidence. In other words, actual recidivism seems to more or less match predicted recidivism. One of the earliest and most versatile of these devices was the Hare Psychopathy Checklist Revised. However, even though this method was considered generally accepted and reliable in the field of forensic psychology, it was not without its critics. One argued that given its high rates of false positives, the checklist should never be used in the forensic or clinical setting if decisions involving life and liberty were at stake and claimed that while it might be the strongest tool available, it was by no means a reliable device for predicting future dangerousness.

What strategic and what tactical moves do prosecutors use in insanity defense cases?

The prosecution may try to employ several strategies to argue that the defendant should be held responsible for a crime. When the burden of proof is on the defense to prove that the defendant was not sane at the time of the crime, the prosecution may try to find evidence that suggests the defendant was sane at the time. This may include showing that the defendant made a well thought out plan or that he took logical steps to avoid being deterred from or detected during the crime he was committing. It may also include finding a distinct and logical motive for the crime, which would also rule out the irresistible impulse theory. Even if the defendant has had a history of mental illness or if experts testify that the defendant suffered from mental problems, this alone would not be enough to satisfy the requirements for a finding of not guilty by reason of insanity.

Another important tactic that the prosecution may use is to discredit defense experts, as was successfully done by the prosecutor in the Ralph Tortorici case. By diminishing the professional credibility of the experts, the prosecution may cast doubt on the significance of the defendant's mental illness. The prosecution may then investigate the defendant's background and childhood in order to find a reasonable cause for the crime, such as abuse or retaliation. By giving alternate explanations, the prosecution may try to downplay the importance of the defendant's illness in favor of playing up exaggerated responses to conditions that many people have experienced. This would place responsibility back on the defendant. Finally, during defense examination of witnesses, the prosecution may raise objections to certain questions or testimony that would support the defense's positions.

What strategic and what tactical moves do defense counsel use in insanity defense cases?

Arguing an insanity defense case, especially a high-profile one, can be an uphill battle for the defense lawyer. Often, jurors come into the trial already set on what they believe about mental illness. The defense must find a way to get jurors to reconsider their opinions in order to secure a favorable view of the defendant. Further, the defendant is often medicated and treated when placed in custody so that when the jury views a more reasonable appearing defendant, they may not understand how the insanity defense could be suggested in the first place. To combat this problem, some defense attorneys take their clients off medication before the trial so that jurors can see the defendant's state before treatment. This is especially effective for schizophrenics and those suffering from various other psychoses. To convince the jury that the defendant is indeed mentally ill the defense attorney may put the defendant on the stand to testify. Yet, if the defense does not appear to be well informed or certain of the nature of the illness, the jury may become even more skeptical. Furthermore, if the defense lawyer is pitted against a relentless prosecutor, he must be vigilant in raising objections and countering the information that the jury receives.

When the prosecution has the burden of proving the defendant sane, defense counsel have an easier time in insanity defense cases. Their task is more difficult when the defense has the burden of proving the defendant was insane and therefore not responsible for his actions at the time of the crime. This would include proving that mental illness or defect led the defendant to commit the crime and prevented him from realizing his wrongdoing or from realizing that his act was wrong. This is no easy task, especially when the majority of the public is skeptical of mental illness in the first place.

The defense must rely heavily on expert testimony that favors the defendant and supports the insanity defense. If experts cannot persuasively convince the jury that the defendant was not responsible for his actions because of mental illness, then the insanity defense will not be successful.

How important is the lawyer's advocacy to the success of the insanity defense?

Because of the complicated nature of mental illness, the disjunction between psychological and legal notions of responsibility, the adversary nature of the expert psychological testimony, the varying demands of burden of proof, and the skepticism of the public at large, the advocacy of both prosecution and defense lawyers is especially important in cases involving the insanity defense. A prosecutor who mistakenly thinks the case is open and shut because the defendant has clearly committed some proscribed act and therefore does not advocate effectively may well lose his case. A defense attorney who mistakenly thinks the case is open and shut because the defendant has a history of mental illness and therefore does not advocate effectively may well lose his case. Convincing a jury in an insanity defense case, especially when it is high-profile and the act was particularly heinous, may mislead both the prosecution and defense attorneys. A clear approach and a strong advocacy are both essential to success.

On what do prosecutors and defense counsel agree concerning the insanity defense?

There is virtually no agreement regarding the insanity defense among prosecutors and among defense attorneys, let alone between these two sets of lawyers. About the only common sentiment is that the insanity defense, as it stands now, is far from perfect. While some believe the insanity defense should be abolished, others contend that it should be reformed.

On what do psychologists and psychiatrists agree concerning the insanity defense?

When psychologists and psychiatrists testify at a trial as expert witnesses, they are often seen more as partisans of one side or another than as scientists. Since psychologists and psychiatrists testify for both prosecutors and defense attorneys, disagreements about the insanity defense do not generally split along the psychologist psychiatrist divide. Psychologists and psychiatrists disagree widely with each other about the nature of culpability, about the validity of the insanity defense, and similar issues. As with lawyers, about the only common sentiment is that the insanity defense, as it stands now, is far from perfect. A large part of this is attributable to the fact that insanity is a legal concept, not a scientific concept. Thus, psychiatrists and psychologists must fit their conceptions of an individual's mental health into the legal framework.

How important is the judge's attitude toward the insanity defense?

A judge's attitude toward the insanity defense can affect the tenor of his instructions to jurors. For instance, after some courts adopted the Durham rule in the 1950s, some critics said some of them continued to issue instructions fitting the M'Naghten test due to their disapproval of the Durham rule. Such actions could greatly have influenced the outcome of jurors' deliberations. Many commentators have believed that several Supreme Court decisions permitting the limitation of the rights of insanity acquittees have reflected a distaste for those who employ an insanity defense. In many instances judges' attitudes toward the insanity defense have the potential to have a very appreciable impact.

How important are jurors' attitudes toward the insanity defense?

Jurors' attitudes toward the insanity defense can be enormously important, as reflected by the fact that the attorneys in cases involving an insanity defense often conduct extensive questioning of potential jurors on their outlook on the insanity defense. Studies have concluded that judges' instructions and the particular insanity standard in place for a given trial often have minor impacts on jurors' decision-making. This lends credence to the belief that jurors' attitudes about the insanity defense, and its compatibility with each juror's respective conception of justice, have an enormous impact on how receptive they will be to an insanity plea.

Case Examples

8

Collective Cases

Ralph Tortorici

What was the Frontline documentary A Crime of Insanity?

In 2002, Frontline produced a documentary on the case of Ralph Tortorici. Along with a summary of that case, it argued strongly that the case of Ralph Tortorici represented a miscarriage of justice. A summary of the documentary follows.

On December 14, 1994, Ralph Tortorici, a twenty six year old psychology major, took a class hostage at the State University of New York at Albany. Armed with a high-powered rifle and a hunting knife, he tied together the doors to the classroom so the police could not enter, and said, because of a computer chip implanted in his brain and in his penis, that he wanted to speak with the president about a plot. In an ensuing struggle, he seriously injured in the leg and groin Jason McEnaney, a nineteen year old student who attempted to disarm him. Arrested, Tortorici was charged with felony counts of kidnapping, aggravated assault, and attempted murder. He pleaded not guilty by reason of insanity. Tried and found guilty in 1996, he was sentenced, in a large part because of the thirty-seven victims in the classroom, to the maximum of twenty to forty-seven years in prison. Sent to a maximum security prison he was housed in the mental health unit in his own cell. Three weeks later he tried to kill himself by hanging with a bed sheet. Three years later his appeal was denied. During his time in prison he moved back and forth between it and short stays in a psychiatric facility. Finally he spent a year in that facility before he was returned to prison. Shortly after, on August 10, 1999, he committed suicide in the Sullivan County Correctional Facility by hanging himself with a bed sheet in his cell.

The Frontline documentary made clear its thesis by its title and at the outset. The prosecutor Cheryl Coleman said she knew Tortorici was insane at the time of his hostage taking and did not want to prosecute him. Her superior, the chief assistant district attorney Lawrence Wiest, said his obligation was to the victims and to the community, and he wanted Tortorici prosecuted. She concluded that everything that seemed to be right in her prosecution of the case turned out to be wrong. The narrator concluded that the case demonstrated ethical dilemmas in a crime of insanity.

Besides the prosecutor, other important participants in the case were interviewed in the documentary. Tortorici's father and brother spoke of his straight-arrow behavior until age fifteen at which time he became isolated and antagonistic. A year later signs of serious mental illness surfaced as he talked of a conspiracy against him, of police following him, of hearing things in his razor, of knowing that there were listening bugs in lamps. Born with a defective urethra, he became convinced that a tracking microchip device had been implanted in his penis during many operations. Full body x-rays could not convince him that his belief was untrue. He considered doctors to be part of the plot. He was diagnosed with paranoid schizophrenia.

After the hostage taking, the prosecutor was unable for six months to locate a psychiatrist willing to testify for the prosecution. She finally found Dr. Lawrence Siegel who concluded after interviewing him that Tortorici was not competent to stand trial. The trial judge, Lawrence Rosen, had found Tortorici competent, and said that Dr. Siegel's psychiatric report was not responsive to the issue of insanity at the time of the hostage taking, and that the case was ready to go to trial without delay.

Ralph Tortorici refused to attend any court sessions. His defense attorney, Peter Lynch, called law enforcement and family members as witnesses, as well as four psychiatric experts. They all testified to incidents demonstrating the defendant's paranoid schizophrenia, and the experts concluded that he was seriously mentally ill and fit the definition of insanity. The prosecutor, having no psychiatric witnesses of her own and having thoroughly researched prior testimony by the defense experts in their previous cases, ridiculed and called into question their expertise. She argued that Tortorici proceeded during the incident in a logical, organized way, as shown by his bringing the gun and sufficient ammunition, and tying the doors together to prevent the police, who he knew would be called, from entering. She concluded that he knew what he was doing and knew that it was wrong. Further she said a dispute he had with the university and traces of cocaine in his system provided motivation for his behavior.

In their summations Peter Lynch, the defense attorney, argued that Ralph Tortorici had a fixed delusional belief which made him mentally ill and legally insane. Cheryl Coleman, the prosecutor, argued forcefully and persuasively that the defendant knew what he was doing and that it was wrong. After eight days of testimony and thirty-one witnesses, and a two and a half hour charge by the judge to the jury, the jury deliberated about an hour and found Tortorici guilty as charged.

According to Peter Lynch, Judge Rosen later told him that, given the verdict in this case, the insanity defense was essentially dead in the jurisdiction. In essence, the documentary suggested, Tortorici must have been viewed by the jury as a terrorist who was not even present during the trial. A month later, Tortorici did appear in court at his sentencing, and made a rambling statement about microchips and Jews and advanced technology. The judge sentenced him to the maximum allowable term in prison.

As the documentary concluded, Judge Rosen did not question himself, for the jury had made the decision. Lawrence Wiest, the chief assistant district attorney, said his office had done the right thing and congratulated the prosecutorial team for providing justice for the victims and the community. Dr. Siegel, the lone possible prosecution psychiatrist, said the verdict surprised him. Only Cheryl Coleman, the prosecutor, was in shock. She said she felt responsible for Tortorici's death because she had convicted him. She felt ashamed. She left the job, entered private practice, and later was appointed to be a judge. The documentary ended with the questions of what is right and of what is legal and of what is their relation to each other. The documentary strongly sided with the prosecutor Cheryl Coleman's conclusions concerning the case, that it was a miscarriage of justice and a crime of insanity.

What follows are the questions raised by the contributors to this volume on initially viewing the documentary and their responses to their own questions.

Was justice served in the trial of Ralph Tortorici?

Even after Ralph Tortorici killed himself three years into his prison sentence, the chief assistant district attorney claimed that justice had been served for the victims in the case and for the community. My initial reaction to this was to think that the chief was merely rationalizing his decision to follow through with the case even when it was clear that Tortorici was mentally unstable. By claiming that justice had been served, the chief absolved himself of responsibility for Tortorici's death because it was an after-effect of achieving a greater good. While this analysis of the chief's statement may be true, it is also worth examining the role of justice, or lack thereof, in Ralph Tortorici's case. Had Ralph Tortorici gone to a rehabilitative hospital for two years and been released as no longer psychotic, justice would not in my view have been served. Regardless of whether Tortorici knew right from wrong, he seemed to know what he was doing, and he seemed to know what effect his actions had on others. We know this because he explicitly claimed that he was taking the class hostage and knew that he could get the government to respond to his actions because the government would want to help save the hostages from him. Thus, although Tortorici is clearly mentally ill, his mental illness may not have actually been the direct cause of his actions. Rather, taking the class hostage could have been the way in which he sanely chose to handle his paranoia. In this respect, he is responsible for his actions and justice would deem that, while he should receive psychological help, he should also be punished for his actions.

It is important to note the difference, then, between a crime of insanity and a crime that results from insanity. The main difference may be better explained through an analogy. A woman is walking down the street and sees an armed man walking towards her in a threatening manner. There is a manned police car within yelling distance that the man does not see. However, the woman decides to take a revolver out of her purse and shoot the armed man dead. Although the woman could claim that she acted in self-defense, shooting the man was not her only option. Thus, while the woman faced an extreme situation, that extreme situation does not entirely absolve her of responsibility for her choices. I believe that this may hold true in Ralph Tortorici's case. While he certainly faced an extreme environment, taking aggressive and violent action against others was not his only choice. Others in his situation, knowing that their actions would be detrimental to others, as he did, may have tried to be more creative in their approach to the situation. His actions were not a result of his mental illness, but a means of dealing with his mental illness. Since there were other means available, his actions were punishable.

What were the main weaknesses in the defense's approach that led to a guilty verdict for Ralph Tortorici?

A criminal suspect is always legally presumed innocent until proven guilty. In many cases, however, the media can create a bias that reverses the burden of proof, making it an uphill battle for the defense. The defense team for Ralph Tortorici had plenty of material with which to overcome this obstacle. Tortorici's case was theirs to win, for although the facts of his crime were obvious, so was his apparent psychosis. He had a well-documented history of suspicious and abnormal behavior that would lead even an uneducated observer to a confident schizophrenia diagnosis. In addition, the prosecution's expert went so far as to state that Tortorici was completely psychologically unfit to stand trial. The cards seemed to be stacked up in the defense's favor from the start of the case. So what did the defense do to lose this case?

First, the defense did not force their defendant to be present in the trial. Tortorici refused to step foot inside the courtroom for reasons of irrational paranoia, and the subsequent lack of a human element for the defense was devastating to their case. The jury was not judging a man, but a crime. They were not ending a life, but merely expressing their disapproval for an act. The defense should have made more of an effort to involve Tortorici in the case, explaining to the judge that they could not continue without their client's presence or just frequently referring to the fact that he was downstairs in a holding cell because he was insane. Furthermore, the defense could have brought in more of his relatives than just his grandmother with the hopes of tugging a bit on the jury's heartstrings. Without countering the prosecution's human element with their own, the defense had no hope of winning over a jury.

Second, the defense team should have more effectively diffused prosecutor Coleman's cross-examination of the defense's expert witnesses. While cross-examination can be damaging to the credibility of a witness, damage control on their behalf can help to restore the value of their testimony. The defense should not have allowed Coleman to single-handedly discredit the entire psychological profession in this trial. If the defense's rebuttal was not sufficient, they should have called more witnesses to testify about the scientific basis of psychology and specifically schizophrenia. The defense allowed the prosecution to dismantle the credibility of the insanity defense before their very eyes.

Finally, the defense should have focused more on motive as a way to show Tortorici's psychosis. The prosecution had the burden of proof to show that Tortorici, if he was sane, committed this act for sane reasons. They brushed upon a few possible motives for the act, but never picked one and often tried to divert the jury's attention away from that weakness in their case. Had the defense focused more on Tortorici's lack of sane motivation, they might have been able to convince the jury that he was in fact insane.

Everyone, including the chief assistant district attorney, knew that this was the defense's case to win. The defense failed Tortorici by not effectively presenting his case. And while prosecutor Coleman said that she felt responsible for his death in jail, Tortorici's inept defense attorneys should help shoulder that burden.

What evidence of Tortorici's sanity was present at the time of the shooting and how did the prosecution present this to the jury?

Though clearly insane as a schizophrenic person at the time of trial, it proved difficult to prove Ralph Tortorici criminally insane at the time of his classroom takeover and subsequent shooting in Albany. Despite a lack of availability of willing psychiatrists or psychologists to diagnose Tortorici before the trial, the prosecutorial team was finally able to secure one willing doctor to evaluate him in his jail cell. That psychiatrist found him to be a paranoid schizophrenic at the time of the evaluation, months after the incident at the university, but did not give a diagnosis of the patient at the time of the shooting because he concluded that Tortorici could not cooperate in the evaluation.

The strongest evidence working against an insanity defense for Ralph Tortorici stemmed from his premeditation. Tortorici carried with him a gun and knife, items he had to think of before hand to bring with him to the classroom. He attempted to tie off the lecture hall doors, an indication that he was expecting the police, a very rational way of thinking. While his message to the students may have been off the wall, describing the government's conspiracy against him, his actions leading right up until the time of the shooting show a reasonable and rational Ralph Tortorici, simply an armed graduate student starved for attention and an audience.

While the defense presented evidence of his schizophrenia from a young age, such as his references to voices in his head, and his constant dissertations on a government monitoring his every move, the jury's decision focused upon the moment the crime was committed. Emotional testimony from the victim of the shooting, as well as a spirited closing argument from the prosecution pointing to the presence of intent on the part of Tortorici when pulling the trigger, proved important in sealing his fate. An emotionally charged jury, and recall that one fainted during testimony, found their decision that much easier when Ralph failed to show his face in the courtroom. Having no one to feel sympathy for except a maimed student victim, a faceless Ralph Tortorici was that much easier to convict.

Ralph Tortorici's evident preparations before his assault, the lack of circumstantial evidence of his insanity at the crime scene, and the context of the courtroom action all helped contribute to rejection of his insanity plea and to his conviction. The failure of the jury to recognize his mental problems and to treat him accordingly led to his eventual demise. The expediency and haste of the Albany courtroom revealed a serious defect in the justice system, one that cost the life of Ralph Tortorici.

What role, if any, did politics play in the trial of Ralph Tortorici?

The case of Ralph Tortorici was a highly publicized event. Tortorici taking a class of students at the State University of New York Albany hostage was a major event that naturally triggered public outrage. That Jason McEnaney, a student who tried to disarm Tortorici, sustained serious injuries only added to the community cries for justice. That Tortorici showed little remorse, as illustrated by his statement when he was arrested that he did what he had to do, made him even less of a sympathetic defendant. Clearly, many people in the community, especially those whose family members were taken hostage, wanted Tortorici punished for his crimes. Whether or not he was insane and thus not responsible for his actions was more of an afterthought to the people affected by Tortorici's actions. The chief assistant district attorney in Albany during the Tortorici trial, Lawrence Wiest, understood this.

Wiest acknowledged that Tortorici likely met the criteria for not responsible due to mental defect, yet his idea to prosecute seemed to have been tainted by his feeling that Tortorici's conduct was viewed as repugnant. Wiest's position was an elected position. Consequently, one of his main concerns was ensuring that he did not alienate the voting public. Therefore he was likely to act in a manner that would satisfy as many voters as possible and give him the best chance of re-election.

Another person whose actions can be traced to political motives was Judge Rosen. Once again, his position was subject to public scrutiny. As a result, he did not want to make a decision that could potentially cost him public support or question his judicial ability. This could explain why, even after the psychiatrist for the prosecution, Dr. Siegel, wrote a document questioning Tortorici's competency Rosen chose to go ahead with the trial. His justification was that if he postponed the trial the defense could later say that he was giving the prosecution more time to find medical experts. However, if the defense had agreed to postpone the trial, Judge Rosen could easily have guarded against this contingency. Thus, his motives for continuing with the trial could also be called into question.

What would have happened to Ralph Tortorici if he had been found not guilty by reason of insanity?

Though it is nearly impossible to answer this question with certainty, based on a number of factors one can conclude what would have likely happened to Tortorici if he had been found not guilty by reason of insanity. Under the New York American Law Institute test he would have been found not responsible by reason of mental defect. He then would have been evaluated for his dangerousness at that time by reason of mental illness, the standard used for determining whether someone can be committed against his or her will to a psychiatric facility. In the case of Tortorici, based on the actions of Judge Rosen in sentencing him and on the views held by everyone working on the case, that Tortorici was insane because of his serious mental illness, it is extremely likely that Tortorici would have been sent to a psychiatric facility and would have remained there for a lengthy period of time.

This raises the issue of why the jury found Tortorici guilty when even the prosecutor felt he was severely mentally impaired. And though the guilty verdict could be credited to many things, such as Tortorici's decision to not appear in court, perhaps the jury was swayed towards a guilty verdict because of the judge's instructions, or lack thereof. Judge Rosen gave an extensive two and a half hours worth of instructions to the jury, but was legally unable to tell them what would likely happen to Tortorici if he were found not guilty.

Additionally, because the jury did not have a guilty but mentally ill verdict as an option in New York, such a verdict requiring a person to begin their sentence in a mental facility and after being cured to complete their sentence in prison, they may have felt that letting Tortorici go free, which would have been very unlikely to happen, was not a viable option.

Why did Ralph Tortorici stand trial despite the fact that he seemed to suffer from acute psychosis?

Before the trial began, the court had to determine if Tortorici was competent, in light of his previous mental health issues, to stand trial. Did he have the cognitive and affective ability to cooperate in his own defense? In New York State, competency implies that the defendant understands the charges against him and is able to help with his own defense. Two court-ordered psychiatrists found Tortorici incompetent, and he was committed to Mid-Hudson Psychiatric Center.

Though Tortorici refused medication, he was deemed competent to stand trial by March 1995. However, the threshold for being deemed competent is so low that it is a great rarity for a defendant to be diagnosed incompetent. This low threshold is intended to give as many people a trial as possible unless the defendant may be so sick that he cannot understand what is going on around him. Although he may not have been competent in the so-called spirit of competency, he was viewed as legally competent.

Dr. Lawrence Siegel evaluated Tortorici in January 1996 and found him to be suffering from acute psychosis. He did not believe that Tortorici was competent to stand trial and recommended medication and hospitalization. Dr. Siegel found Tortorici to be disordered in his thinking and delusional. However, Dr. Siegel did admit that most of the conversations about his legal situation were coherent, and that Tortorici was aware of when and where he was, as well as the general outline of the trial procedure.

According to Peter Lynch, Tortorici's defense attorney, there was no doubt in anyone's mind that the defendant was mentally ill. However, Lynch never tried to have Tortorici deemed incompetent again because it was against his client's wishes. Although Tortorici knew he was mentally ill, he did not want to return to the psychiatric center and decided to proceed with the trial. Because these conversations between the lawyer and client were generally rational and reasonable, Lynch could not override this wish.

Tortorici again displayed unusual behavior when he refused to attend his own trial, an action that should have warranted Judge Rosen to have the defendant reevaluated for competency. Instead, Rosen chose to continue with the trial without even talking to Tortorici about the decision.

How did psychologists and psychiatrists affect the outcome of the Tortorici trial?

In cases of mental illness or insanity, such as Ralph Tortorici's, psychologists and psychiatrists are often used as expert witnesses for the defense or the prosecution. Usually, the prosecution has no problem finding at least a few people who are willing to testify as expert witnesses. However, the Tortorici case was unusual in that prosecutor Cheryl Coleman could not locate anyone to testify. This was because professionals she contacted did not believe that Tortorici was responsible given his mental health history. Others worried about losing respect among their colleagues. After six months, Coleman finally found psychiatrist Lawrence Siegel to examine Tortorici. However, he recommended that the trial be postponed because he did not think that Tortorici was competent. Despite this, Judge Rosen ruled to go ahead with the trial.

The defense, too, began to line up psychiatrists to testify that Tortorici was not responsible for his actions because he was insane at the time of the crime. Tortorici's well-documented history of mental illness eliminated the possibility that the defendant was faking his situation. The defense had no difficulty locating psychiatric experts.

The prosecution knew that without an expert witness to testify, it would be difficult to convict Tortorici. Therefore, Coleman made it a priority to discredit the professional witnesses for the defense. This would play into the jury's natural skepticism about psychiatrists and their views about mental health. In particular, she attacked one of the defense's main experts, Dr. Klopott, who had testified in a 1979 murder trial that the defendant had become a serial killer because he had trouble potty training. This bit of information largely discredited Klopott in the minds of the jurors, and the fact that the psychiatrist considered Tortorici to be insane had no meaning. Even though Klopott was not the defense's only psychiatric evidence, Coleman effectively called their expertise into question.

Furthermore, Tortorici's cocaine abuse came to be a major issue for the prosecution. Even though Siegel ruled out cocaine induced psychotic disorder, he did confirm alcohol and cocaine abuse. This hurt the defense's argument that Tortorici was just suffering from delusions caused by mental illness. Coleman also made it a point to emphasize that Tortorici acted in a methodical and reasonable way during the crime. This too helped to discredit the psychiatric evidence brought forth by the expert witnesses and past evaluations.

What methods did the prosecution use to convince the jury that Tortorici was legally sane?

In order to convince the jury that Tortorici was sane at the time of his crime, the prosecution first had to demonstrate that Tortorici could comprehend that his actions were morally reprehensible and that he understood the consequences of his behavior. Prosecutor Cheryl Coleman described how Tortorici had hidden his weapons in his coat, indicating that he knew that his possession was wrong and that he must be secretive. Once he took the classroom hostage, Tortorici quickly made sure the doors were tied shut, which suggested that he intentionally wanted to keep the police out of the classroom and that he knew what he was doing was wrong. Witnesses also testified that Tortorici used his weapons to threaten them, which suggests that he understood the potential of harm.

The prosecution was also able to capitalize on the victim of the crime, Jason McEnaney, who was shot in the groin. He was a powerful witness who moved the jury to such an extent that one person even fainted while listening to his testimony. By shifting the attention of the jury from the question of Tortorici's sanity to the suffering of McEnaney, the jury possibly felt compelled to honor the victim's need for retribution.

Despite all their best efforts, however, it was impossible to ignore that the prosecution was unable to secure one psychological expert able to testify that Tortorici was sane at the time of the crime, while the defense had several. As a result, the prosecution extensively researched the cases that each expert had participated in and manipulated it in such a manner that it appeared that the experts were financially motivated to participate in the defense of Tortorici.

What role did Judge Rosen play in Tortorici's case?

Before the trial began, Ralph Tortorici's competence to stand trial had to be evaluated. Competence to stand trail simply means that the defendant understands the nature of the charges and can aid in his defense. During the first evaluation, psychologists at a secure mental health facility called Mid-Hudson deemed Tortorici incompetent to stand trial. After several months the psychiatrists felt his paranoid schizophrenia had stabilized and that the trial could move forward. Yet the defense remained concerned that Tortorici would not be able to aid his defense and that they were unable to effectively serve the needs of their client while he was incompetent. The prosecution's psychological expert, Dr. Lawrence Siegel, suggested that the trial be postponed because it was impossible to evaluate Tortorici in his current condition and he was therefore incapable of standing trial. Judge Rosen, however, did not want the trial to endure any more delays and chose to follow the previous psychiatrists' recommendations. He deemed Tortorici competent to stand trial.

Judge Rosen also allowed Tortorici to waive his right to be present for his trail. He interviewed Tortorici to ensure that he understood that he was voluntarily waiving his constitutional right and the potential consequences of his action. Finally, during the sentencing, Judge Rosen listened to a crazed, delusional Tortorici give a bizarre statement before giving Tortorici the maximum punishment of twenty to forty-seven years in prison.

How might the option to find the defendant guilty but mentally ill have affected the outcome of the Tortorici case?

The statutes concerning the insanity defense differ from state to state. Starting in 1976, some states adopted laws allowing juries to return a verdict of guilty but mentally ill, or guilty but insane, in insanity cases. Such a verdict would result in sentencing the defendant as if he or she were found guilty of the offense, but would signal that the defendant needed special help for a mental disorder. Thus, a defendant might begin his or her prison term in a hospital instead of in jail. However, the trial of Ralph Tortorici took place in New York, where no such option existed.

If the guilty but mentally ill verdict were available in the Tortorici case, it is very likely that the jury would have implemented it. The Frontline interview with Norm LaMarche, a juror in the trial, revealed that while the jury did not find Tortorici not guilty by reason of insanity, there seemed to be a consensus among the jurors that he had a serious mental illness. LaMarche noted that there were concerns aired in the jury's deliberation on what kind of prison Tortorici would be sent to and whether or not he would receive adequate help. However, despite belief that he had a serious mental illness, the jury was unwilling to rule that Tortorici was not responsible for his actions. As a result, they had no choice but to trust the judge and the system to provide him the necessary treatment for his illness. Prosecutor Cheryl Coleman describes this situation as a failure of the all-or-nothing nature of the system. She was an advocate for introducing the guilty but mentally ill option for juries as a middle ground, holding defendants responsible for their actions while trying to insure that they will get help and attention for their mental problems.

However, controversy surrounding the implementation of the guilty but mentally ill verdict suggests that such an option may have had little effect on the outcome of the Tortorici case, past altering the description of the guilty verdict. First of all, studies in states that have added a guilty but mentally ill verdict have shown that in the majority of cases there is very little difference between what happens to those who are simply found guilty and those who are found guilty but mentally ill. For example, a study in Michigan found that seventy-five percent of those found guilty but mentally ill were sent straight to prison without any special treatment. Thus, it is quite possible that Ralph Tortorici would not have received significantly more treatment had he been found guilty but mentally ill, and thus such a verdict would not necessarily have prevented his suicide.

The outcome of Ralph Tortorici's case would probably have been different, therefore, in name only had there been an option of a guilty but mentally ill verdict. This is primarily due to the problems associated with implementing such a verdict, or even having such an option. These problems include overcrowding in hospitals, limitations in resources to treat the mentally ill, and the confusion that the guilty but mentally ill verdict adds to the already difficult distinction between the medical issue of mental illness and the legal issue of insanity.

What effect did the prosecution's failure to find an expert witness have on the Tortorici trial?

One of the unusual aspects of Ralph Tortorici's case was the inability of the prosecution to find an expert witness to testify on his behalf. In other words, they could not find a psychiatrist who was willing to testify that Tortorici was mentally capable of understanding the nature and wrongfulness of his crime at the time of the offense. All but one of the psychiatrists contacted by the prosecution refused to participate because they did not want to have their name attached to the trial, believed that Tortorici was not responsible, or feared that it would negatively impact the reputation of the field. On the other hand, the defense had secured several psychiatrists willing to argue that Tortorici had a well-documented history of mental illness and was not legally sane when he committed the crime.

Such an imbalance of expert witnesses was a huge disadvantage for the prosecution. In general, hearing uncontradicted testimony from an expert is among the most likely factors to lead a jury to vote in favor of the verdict not guilty by reason of insanity. In addition, prosecutor Cheryl Coleman noted in her interview with Frontline that a lawyer is supposed to call an expert to testify about any scientific or medical evidence or position that is beyond what the average person should know and understand.

Despite this disadvantage for the prosecution, the jury returned a guilty verdict. An interview with a juror, Norm LaMarche, helps explain why the testimony of expert witnesses did not make a bigger impact in the trial. These reasons include the effective prosecutorial cross-examination of experts for the defense, the instructions of Judge Rosen against ultimate opinion testimony, and some possible confusion concerning the differences between competency and insanity on the part of the jurors.

Cheryl Coleman seriously mitigated the potential effects of the defense expert witnesses by undermining their credibility and the credibility of their profession in general. By bringing up previous cases in which the experts had testified in different ways, she tried to make it look like their testimony could be bought. In addition, she presented testimony that the experts had given in the past that, particularly out of context, would appear funny or unpopular. For example, she tried to make the jurors skeptical about one expert by describing his testimony about bedwetting in a previous trial of a serial killer. In his interview, LaMarche acknowledged that Coleman was effective at lowering the credibility of the witnesses.

LaMarche also claimed that Judge Rosen was adamant about keeping the expert witnesses from expressing an absolute opinion about whether or not Tortorici was legally insane at the time of the crime. Judge Rosen was following the Insanity Defense Reform Act of 1984 which prohibits experts from giving ultimate opinion testimony. As a result, the witnesses can give their opinions about mental illness and how that might affect the defendant's actions, but their inability to give an ultimate opinion about insanity may have lessened the impact of their testimony.

Finally, when questioned about the lack of an expert witness for the prosecution, LaMarche implied that the fact that Tortorici had been found competent to stand trial somehow diminished the need for an expert witness for the prosecution. This response called into question the jurors' understanding of the legal definitions of insanity and competency and the distinctions between the two. This confusion, in conjunction with the other factors discussed above resulted in the jury putting very little weight on the testimony of expert witnesses, and lessened the impact of the prosecution's lack of expert testimony.

Does a documented history of mental illness provide evidence for a plea of not guilty by reason of insanity?

While the existence of past or present mental illness certainly can raise questions about a defendant's sanity at the time of the crime, even a well-documented history of severe mental disturbance does not necessarily indicate that the person was insane while the crime was committed. As insanity is a legal concept and not a psychiatric diagnosis, no psychological impairment automatically provides evidence for an insanity plea. Rather, it is up to each individual defendant whether to plead not guilty by reason of insanity and how to meet the law's burden of proof of insanity in his particular jurisdiction.

The fact that severe, documented mental illness does not necessarily translate to insanity in a court of law is illustrated by the example of Ralph Tortorici, a twenty-six year-old university student who took a class hostage and shot and injured one student in 1994. Tortorici's defense claimed he was insane and presented documented evidence of psychological distress dating from at least two years before the crime. Specifically, in 1992 he had sought medical treatment regarding a microchip that he baselessly believed had been implanted in his penis so that the government could monitor his actions. The medical staff transferred him to a psychiatric facility. Several months later, he entered a police station to seek help with the implant, reporting that the device was issuing him commands. The police officer with whom he spoke feared that Tortorici would do something dangerous and transported him to the psychiatric facility. According to the center's report on Tortorici, he had been suffering from these delusions for eight years.

Despite the defendant's documented history of believing that a nonexistent microchip was issuing him commands to commit crimes, the jury rejected his insanity plea and found him guilty of all charges. One juror noted in an interview that Tortorici was obviously mentally ill but that the jury found him guilty because of the evidence that the crime was planned, which indicated that he had understood the wrongfulness of his conduct and the possible consequences. As the Tortorici case exemplified, a defendant can be seriously mentally disturbed beyond a doubt, yet still be found sane in the eyes of the law.

Although mental illness does not automatically equate with insanity, it is important to note that substantial psychiatric histories could play a role in juries' decisions. For example, a number of studies have indicated that jurors are more likely to acquit a defendant by reason of insanity when they believe him or her to suffer from a severe mental disturbance, especially when it interferes with the defendant's ability to plan and to control his actions. Furthermore, most defendants found not guilty by reason of insanity suffer from psychosis, which is an especially serious and debilitating mental condition. Thus, while the existence of a mental disorder does not necessarily denote insanity, the severity of the disorder does appear to predict the likelihood of success of the insanity defense.

Does an unsuccessful plea of not guilty by reason of insanity produce a bias against the defendant?

In a perfect legal system, defendants would have the freedom to utilize any and every defense available to them, without fear of retribution by judges or jurors. In reality, courts are composed of human beings, who are susceptible to forming unfair prejudices in response to defenses presented by a defendant. Considering that the insanity defense elicits massive disapproval among the American public, who generally believe it to be a loophole for guilty criminals, defendants and their counsel should be concerned about possible repercussions from a failed not guilty by reason of insanity plea. In the end, no matter what instructions the jury receives, certain personal biases, such as disapproval of the insanity plea, may influence the verdict.

Ralph Tortorici, for example, pleaded not guilty by reason of insanity after taking a university class hostage and shooting and injuring a student. The jury rejected this defense and found him guilty of eleven charges of kidnapping and aggravated assault. When he returned to the courtroom for sentencing, an obviously psychotic Tortorici launched into an incoherent diatribe against the supposed governmental conspiracy against him. After letting him speak, the judge ordered the ranting Tortorici to be silent. He subsequently sentenced him to the maximum penalty available, twenty to forty-seven years in prison. The fact that this defendant received the maximum sentence suggests that he may have been the subject of discrimination on the basis of his failed not guilty by reason of insanity plea.

In other cases, however, defendants had unsuccessfully pled not guilty by reason of insanity but still received lighter punishment. Richard Herrin, a Yale graduate who bludgeoned to death his college sweetheart Bonnie Garland, was defended at trial with an insanity plea. The jury rejected the insanity defense in his case, but it convicted Herrin of manslaughter instead of murder, thereby sparing him the stiffer penalties of a murder conviction. Thus, it would seem that whether a defendant will face adverse discrimination following a failed not guilty by reason of insanity plea depends upon the individual case.

Researchers have extensively studied the impact of successful insanity defenses on punishment, finding that not guilty by reason of insanity verdicts may not produce lighter periods of confinement. It was found that four of the seven states investigated had shorter average confinement periods for not guilty by reason of insanity defendants than for convicted defendants, while the remaining three states had longer confinement periods for those defendants. The results of such studies indicate that a successful insanity defense is not necessarily a ticket to a lighter sentence. The research, however, appears to have neglected the implications of failed not guilty by reason of insanity pleas on sentences served. A large-scale analysis of cases in which the insanity plea failed is needed in order to determine whether defendants suffer discrimination from judges and juries when their pleas are rejected.

Did Tortorici appreciate what he was doing or was he insane at the time of the shooting?

The facts of the incident are fairly clear: Ralph Tortorici entered a lecture hall with a loaded gun, took the room hostage, and made several demands before a scuffle ensued during which Jason McEnaney was shot. What remains unclear was whether Tortorici should have been legally held responsible for his actions, whether or not he was insane at the time of the shooting. This is an interesting issue especially because insanity is a legal concept and, despite any sorts of disorders, if the defendant knew the difference between right and wrong, often he can be found sane.

On the one hand, there are items that the prosecution argued that indicated that Tortorici in fact knew what he was doing was wrong and was legally responsible for his actions: he ordered the doors to be barricaded, he showed his hostages bullets for his gun so that they knew he was not joking, he made attempts to have his hostages as human shields in case the police burst in. In her closing statement, the prosecuting attorney Cheryl Coleman used many of these examples to convict Tortorici, making constant reference to the fact that he knew his actions were wrong.

On the other hand, drawing on the years of evidence during which Tortorici had serious delusional episodes and believed that the government was using him as the guinea pig for some experiment, the defense attorney Peter Lynch said in his closing statement that Tortorici was not sane because of his mental state at the time, which was severely troubled. Ralph Tortorici apparently thought that he was being controlled by the government and that the act that led to the shooting of McEnaney would put an end to the experiment; in a note that he wrote just prior to the incident, Tortorici said that he thought his actions were necessary to somehow fix his life. This demonstrated that, unless Tortorici wrote the note in an attempt to exonerate himself from culpability, the roots of his actions were deeply delusional. However, as the law is written, his being delusional did not mean he was necessarily legally insane; to me, this exposed a weakness in the law, for Tortorici was clearly mentally ill at the time of the incident. Although legally he could have been, and indeed was, found responsible for his actions, Tortorici demonstrated enough evidence that he needed severe rehabilitation and not just imprisonment.

Considering the fact that Tortorici was initially found not competent enough to stand trial, should the trial even have begun?

According to standard definition, competence refers to the ability of a defendant to function affectively and cognitively in the legal setting. Despite the fact that Ralph Tortorici was initially found incompetent to stand trial, and then found competent, and then, on later examination by the prosecution's own psychiatrist, found incompetent, the trial nevertheless began.

Dr. Lawrence Siegel's letter clearly explained that Tortorici should not have been put on trial, as he was not capable of participating rationally in the courtroom. When such a report was coupled with the fact that Tortorici refused to even be in the courtroom during the trial, which was a clear indication that he was incapable of appreciating his role in the proceedings and making legally relevant decisions, it became evident that the trial proceeded not because it was the correct course of action, but because the judge wanted the trial which had partially begun to continue.

There was no lack of evidence of mental instability in Tortorici in the decade leading up to the shooting of Jason McEnaney, and it seems highly unlikely that Tortorici was feigning mental illness the entire time in order to set up such an event. Indeed, in the aforementioned letter Dr. Siegel stated that it was highly unlikely that Tortorici suffered from a psychotic disorder during the shooting and not during the trial. When one takes into account the historical reports of his family as well as those of unbiased third parties, his outrageous claims of government conspiracy, and the very act that led to the shooting of McEnaney, the chances of Tortorici actually being fit to stand trial were remote. It follows that the trial should not have even gotten underway when it did.

Should Tortorici have been medicated against his will in order to assure a more just trial?

In December 1992, two years prior to his arrest, Tortorici was admitted involuntarily by the Mobile Crisis Unit for a period of three days. During this time, he was given anti-psychotic medication. However, the side effect of impotence greatly worried him, and he discontinued its use. After his arrest in January 1995, he was admitted to the Mid-Hudson Psychiatric Center, where he refused medication. Despite Dr. Siegel's adamant claim that Tortorici was incompetent and the fact that his paranoid and delusional thoughts stopped him from attending his own trial, he was judged fit to proceed.

In most states, defendants who have been found incompetent to stand trial have been required by law to receive treatment to restore them to competence, even if taking medication is against their will. Although Tortorici was not incompetent to stand trial according to Judge Rosen, anti-psychotic medication may have been helpful for his case. It is unclear if defense attorney Lynch should have requested that his client be medicated against his will in order to assure a fair trial, given his refusal to attend. However, it is highly doubtful that Judge Rosen would have allowed it.

If Tortorici had been taking anti-psychotic medication, his delusions may have been suppressed, allowing him to make the practical decision to attend his own trial. In Frontline's *A Crime of Insanity*, Tortorici's absence was mentioned as a prime reason for the jury's decision to convict him on the grounds that they lacked a defendant to empathize with. However, it is also possible that if Tortorici attended the trial, tranquilized by medication, the jury would not have been able to witness the level of his true psychosis, thereby undercutting an insanity defense. In *Riggins v. Nevada*, the Supreme Court allowed the defendant to refuse medication as a tactical decision to advance the credibility of his insanity plea. Of course, in Tortorici's case, this issue was a catch twenty-two. If medicated, he would most likely agree to attend the trial and may have even realized that it would be in his best interest to attend the trial while off his medication. However, as soon as he stopped the medication, he would again refuse to attend the trial.

I believe that Tortorici should have been medicated against his will in order to allow him the rational decision to attend his own trial, even if the jury would not be able to witness the extent of his psychosis. It does not seem just for a defendant to be tried and convicted without being present at his own trial because of fears of conspiracy against him, legitimate or not. Tortorici's attendance may or may not have changed the verdict, but the adversarial process would have benefited.

According to accepted legal standards of competence, should Ralph Tortorici have been found incompetent to stand trial?

In the opinion of prosecuting attorney Cheryl Coleman, Ralph Tortorici was not truly competent to stand trial, but was legally found competent because of the horrifically low assessment standards. This low threshold for competency, to which I assume Ms. Coleman is referring, is a simple yes or no test of a defendant's ability to understand the basic elements of the adversary process. Judge Rosen's decision to find Ralph Tortorici competent to stand trial was obviously based on this simple test. Even in Dr. Lawrence Siegel's letter arguing against the court's finding of mental competence, he admitted that Tortorici did indeed possess, at the very least, a rudimentary understanding of legal proceedings and is aware of the charges against him. Dr. Siegel also reported that Tortorici was oriented to time and place and was able to accurately describe the roles of the judge, jury, prosecutors, and defense attorney. Although this basic knowledge of the legal process was sufficient proof of competence for Judge Rosen, it would not be enough to meet the standard for adjudicative competence as defined by the Supreme Court in *Dusky v. United States.*

According to the *Dusky* standard, recognized in courts of law with few modifications, the accused is deemed competent to stand trial if he is sufficiently capable of consulting with his lawyer with a reasonable degree of rational comprehension, and a rational as well as factual understanding of the proceedings against him. Here, Tortorici fell short of the standard. Although he possessed knowledge of the proceedings, his understanding of them was so severely tainted by his psychosis that he was unable to participate in the criminal justice system in a meaningful way and was incapable of defending himself against the charges by the state.

Tortorici's deteriorated psychotic state skewed, if not completely destroyed, his understanding of the true nature of the criminal proceedings. His understanding of the case against him was riddled with delusional thought, and could in no way be considered rational or factual. He was convinced that the government plotted his arrest and the case against him. He informed Dr. Siegel that external government forces were influencing and manipulating every mind in the courtroom through airwaves and power waves. In his delusional mind, this trial was not going to be justice carried out as usual, but would be the culmination of the government's grand conspiracy to control him since adolescence. He referred to the trial as his graduation party prior assuming his role as leader. These recorded statements show that Tortorici was existing in a world completely devoid of reality during the time of and directly prior to the trial.

Tortorici's delusional system left him unable to logically and rationally communicate with his attorney or assist in planning an adequate defense. Although Dr. Siegel reported that Tortorici was capable of forming a relationship with his attorney, he viewed Tortorici as incapable of joint understanding and consideration of beneficial legal advice. In *A Crime of Insanity,* prosecutor Coleman stated that Tortorici was not able to aid his attorney in any way. He was unable to appreciate his role in the proceedings or make legally relevant decisions. His fervent refusal to attend what he considered his own party ultimately aided in his own demise and diminished the jury's ability to arrive at a just verdict.

Was the prosecution right to press charges against Tortorici?

The question of a defendant's competence and guilt normally rests with the court and jury. However, because the purpose of the prosecution is to seek justice, rather than simply to prosecute as vigorously as possible, the prosecution has some discretion in whether to press charges and whether and how present a case. For this reason, the prosecution can elect not to charge someone it believes is not guilty or should not be on trial, due to incompetence, for instance. Thus, the prosecution in Tortorici's case could have chosen not to press charges if it believed that Tortorici was either incompetent to be tried or not guilty. However, the prosecution did press charges. Was it right in doing so?

The prosecution had some misgivings about Tortorici's guilt. While, at first, the prosecution doubted Tortorici's insanity, it only took one meeting with Tortorici to convince the prosecutor, Cheryl Coleman, that Tortorici was seriously mentally diseased. This insanity made her wonder whether Tortorici was actually guilty, whether he appreciated the nature of his actions. Furthermore, Coleman doubted that any jury that saw Tortorici the way she had could convict him.

Moreover, Tortorici's mental disease caused Coleman to question his competence to stand trial. While she realized that under the narrow letter of the law, she might be able to persuade the court that Tortorici was competent, she believed he was not competent to assist in his defense in the way that common sense and the spirit of the law would suggest. Tortorici would later prove his incompetence to assist in his defense by exempting himself from the courtroom during the trial, thus voiding the main reasons, Tortorici's appearance and behavior, that Coleman believed he would be acquitted. Thus, the prosecution had to decide between the strict letter of the law on one hand and the spirit of the law on the other. In the end, the prosecution chose to favor the narrow letter of the law by arguing for Tortorici's competence and guilt.

In the end, the prosecutor's boss, the chief assistant district attorney, decided to press charges. Part of this decision rested on a desire to allow the judge and jury to decide Tortorici's guilt and competence. Another part of this decision, perhaps a greater part, arose from political motivations, upcoming elections, and a desire to show deference to the victims in this case. Expecting Tortorici's probable acquittal, some in the district attorney's office viewed prosecuting Tortorici as a necessary formality.

Once the decision had been made to prosecute, Coleman laid aside her hesitation and focused only on winning the trial. Given in large part to Coleman's skilled performance and Tortorici's unexpected decision to exempt himself from the courtroom, Tortorici was convicted. This surprised almost everyone, especially Coleman herself. After the conviction, she began to question her role in the trial, thinking that the prosecution perhaps should not have pressed charges against Tortorici. This made her feel responsible for Tortorici's conviction and eventual suicide in jail.

To be fair, Coleman and the prosecution did not bear full responsibility for determining Tortorici's guilt and competence. This responsibility also rested with the judge and jury. However, the prosecution did share some responsibility for its role in prosecuting Tortorici. Thus, while Coleman might not have been correct in deciding that the prosecution's decision had been wrong, she was right to seriously consider whether the prosecution perhaps should not have tried Tortorici in the first place.

What was the burden of proof in the Tortorici case?

In the widely publicized John Hinckley, Jr. case, the prosecution bore the burden of proving him to be sane. Many considered that factor as crucial to the jury's finding him not guilty by reason of insanity in his attempted assassination of President Reagan. As a reaction to that verdict of not guilty by reason of insanity, the federal Insanity Defense Reform Act of 1984 shifted the burden of proof in insanity defenses from the prosecution to the defense in cases where it applied. Many states also reconsidered and most of those who had not now put the burden of proof of insanity on the defense. In this case Tortorici and his attorney bore the burden of proving him not guilty by reason of insanity. The defendant had to meet a clear and convincing evidence standard, which is a lower standard than beyond a reasonable doubt standard. Nonetheless, it becomes for many defendants especially difficult to meet this burden when many are indigent, or relying on overworked public defenders. Additionally, studies have shown that jurors are not very receptive to pleas of not guilty by reason of insanity. In approving the Insanity Defense Reform Act, Congress was probably responding at least in part to the aversion to the insanity defense held by the very same public that winds up serving on juries. Thus, the legislation made insanity defenses substantially more difficult to succeed. While this did not appear as especially significant in the Tortorici case it may have been a factor, for it has reflected more widespread displeasure with the insanity defense in general, particularly the acquittal of John Hinckley Jr., who shot President Reagan and others.

Should jurors be instructed about the consequences of an insanity acquittal?

In the Tortorici case, the judge was prohibited by law from telling the jury that if the defendant were found not guilty by reason of insanity, he would probably spend as much time in a secure mental institution as he would in prison if he were found guilty. In my view, there were at least three reasons why the judge should have informed the jury of this fact, and, generally, of the consequences of an insanity acquittal.

First, it is likely that when the members of the jury voted to convict Tortorici, they were doing so because they feared that he would be freed and could pose a danger to society a second time. If they knew, however, that this fear was probably unfounded, they would probably have been more willing to change their verdict to not guilty by reason of insanity. As cross-sections of populations, jurors do not render verdicts in a vacuum. Their personal prejudices and fears play into their verdicts, and if they had this extra piece of information, their fears would likely have become less important in their decision-making. There was no reason to believe that this particular fear held by jurors was an important one for them to hold, and that it should therefore have been shielded from information that would dispel it.

Second, enabling the judge to assuage this fear would have allowed the jurors to set aside their concerns about incapacitation and instead to concentrate on treatment. They would have been able to focus their considerations on whether a secure mental institution would have been a better place for Tortorici to be than a prison. This could have increased the probability that Tortorici would have been sent to a place where he would have been treated more effectively. This could have saved his life.

Third, failing to inform the jury of this fact shows a lack of trust in the jurors' ability to weigh that information properly. If lawmakers are concerned that jurors would be less likely to convict if they were aware of this information, it indicates that the same people who are empowered to determine another's guilt would not be fit if they knew what would happen to the defendant. The notion that additional information would render a jury unfit to administer justice undermines the very concept of the jury system.

But there are also several reasons why the judge should not inform the jury of this fact. First, the jury should not be concerned with what will happen to the defendant after he is found guilty or not guilty. The jury's task should only be to consider whether he is guilty or not guilty. In the Tortorici case, the sentencing was left to the judge, not the jury. Planting sentencing concerns in jurors' minds blurs the clear division of responsibilities between the judge and the jury, and distracts jurors from the facts of the case, which is what they should be working on.

The second reason can be illustrated by Judge Rosen's comment in A Crime of Insanity to the effect that judges love juries because then judges cannot be blamed when someone is convicted and then given a harsh sentence. Judges do not decide guilt. They simply apply the law in sentencing. The division of duties is important for ensuring that no single individual is wholly responsible for the defendant's penalty, and thus no single individual can be wholly blamed for any faults later discovered, such as when a convicted defendant commits suicide in an apparent fit of insanity.

Third, by going out of his way to inform the jury of this fact, the judge might lead the jury to attach special, undue significance to this fact. After all, a judge does not inform the jury of the probability that someone convicted of the same crime in the same jurisdiction will receive parole, or that he will wind up in a prison with a reputation for being violent. Why, then, should the judge inform the jurors of this fact?

And fourth, it is not guaranteed that the defendant would spend equal amounts of time in prison or in a secure mental institution. If he were to spend less time in a mental institution than he would have in a prison, is then released, and goes on to shoot another person, it is likely that the judge would have subverted the jurors' legitimate concerns about incapacitation.

Is a jury qualified to make decisions on whether a defendant is mentally ill?

When an insanity defense was presented, the jury was instructed to rule on whether the defendant was not responsible for the crime by reason of insanity. The jury in the Tortorici case was asked to evaluate whether the defendant understood what he was doing and whether he knew that what he was doing was wrong.

It was my view that the jury should not have had the power to make such decisions. As Judge Lawrence Rosen stated, it should not have been the responsibility of twelve average people with little, if any, background or professional knowledge to decide whether a defendant was mentally ill.

Granted, the principle of having the people decide is foundational to the criminal justice system. In fact, after being informed of Tortorici's death, Judge Rosen denied responsibility for the death since the ruling was the people's decision. Having community members decide the verdict was reasonable considering that the public was regarded as the victim of the crime.

But though the people may have been receiving justice under this system, was the defendant equally receiving justice? For instance, when asked if he thought the jury was capable of making decisions about Tortorici's state of mind, one of the jurors confidently answered that the jurors felt they were equipped to make decisions that were comparable to their own life experiences. The juror mentioned that he and the rest of the jury did not place much value on the opinions of the psychiatric experts who testified during the trial, but instead they based their verdict on common sense and their personal lives and life experiences. Were these the standards by which a defendant's mental health could have been accurately and fairly judged? I would answer no because members of the jury were inadequately equipped to handle the complexities involved with mental illness.

The jury should have simply decided whether the defendant was guilty of the crime, and if so, whether the defendant was responsible for the crime aside from mental health considerations. After the jury's conclusion, an expert who had more experience with mental health should have assessed the defendant's mental state and offered recommendations as to whether the defendant should have been placed in a psychiatric facility or prison. The judge should then have considered the jury's verdict and the expert's informed opinion while he was rendering his sentence. This type of bifurcated trial would have enabled members of the community, as well as the defendant, to each find justice.

Is the basis by which a jury accepts an insanity plea valid?

The jury in the Tortorici case was directed by the judge to consider the insanity defense according to the M'Naghten rule. The M'Naghten rule stated that the defendant was not responsible for the crime if the defendant did not know what he was doing and that what he was doing was wrong. Moreover, regardless of the defendant's mental history, the defense had to show that the defendant was mentally unfit at the time of the crime.

Prosecutor Cheryl Coleman skillfully seemed to demonstrate that Ralph Tortorici was in fact aware of his actions and that he realized the wrongfulness of these actions, and therefore was not legally insane at the time of the crime. For example, she cited Tortorici's comments, such as his threat of having enough ammunition to kill many cops, as evidence that he understood his actions. Coleman also reminded the jury of how Tortorici hid his gun in his coat while walking to the classroom to prove that Tortorici knew that his actions were wrong.

However, even under the assumption that Tortorici failed the M'Naghten rule, my view was that there needed to be further consideration of his mental state at the time of the crime. The directives given to this jury ruling on the insanity plea were not adequate. Even if Tortorici knew that holding a classroom hostage with dangerous firearms was wrong and had legal consequences, the reason for his crime in the first place was because he truly believed that the government had implanted a tracking chip in his penis. This showed that his frame of mind was unstable. In other words, though the defendant's action B and action C may have been sensible, the original reason A that caused his actions B and C was completely nonsensical. Therefore, the insanity plea should not have been so easily rejected. Other factors should also have been considered. And if the standard had been whether Tortorici was unable to appreciate the wrongfulness of his actions or to conform his actions to the law, he may well have been found not guilty by reason of insanity.

Richard Herrin

What was the case about?

This case has been extensively detailed in Willard Gaylin's *The Killing of Bonnie Garland*. The answers to the questions which follow rely on his presentation of the facts for the legal, religious, and psychosocial elements of this case.

The victim in the case was Bonnie Garland. Her boyfriend, Richard Herrin, killed her, confessed to the killing, then pleaded not guilty by reason of insanity. His lawyer, Jack Litman, argued that Herrin was under severe emotional stress at the time. Though he avoided a murder conviction, the jury convicted Herrin of manslaughter. Nonetheless, the insanity defense and the psychological testimony it evoked were both important to a case which detailed the differences among a defendant's, the victim's, and society's rights.

What were the defendant's early years like?

Richard Herrin was a poor Mexican American boy raised in a minority ghetto in Los Angeles, California. His biological father was an alcoholic and abandoned Herrin and his mother, Linda Ugarte, when the boy was only three years old. At age seven, his mother remarried. Herrin's stepfather was not particularly supportive. In fact, he forced his stepson to work at age eight and frequently ridiculed and scolded him. Herrin was plagued by the public humiliation of such scoldings for years to come. This type of psychological abuse may have been why Herrin was overwhelmingly concerned with image, especially in his relationships through early adulthood.

As a boy, Herrin suffered from eczema and was a chronic bed wetter. He described his own childhood as isolated and lonely. He reluctantly attributed not having many kids to play with as a youth to his mother being a bit smothering. Throughout grammar and high school, Herrin was a disciplined student. He graduated number one in his class, and received full financial aid to attend Yale University in 1971.

When did he first start having problems?

There was debate surrounding what constituted problems in the case of Richard Herrin. Some claimed that signs of his personality problems began in childhood, while others argued that the college years were when Herrin's behavior became the most unusual. However, this was a difficult question because most would agree that any problems exhibited by Herrin would be considered within what constituted normal limits until the very unexpected act of killing in July 1977.

What was the nature of those problems?

One of the psychoforensic experts, Dr. Train, claimed that Herrin's personality problems were due to his development, and that his isolation and bedwetting to age fourteen were signs. Dr. Train also claimed that Herrin suffered from model boy syndrome, and was therefore unable to express anger and felt the need to ingratiate due to fear of abandonment.

But the more rapid deterioration of Herrin's psychological state was evident throughout his college years. Upon entering Yale, Herrin began to feel extremely inadequate and did not do well academically or socially. His commitment to causes was minimal and his personal attachments were unsubstantial. In his only two relationships, first with a girl named Ginny and then with Bonnie Garland, he was emotionally indifferent, overly concerned with image, and ignored the reality of the relationships coming to an end.

In *The Killing of Bonnie Garland*, Willard Gaylin described what he had gathered from long interviews with Herrin concerning what Gaylin termed his pathological nature. Gaylin believed Herrin displayed a withdrawn and rigid personality, flatness of affect, isolation from his own emotions, immature sexuality, strong dependence on denial, ideas of reference with a paranoid strain, and concreteness.

When was the defendant first considered mentally ill?

It was debatable whether or not Herrin had the necessary impairment to be considered mentally ill. His mental state did not really come into question until he bludgeoned his girlfriend, Bonnie Garland, with a hammer while she slept. According to Gaylin, even the definition of mental illness itself can be debated. Professional opinions range from one extreme that everyone suffers some kind of mental illness to the other that mental illness is a myth. Herrin was evaluated by several doctors who all came up with different conclusions explaining his mental state.

What was the nature of that mental illness?

Many professionals considered Herrin to be mentally ill. Dr. Train believed that Herrin suffered from a severe mental illness classified at that time as a transient situational reaction, which described individuals who appeared to be relatively normal, but were really unstable and not functional at an appropriate level. Dr. Train also suggested that his mental state reached psychotic proportions at the time of the killing and even mentioned the beginnings of dissociation.

Another expert, Dr. Rubenstein, also testified for the defense, describing Herrin's personality as borderline and paranoid. Although Dr. Rubenstein said that he could not make a case for schizophrenia in court, he did believe Herrin exhibited a defect of ego function, a disturbance in capacity for empathy and an inability to form mature love relationships. Dr. Rubenstein reported to Gaylin that Herrin's mental state approximated psychosis, but was not quite there. Another expert, Dr. Abrams, reported that he found no psychotic manifestations or mental disease or defect in his examination of Herrin. And still another expert, Dr. Schwartz, concluded that Herrin was undergoing depersonalization symptoms, including difficulty in recognizing things about himself accompanied by feelings of unreality, vagueness and confusion, which he described as a condition not a disease.

Was there a diagnosis?

The psychiatrists who evaluated Herrin never attempted to arrive at a consensus concerning diagnosis. All the psychiatrists presented contrasting opinions.

Was he referred for psychological treatment?

Herrin received psychiatric evaluations, but was not referred for treatment. Herrin had never believed he needed psychiatric treatment, even when, a bit prior to his killing her, Garland suggested that he required therapy, Herrin refused, believing that he was the type of person who was free from such psychological problems.

Did he have treatment?

No.

What was the nature of the treatment? Did the treatment involve medication? How consistent was the treatment? To what extent did he comply with treatment? What was the outcome of the treatment?

Not applicable in this case.

What have various people said about his early life?

Gaylin argued that Richard Herrin's childhood was not terribly traumatic despite what the defense's expert psychiatric witnesses had claimed. Dr. Train often mentioned Herrin's early life in order to explain his bizarre behaviors and the eventual killing. Dr. Train said that the unstable elements of Herrin's personality were due to a continuation of the feelings he had never gotten over in his childhood. Gaylin disagreed. He said that Herrin's childhood was not all that unusual as Train would have liked the jury to believe. Gaylin also felt that Train manipulated childhood events in order to fit a sympathetic story of Herrin.

Charges in the case

Richard Herrin had been dating Bonnie Garland for two and a half years when she went to Europe for a Glee Club tour in the summer of 1977. He had met her at Yale and had graduated before her, but kept in touch with her. For that tour, Herrin had a copy of her itinerary and wrote a letter to her that she would receive in each of the cities on the tour. Herrin and Garland had written each other in this manner two years earlier when she had gone on a previous tour. Unlike the first tour, however, this summer Herrin did not receive any letters during her time in Europe. He became very anxious. When he called her house upon her return to the states, he was told that she had gone to New Haven. He also received a letter that she had written from Norway in which she had said that there was somebody else and had expressed interested in seeing other people.

Herrin flew out to see her and try to work things out in early July of 1977. After spending a couple days at a friend's house, he stayed with her for a couple days in her house in Scarsdale, New York. During his visit, she made it clear that she intended to see other people and did not want to remain in a relationship or unofficial engagement with him. However, on the first night they ended up sleeping together, and on the second night she invited him to stay with her in her bed once again. Garland had been a bit sick, and so she went to bed early. Herrin said he would come to bed shortly.

After she had gone to bed he made the decision that both of them were going to die that night. He spent some time considering how they should die and searching for an appropriate means of killing her. He found a hammer in the workshop in the basement and wrapped it and some rope in a towel. He left the towel in the hallway outside her room while he went in to check to make sure she was asleep. Then he went back into the hallway and got the towel and the hammer. He leaned over her, raised the hammer over his head with both hands, and struck her in the middle of the temple. After this first blow the skull and skin were not broken, but blood began to come out of her ear, her body jerked, her eyes rolled back, and she started making a guttural noise. He paused after the first blow, lifted her head, and said her name. Then he continued to hit her head with the hammer, now breaking the skin and skull and penetrating the temple area.

Bonnie Garland continued to make noise and Richard Herrin claimed that he felt the need to get away from the house because he feared that people would wake up and prevent him from killing himself. He hit her in the throat and chest and tried to strangle her in an attempt to stop the noise. But the noise continued, so he took the keys to the car and left.

Richard Herrin drove around thinking about the various ways he could kill himself. He considered driving the car off a mountain, into oncoming traffic, or into a lake. When he saw a sign for Van Winkle Bridge he went to it, got out of his car, and considered diving off it. When he could not bring himself to do it, he continued to drive and consider possibilities for suicide. Finally, he turned the car around and went back to Coxsackie, a town with a church he had passed earlier. At 6:00 a.m., he parked outside the church and fell asleep on the stairs. He woke up about an hour later, knocked on the door of the rectory, and confessed to Father Tartaglia that he had killed Bonnie Garland and wanted to turn himself in. The priest called the police who arrested him and went to the Garlands' house where they found her still alive. They took her to the emergency room where doctors started operating immediately, but she died in the hospital.

How did the case proceed?

Herrin pleaded not guilty at his arraignment.

What rulings did the judge make?

The judge admitted Herrin's suicide note. He released him on bail through funds raised by the Catholic Chaplaincy at Yale.

What prosecution and defense testimony was introduced?

Dr. John Train and Dr. Rubenstein testified as psychological experts for the defense, while Dr. Daniel Schwartz, Dr. Abraham Halpern, and Dr. Leonard Abrams testified for the prosecution.

Was there a plea bargain?

No.

Did the jury decide the case?

Yes.

What comments did jurors make?

The jurors stated that Dr. Schwartz had definitely affected their decision. Though Dr. Schwartz's aim may have been to convince the jury that the defendant was not legally insane, his allusion to the defendant having some sort of condition caused the jury to reduce the conviction to manslaughter. For example, a juror later stated his belief that symptoms are signs of an underlying disease.

One juror claimed that Herrin's Yale degree and difficult childhood did not affect his decision. However, this claim is questionable since the same juror also stated that he did not convict Herrin on murder because the defense attorneys presented a more holistic picture of Herrin. Thus, although Herrin's education and background may not have completely excused his crime in the eyes of the jury, it did reduce his charge.

What sentence was imposed?

The jury charged Herrin guilty of manslaughter. The judge gave him a sentence of eight and a third to twenty-five years.

What factors influenced that sentence?

Many thought that because Herrin was young, attractive, newsworthy, from Yale, and a member of a minority group while still being able to give an impression of being similar enough to any one of the jurors, Herrin received a lighter conviction than expected.

What was the prosecution's view of the case?

District Attorney William M. Fredreck took a very simplistic view of the case. He relied on the fact that Herrin confessed to killing Bonnie Garland. Herrin had admitted that he had the idea, searched for a weapon, and then struck her with the intent to kill her. Fredreck considered this sufficient. Fredreck felt that his job was, quite simply, to show that Herrin was a fairly normal boy who was fully responsible for the atrocious crime he committed. Consequently, Fredreck chose to focus on proving Herrin's normalcy and thus responsibility. He did not feel that details, such as Herrin's background or his relationship with Garland, needed to be explored in any sort of depth.

What did the prosecutor do initially?

Initially, Fredreck assembled a psychiatric team to examine Richard Herrin in order to testify to his healthy psychological state. He brought together Dr. Daniel Schwartz, Dr. Abraham Halpern, and Dr. Leonard Abrams. Among these professionals, Dr. Schwartz was Fredreck's most experienced witness, as he had been involved in many high profile and unusual trials. Fredreck's strategy was to have his expert witnesses theorize on what the defense's psychiatrists would say and come up with counter arguments to refute any claims that Herrin was insane during the time of the murder.

What became the prosecutor's strategy in the case?

One of the main reasons that Fredreck lost this case was because his strategy did not change throughout the trial. He did not change to counter the points made by defense attorney Jack Litman. Fredreck's strategy was to make the case very simple for the jury. He decided to ignore Herrin's emotional state and to focus on his behavior. As it turned out, the flaw in his thinking was that in New York an extreme emotional disturbance was enough to change a conviction of murder to manslaughter, which was what Herrin eventually received. Thus, by ignoring Herrin's emotional state, the very thing Litman was focusing on, Fredreck left many of Litman's claims unchallenged causing the jury to accept Litman's statements as fact. Fredreck also made two key errors during the trial. He allowed Litman's psychiatric witness Dr. Train to talk at great length without interruption and he examined Herrin for less than three minutes. The first error allowed the defense to paint a sympathetic view of Herrin. The second allowed the defense's portrayal of Herrin to go unchallenged. Fredreck tried a few other tactics to prove Herrin's guilt, such as having Herrin admit to planning the murder, thus indicating premeditation, yet he never drove these points home. Rather, he glossed over important points, such as his argument that Herrin could not be emotionally disturbed because, as the defense itself said, Herrin showed no emotion. Fredreck had some potential good points to make, but he never made them clear enough to the jury. While Litman repeatedly drove home the points of Herrin's mental illness, Fredreck merely proceeded with his initial static strategy. He did not adapt to the changing dynamics of the case or respond to defense testimony with refutation testimony. He perhaps had the tools to win the case, yet he failed to utilize them properly.

When was the defense lawyer first involved in this case and was he hired or appointed?

Jack T. Litman was hired by Richard Herrin after Herrin was charged with killing Bonnie Garland. He became involved through the intervention of a Yale friend of Herrin's.

What did the defense lawyer do initially?

Litman interviewed Herrin for a significant period in order to establish his state of mind during the killing. Since the facts of the case were reasonably straightforward, Litman began formulating a strategy that would lessen Richard's sentence to voluntary manslaughter. Though he also argued for insanity, he seemed more confident of the reduced charge of manslaughter.

What was the defense lawyer's view of the case?

The defense attorney, Jack Litman, took a more complicated view of the case. He set out to convince the jury that Richard Herrin was not responsible because he was insane at the time of the killing. Litman believed that Herrin was essentially in a state of temporary insanity because of the traumatic discussion he had had with his girlfriend. He felt that Herrin did not fully realize what he was doing until after he had killed her. He would back this up with extensive psychiatric testimony attesting to Herrin's past and present psychological problems. Should he not convince the jury of Herrin's insanity, he planned to convince them that he was not fully responsible because of his extreme emotional disturbance.

What became the defense lawyer's strategy in the case?

Litman adopted the approach of blaming the victim. He drudged up all of the discussions and memories that Richard Herrin had of Bonnie Garland and their relationship and tried to establish Herrin as the actual victim. Litman claimed that Garland's emotional abuse of Herrin led to his abnormal mental state and eventually resulted in her death. To support this theory, Litman also brought up

Herrin's troubled upbringing and abnormal social life, as well as his apparent remorse following the murder.

When did a psychoforensic professional first become involved in this case?

Dr. John Train examined Richard Herrin for nine hours over two days, August 2 and August 5, 1977. This was within three to four weeks of the murder.

Was the professional a psychologist or a psychiatrist?

Dr. Train was a psychiatrist.

Who appointed or hired the psychoforensic professional?

Dr. Train was hired by the defense.

What did the professional do initially?

While interviewing Richard, Dr. Train probed for causes of the defendant's behavior. By examining his childhood, Train determined that events in his early years contributed to later behaviors. These included having an alcoholic father, a mother who remarried, and a stepfather who was harsh and critical.

What diagnostic conclusions did that professional reach?

Dr. Train created an elaborate diagnosis for Herrin that Gaylin found not fully psychiatrically sound. He testified that Herrin suffered from a severe mental disease called at that time transient situational reaction, which indicated a problem with adjustment. He also testified that Herrin had a model boy syndrome that included his inability to express anger and his need to ingratiate. Finally, he tried to establish that Richard had a symbiotic relationship with Garland and that she became the foundation of his being. On inspection this did not hold up because Garland was not dependent on him in the same way that Herrin was on her. However, Train also suggested a type of psychosis at the time of the murder.

What did that psychoforensic professional do subsequently?

In court, Train played the storyteller, rather than a true psychiatric expert. Gaylin noted that he falsified statistics, altered facts, and basically testified to what the defense wanted. He used examples of letters written between Garland and Herrin to support his claims, as well as exaggerating Richard's childhood problems to make them seem like an adequate cause of the killing.

What other psychoforensic professionals became involved?

Dr. Mark Rubenstein, a psychiatrist, also worked for the defense while Dr. Halpern, another psychiatrist, was hired by the prosecution.

In addition, Lawrence Abt, a psychologist, performed various psychological tests on Herrin evaluating his IQ and signs of psychosis. He concluded that Herrin had a high IQ and exhibited no signs of psychosis.

Dr. Harvey Lothringer also evaluated Herrin the day after the murder and wrote a report for the Forensic Unit at the County Jail and also concluded that Herrin showed no signs of psychosis.

Abrams reviewed both of these reports and mentioned them during his testimony.

Was the subject held in a facility?

Richard Herrin was held and interviewed in the Westchester County Jail in the hospital, or mental health, unit.

Was the subject examined on an outpatient basis?

He was examined in jail by Dr. Train, but he was examined by Dr. Schwartz while he was staying with the Christian Brothers while he was released on bail.

How important was the case to the media?

The case appears to have been of some importance to the media. It involved the combination of a prestigious university like Yale, unrequited love, and murder which make for an interesting story. *The New York Times* ran a long story in 1978, before the end of the trial, entitled "A fatal romance at Yale: The tragic story of the high school valedictorian and the golden Scarsdale girl, and its painful aftermath." Additionally, *The New York Times* ran a handful of other stories on different aspects of the trial, from jury selection through to the sentencing. The intrigue of the case also served as fodder for tabloids like the *Sun* and *National Enquirer*. The case subsequently became the subject of two books, *The Yale Murder* by Peter Meyer and *The Killing of Bonnie Garland* by Willard Gaylin.

What were the majority media responses?

The majority response appeared at least somewhat sympathetic to Herrin's case. In later published stories, Bonnie Garland's name was not mentioned while Richard Herrin's was. Many of *The New York Times* stories devoted more attention to the defense's statements than to the prosecution's. The *National Catholic Reporter* illustrated how a Catholic community had championed Herrin's cause.

What were the dissenting media responses?

The *Sun* and *National Enquirer* published stories based on what they were told by Bonnie Garland's parents. It is difficult to tell from *The Killing of Bonnie Garland* what the dissenting media responses were.

How influential were the media in the outcome of the case?

Willard Gaylin made virtually no mention of the media's influence in the outcome of the case.

How influential were the media in the aftermath of the case?

Again, *The Killing of Bonnie Garland* made no mention of the media's influence in the aftermath of the case.

What did legal commentators say about the case?

Professor Alan Dershowitz examined the effectiveness of the defense's strategy in the Richard Herrin case. Defense attorney Jack Litman, whom Dershowitz praised for his skill, had, he argued, successfully transformed Herrin from the perpetrator into a victim of his circumstances. Rather than considering Herrin fortunate to have matriculated at Yale, Litman persuaded the jury to view this opportunity as an unconquerable hardship. Having come from a disadvantaged background, Herrin was unprepared for the academic, and, more important, social environment he found at Yale. This taxing atmosphere quickly broke down Herrin's poorly developed coping mechanisms, a product of his traumatic youth, and left him essentially powerless to control himself during his crime. Using attorney Litman's own words, Dershowitz demonstrated how the jury was led to the conclusion that Herrin did not intend to kill Bonnie Garland. Considering that Herrin had never been known to show any anger until his single, gruesomely violent deed in her bedroom, the crime was obviously a product not of Herrin, but of a serious mental disorder. The fact that Herrin fled the house half-naked, with no money and no plans further exemplified the defense's claim that the crime was unplanned and unintentional. Given that the jury convicted Herrin of manslaughter instead of murder, which requires a criminal intent that manslaughter lacks, it was probable that the jury was persuaded by Litman's argument that Herrin's crime was unintentional.

What did psychoforensic commentators say about the case?

One commentator addressed the issue of whether mental illness should excuse criminal behavior. He argued that, given the brutal, senseless nature of Herrin's crime against Bonnie Garland, one's first reaction may have been to assume that he was insane when the crime was committed. To be sure, his behavior was not indicative of normal mental processes: most normal people, after all, do not bludgeon their lovers while they sleep. The crime was unimaginable to people familiar with Herrin's quiet disposition and was completely out of sync with behavior that could possibly have been anticipated from him. Yet, something drove him to kill Bonnie. The easy conclusion was that he was insane at the time and had no control over his actions. However, this assumption that he was crazy could be applied just as easily in nearly any criminal case. Arguably, any criminal is not thinking clearly and with a full understanding of the consequences when he commits his crime: otherwise, why would he follow through with it? When too much credence is automatically given to the mental incapacity of defendants, the danger is that no one will be responsible for his crime. The essential judgment of guilt would be taken from jurors and put into the hands of expert psychological witnesses. Although some defendants certainly were driven to crime simply on account of mental illness, it is important to remember that thousands of severely mentally impaired people walk among the ranks of society every day without committing crimes. Mental illness can be a mitigating factor in trials, but more normally, it leaves the patient fully capable of controlling his own behavior.

What did other commentators say about the case?

One commentator analyzed the Richard Herrin case in a philosophical light. He argued that when the religious persons surrounding Herrin were asked whether they could imagine committing a similar act in any given situation, they all replied that, yes, they could imagine themselves committing a horrible crime in certain extreme circumstances. He then considered this question: how would you feel if you had committed Herrin's crime? He proposed that any moral person would feel endlessly guilty and would consider himself deserving of strict punishment. Rather than welcoming cathartic punishment, however, Herrin considered his debt to be paid off and resisted the notion of any imprisonment. Because Herrin did not conform to the guilty feelings of that moral person, he proceeded to question whether Herrin should be subjected to a different standard, thereby accounting for the fact that no one else had been subjected to exactly the same stresses as Herrin was. He answered his own question with an unwavering no. To hold Herrin, or anyone else, for that matter, to a lower standard than one held oneself was inherently discriminatory and condescending because it implied that the person was somehow a lesser human being. Although Herrin may have been the victim of overpowering circumstances, the fact that he felt little, if any, guilt made him culpable.

What do we learn about the insanity defense from this case?

In this case, the acceptance of the insanity defense did not rest simply on the testimony and relative strength of the expert witnesses. Richard Herrin owed his acquittal from the murder charge, although he was convicted of the lesser charge of manslaughter, in large part to the skill of his defense attorney, Jack Litman, and to the inadequacy of the prosecutor, William Fredreck. Litman related the story of Richard Herrin, reaching all the way back to Herrin's childhood, while conveniently steering clear of mentions of Bonnie Garland. Fredreck, the prosecutor, paled by comparison, failing to focus the case on its victim, Bonnie Garland, or to understand the complexity of the case and the importance of a flexible strategy. As a result, the jury seemed to sympathize more with the defendant, Herrin, than with the victim, Garland. That contributed largely to Herrin's murder acquittal.

From this we learn that the insanity defense is not a simple matter of objective evaluation of expert testimony. Many other subjective and human factors, such as a jury's self-identification with the defendant or victim, can influence the success of the insanity defense. This renders the insanity defense subjective and imprecise.

What other issues were involved in this case?

A major issue involved with this case was that of public safety, for Herrin was allowed to enroll in a college under an alias while the trial was pending, and the other students initially were not informed of what he had done. Another was the fact that Herrin was released on bail into the custody of the church. This was important not only because of the issue of public safety but also because of the issue of whether such a release implicitly condoned or exonerated the accused.

Throughout the case, the issue of the role of expert testimony regarding someone's state of mind in the past was in the forefront. Both sides were able to find experts willing to testify that Herrin was or was not psychotic, was or was not insane.

How representative of insanity defense cases was this case?

The case of Richard Herrin could not be thought of as a typical insanity defense case, as it garnered more publicity than most cases of similar natures do and Litman argued for one of two conflicting outcomes: innocence by reason of insanity, and a reduced charge of manslaughter due to extreme emotional disturbance. Further it generated more discussion as books were released and reevaluations took place.

What concluding comments could be made concerning the insanity defense itself?

As is evident from this case, the insanity defense is a very subjective tool, one that can be molded to the whims of the defense attorneys as they see fit; it is, therefore, a rather imprecise method as it is greatly affected by external factors. In this case, the success of the insanity defense rested heavily on the techniques of Litman, and less on the actual facts of the case.

How would you sum up this case in a brief paragraph?

Richard Herrin bludgeoned his girlfriend, Bonnie Garland, to death with a hammer. His motive apparently was jealously, as Garland wanted to end the relationship and see other men. Herrin's defense attorney, Jack Litman, argued that Herrin was not guilty of murder, due to insanity or extreme emotional disturbance. Litman produced experts who testified that Herrin suffered from a transient situational reaction at the time of the crime arising from adult adjustment problem. The prosecutor took a very simple approach to the case, produced some experts of his own, and was largely ineffective. The jury found Herrin not guilty of murder, but guilty of manslaughter.

Dan and Ron Lafferty

What were the essentials of the case?

This case has been extensively presented and analyzed in Jon Krakauer's *Under the Banner of Heaven*. The case presentation which follows relies on his material for the summary of the legal, religious, psychological, and social facts of this case.

Ron and Dan Lafferty, who were brothers, confessed upon capture to killing Ron's sister-in-law, Brenda Lafferty, and his niece, Erica. Their guilt was never an issue. Representation, though offered, was refused by both brothers, as was an insanity plea, as they felt they had done no wrong by murdering Brenda and her daughter, and they wanted their message to be heard as a rational one. The Laffertys believed a greater good awaited them in heaven, and therefore felt no shame in committing murder, or consequently facing the death penalty, as it would only help them get to heaven faster. Dan, particularly, believed his transformation into the prophet Elijah was imminent, as was the destruction of his prison cell. The brothers felt no emotion other than certainty in their futures, and a certainty that the present world was a farce that would cease to exist as Fundamental Mormonism became the only true path to salvation.

What were the facts preceding the acts in this case?

Ron and Dan Lafferty were Mormons who joined the School of Prophets, and became leaders within this community. Ron had just lost his job, been abandoned by his wife and children, and been scorned by his church and community. His religious views escalated until he believed himself to be receiving direct revelations from God, one of which was a command to commit the murder of three people, one of whom was Brenda Lafferty. Ron was angry with his sister-in-law Brenda Lafferty for encouraging his wife to leave him. The other two intended victims were others who had encouraged his wife's separation from him. The reason for baby Erica's death, according to Ron Lafferty, was because she was a child of perdition and because God had also named the baby as one of his victims. Later Ron claimed that God had appointed his younger brother, Dan Lafferty, to be the one to actually commit the murders, although both men were in the house at the time of the crime. After the brothers presented this supposed notice from God to the rest of those belonging to the School of the Prophets and received a strongly negative response, Ron and Dan left the state, eventually driving to Utah County to commit the murders.

What specifically happened in this case?

According to Dan Lafferty's testimony, which is believed to be fairly accurate, on July 24, 1984, the two brothers arrived at their brother Allen's home in Utah County. Their two friends accompanied them. Though at first no one answered the door, on the second attempt, Allen's wife, Brenda Lafferty, opened the door. Brenda did not want to let Dan in, but he pushed his way past her while the other three men stayed in the car. Ron entered the home shortly after, beating Brenda's face badly. Once inside, however, Ron did not want to kill Brenda, so Dan slit her throat after doing the same to Allen's daughter, Erica. Both men left the house in bloody clothes, frightening the two other men in the car. Ron and Dan planned to murder the other two intended victims before the day was over.

After the crime, it was revealed that Allen Lafferty, husband and father to the victims, had received a phone call from Dan during which Dan warned Allen of Ron's violent plans. Allen never informed his wife of the warning. Though Allen was at first a suspect in the case, he was the one who pointed the police in Ron and Dan's direction.

Who were the victims?

Brenda Lafferty, the defendants' sister-in-law, and Erica Lafferty, the defendants' niece, were the victims.

Did the defendants know the victims?

Yes, they were the brother-in-law and uncle of the victims.

What happened immediately after the acts in this case?

Allen Lafferty, husband and father to the victims, came home after work in the evening to find the house eerily quiet. He then saw his wife lying on the kitchen floor in a pool of blood and his baby girl lying in blood in her crib. Since all of the phones in the house were out of order, he called the police at his neighbor's house. Allen Lafferty immediately became a suspect, but was later released after leading police to the actual perpetrators, his brothers Ron and Dan Lafferty. Ron and Dan Lafferty were arrested at a casino in Reno, Nevada, but still denied committing the murders.

How was, or was not, the insanity plea used in this case?

The insanity defense, though recommended by counsel, was not used by either Dan or Ron Lafferty. The brothers thought their thinking completely rational and felt their ideas and predictions would be discredited by pleading insane.

What state did the case proceed in?

Utah.

What was the law in that state concerning the insanity defense?

The not guilty by reason of insanity verdict in the Hinckley trial provoked widespread public concern, prompting various states to implement reforms of their respective insanity defense laws. In 1983, Utah joined Montana and Idaho, becoming the third state to abolish the traditional insanity defense as a means of reducing admissibility of mental disorder evidence. However, Utah replaced the void with the mens rea insanity defense.

What were the legal elements of the insanity defense?

The mens rea insanity defense continued to allow the introduction of evidence of mental illness as a mitigating factor. If the defense could negate mens rea, proving that due to mental disease or defect the defendant did not possess the requisite mind required for conviction of a specific offense, charges against him could be reduced. In Ron Lafferty's case, mounting a successful insanity defense could have meant a reduction from first degree murder to manslaughter.

What were the elements such as burden of proof?

The burden of proof was on the defense to show that the defendant lacked the culpable mental state to be held criminally responsible for a charged offense. Evidence of a personality disorder, although listed in the *Diagnostic and Statistical Manual of Mental Disorders*, could not be used to challenge culpability.

What was the law in that state concerning diminished capacity?

In 1986, the Utah legislature enacted an amendment authorizing the addition of a diminished capacity concept to the mens rea insanity defense. Dan Lafferty's trial and conviction and Ron Lafferty's first trial and conviction occurred a year prior to the enactment of this amendment.

What were the legal elements of diminished capacity?

Utah's mens rea diminished capacity defense was a variant of the insanity plea, allowing psychiatric testimony of the defendant's mental condition at the time of the offense. The accused could still be considered sane, but not responsible for the crime due to a mental state that diminished his capacity to harbor the criminal intent necessary for conviction.

How did the case proceed?

In 1985, Dan Lafferty represented himself at trial, leaving his court-appointed attorneys in an advisory role only. The jury deliberations began five days after the trial began, and lasted nine hours. Ron Lafferty's trial began four months after Dan Lafferty's, since Ron Lafferty had nearly committed suicide by hanging and had to be examined for brain damage. At the trial, Ron Lafferty disallowed his court-appointed attorneys to base his defense on the claim that he was suffering from mental illness, stating that that would appear tantamount to an admission of guilt. Ron Lafferty extended his stay on death row to over seventeen years through appeals and other legal strategies, which included appealing to several different courts. The U.S. Court of Appeals ruled years after his original conviction that Ron Lafferty was not initially competent to stand trial, and the conviction was overturned. In 1992, doctors determined that Ron Lafferty was not fit to stand trial again, and so he was sent to a hospital and treated for mental illness. In 1994, Ron Lafferty was deemed competent to stand trial again. At the new trial in 1996, Ron Lafferty's lawyers employed an insanity defense. He was again found guilty of first-degree murder.

What rulings did the judge make?

A judge ruled in 1994 that Ron Lafferty was competent to stand trial after having stayed in a hospital to be treated for mental illness.

What prosecution or defense testimony was introduced?

Due to his refusal to use an insanity defense, Ron Lafferty's attorney could not call upon any expert witnesses he had planned to have testify on his client's mental stability. In his retrial in 1996, Ron's lawyers called to the stand one psychologist and three psychiatrists who testified that Ron suffered from mental illnesses, while the prosecution called upon one psychiatrist and three psychologists to refute the defense witnesses' claims.

Was there a plea bargain?

Authorities told Chip Carnes that he would be charged with capital homicide and could face the death penalty if he did not provide testimony that could assist with first-degree murder convictions for Dan and Ron Lafferty. Carnes and Richard Knapp also helped police recover evidence and provided them with a lead in pursuing the Lafferty brothers, in exchange for leniency from the police.

Did the jury decide the case?

Juries convicted Dan and Ron Lafferty in 1985, and also sentenced Ron Lafferty to death at the time. At his retrial in 1996, the judge sentenced Ron Lafferty to death.

What comments did jurors make?

In Dan Lafferty's 1985 sentencing, the jury foreman said the defendant escaped the death penalty because he had seduced through non verbal signals a woman on the jury.

What sentence was imposed?

In 1985, after Dan Lafferty escaped the death penalty on a ten to two jury vote, the judge sentenced him to two terms of life imprisonment. That same year, Ron Lafferty was sentenced to death, either by lethal injection or by firing squad. In his retrial, in 1996, Ron Lafferty was again sentenced to death.

What factors influenced that sentence?

While sentencing Dan Lafferty, the judge commented that Lafferty showed very little remorse or feeling.

What role did the lawyers play in this case?

By the time of the retrial, Ron Lafferty's brother Dan had accepted that he would spend his life in jail, and therefore he became much more open to talking about the murders. Because of his testimony, the only option left for the defense was to plead insanity. Thus, the prosecution, a team of lawyers which included Attorney General Mark Shurtleff and Assistant Attorney Generals Kris Leonard, Creighton Horton, and Michael Wims, set out to show that Ron Lafferty was sane and had known what he was doing when he took part in the murders of Brenda and Erica Lafferty. Members of the prosecution expressed doubt in the sincerity of Ron

Lafferty's outbursts in court and religious proclamations and thought he may have been trying to fake insanity.

The prosecution assembled a group of expert witnesses including one psychiatrist and three psychologists to argue that Ron Lafferty was legally sane at the time of the crime. These witnesses included psychiatrist Dr. Noel Gardner, and psychologists Drs. Wootton, Golding, and Cohn.

Their strategy was to show that he was sane through comparison with other individuals. First, they pointed out all the similarities between his fundamentalist religious beliefs and the religious beliefs of people with ordinary religious faiths. By doing so, they made his seemingly outlandish claims and ideas seem much more normal. For example, Dr. Gardner compared Ron Lafferty's belief in reflector shields to belief in guardian angels. This strategy was effective because it forced anyone who was willing to consider whether he was insane to also consider the larger question of whether any religious person is insane. Dr. Gardner emphasized that false beliefs are common in religion, for example, and are not necessarily the basis of mental illness. Dr. Gardner also noted the importance of the roots of his beliefs in ideas he learned from his family and community when he was young. As additional support in this prong of the prosecution's strategy, they hired Richard Wootton, a practicing Mormon, as a witness. Wootton acknowledged that Ron Lafferty's beliefs were somewhat connected with ideas in Mormonism and did not seem that much stranger than Mormonism itself may seem to an outsider.

The second strategy of the prosecution was to point out the differences between Ron Lafferty and people who suffer from mental illnesses. For example, Dr. Stephen Golding testified that Ron Lafferty bore very little resemblance to schizophrenics. Schizophrenics, he said, generally do not share humor or seek out relationships. Instead, they are often lonely, isolated, and self-contained. According to Golding, Ron Lafferty did not share these common characteristics of the seriously mentally ill.

The prosecution's final strategy was to admit that Ron Lafferty seemed to exhibit signs of narcissism. However, they argued that most narcissists do not murder or claim to be prophets of God. Thus, they asserted while he may have been narcissistic and devoutly religious, he was not insane.

The judge involved in the case was Judge Steven Hansen. After the jury brought back a guilty verdict, Judge Hansen sentenced Ron Lafferty to death by firing squad or lethal injection. Ron Lafferty chose the firing squad, as incidentally had Gary Gilmore, also in Utah, the first person executed after the U. S. Supreme Court reconsidered capital punishment and found it constitutional.

When did a psychoforensic professional first become involved in this case?

After the murders and apprehension, a psychoforensic professional became involved in the case, and several others would soon follow. The exact time between apprehension and examination is unclear but the time in question seems to have been fairly short.

Was the professional a psychologist or a psychiatrist?

The professional was C. Jess Groesbeck, a psychiatrist.

Who appointed or hired the professional?

The defense team hired Groesbeck, and they called him as their first expert witness to testify that Ron Lafferty was deranged.

What did that professional do initially?

Groesbeck examined Lafferty and interviewed him in order to gain a sense of why he did what he did, trying to establish whether or not he was insane.

What diagnostic conclusion(s) did that psychoforensic professional reach?

Groesbeck reached the conclusion that when Ron Lafferty's wife left him, he could not deal with such a loss, and the act triggered a schizoaffective disorder or a delusional disorder. The departure of his wife led Lafferty to create an entirely new reality for himself, one not bounded by rationality, and for this reason, Groesbeck argued that Lafferty was unable to realize the charges against him.

Was there ever a question of competence to stand trial?

After extensive psychological evaluation before his first hearing, Ron Lafferty was deemed competent to stand trial. According to the psychiatrist, he was quite aware and seemed to understand the charges brought against him. The trial proceeded accordingly.

However, in 1991 the Tenth U.S. Circuit Court of Appeals in Denver, Colorado, reversed Ron's previous convictions on the grounds that the courts used a faulty standard to determine competency in his original trial. The Court of Appeals claimed that Ron Lafferty could not interpret the charges against him in a realistic way as a consequence of his paranoid delusional system. The court believed that Ron Lafferty's claim that he appealed to a higher law showed that he did not understand the complexities of the legal system, and they asserted that if Utah wanted to keep him in jail, they would have to prove that he was in fact sane.

In 1992 three psychological experts helped convince the courts that Ron Lafferty was not fit to stand trial. He was transferred from Death Row to a Utah State Hospital. In February of 1994, after sixteen months of therapy, he was finally deemed fit to stand trial once more.

What other psychoforensic professionals became involved?

Three psychiatrists and one psychologist testified for the defense, and three psychologists and one psychiatrist for the prosecution.

What diagnoses did the other professionals make?

The defense claimed that Ron Lafferty had slipped into delusional disorder when his wife left him. They claimed that his was a false and distorted view of the world. The prosecution's experts claimed that his beliefs were consistent with what he learned as a child.

What did psychoforensic commentators say about the case?

The psychological community was divided on its take on the Lafferty murder case. Some believed that the Laffertys were mentally ill while others did not. Many thought that there was evidence of delusional behavior, especially in Ron Lafferty, as he believed that the angel Moroni was trying to invade his body, that he heard Christ speak to him, and that he heard buzzing sounds and saw sparks flying from his fingertips. However, others countered that these beliefs were in accordance with what Lafferty had been taught to accept from childhood, and whether they were real or not in actuality, they were reality to him. This would oppose the theory that Lafferty was suffering from any kind of schizophrenic or delusional disorder. Religious beliefs do not indicate mental illness in and by themselves, and since Lafferty shared a reality with others, he could not be classified as schizophrenic.

Despite the opinion that Lafferty did not suffer from schizophrenia, though, some psychologists did think that he exhibited symptoms of narcissistic personality disorder. His exaggerated sense of self-importance, his lack of empathy, and his arrogance all led them to this diagnosis. They concluded that Lafferty may have used his religion to create soothing ideas so that pain was less of a reality for him. However, it should also be noted, few narcissists are actually murderers, and this diagnosis would not relieve him of the responsibility for his crimes. Neither Ron Lafferty, nor Dan Lafferty, fit the description of insanity, and few psychologists believed that this defense should be used in this case.

What did legal commentators say about the case?

Legal commentators were very intrigued by the Lafferty case. Here were two people being tried for a violent crime against their own family, yet neither was willing to be tried as mentally ill or insane. Both Dan Lafferty and Ron Lafferty, despite the nature of their crimes, communicated with their lawyers fairly well. Because of their reasonably normal actions before the trial, both Laffertys were never really considered unfit to stand trial. Yet, both acted fairly aggressively and unpredictably when dealing with their attorneys and the police. They showed no remorse and even claimed that they would kill the police officers in the room if God instructed them to. What intrigued lawyers looking at the case from the outside was the seeming paradox confronting those involved with the case: How does one argue insanity for clients who emphatically argue against insanity and whose only seemingly insane actions were feeling that God instructed them to commit their crimes?

This question would have been less difficult if the defendants had claimed to hear instructions from voices in their head, or from another source. But they did not. The component in this trial that fascinated legal commentators was that God, and the Mormon religion, were interwoven into the case. Religion was the basis for the Lafferty brothers' lives, and they held extreme views within their religion. But the case raised the question whether their extreme beliefs made them insane. This was the issue that faced legal commentators and it split them into two camps, with most favoring the view that the Laffertys were not insane during the time of the murders.

Though some commentators felt that the Laffertys were insane, that anyone with such extreme religious views, who, for example, hear God talking to them, are mentally ill and not responsible for their actions, most legal scholars felt that their religious beliefs alone did not make them legally insane. They concluded that the brothers were rational and forward thinking during the time of the murders and should not be able to hide behind a defense intended for the severely mentally ill. They argued that both brothers were very aware of what they were doing as illustrated by how the crimes were committed and how the brothers acted after the crimes. Even when charged, as an example, both brothers adamantly claimed that they were pleased with their actions and would repeat them again if ordered by God. This complete lack of remorse and eagerness to murder again, if directed by God, compelled most legal commentators to judge both Dan and Ron Lafferty legally sane, even if morally and ethically deficient.

What did other commentators say about the case?

The main category of other commentators belonged to the leaders of the Mormon church, and, to a lesser extent, other religious leaders. Unlike psychological and legal commentators, the leaders of the Mormon church were fairly unified in their view of the trial of the Laffertys. If the Laffertys were judged to be insane because God talked to them and gave them orders, every Mormon follower would be judged as insane because the crux of the Mormon faith is that God communicates to his followers. Consequently, followers of the Mormon faith felt that the Laffertys should not be judged as legally insane. They felt that although their views lead them to commit illegal actions, there was nothing intrinsically wrong, or insane, about a devout follower of the religion feeling that God has spoken to them.

How important was the case to the media?

Due to the savageness of the crime and the victims' innocence, as well as the killers' cold-heartedness and shockingly extreme fundamentalist religious beliefs, this case captivated the media. Within a couple of days, the case began to capture headlines and front pages in the local papers, including the *Salt Lake Tribune*, before spreading to the rest of the national media.

What were the majority media responses?

The majority media responses condemned the killings and focused on the bizarre religious motivations of the killers. While most of the media did not take a definite position as to whether their particular religious beliefs made the killers legally insane, most at least showed some skepticism about such claims.

What were the dissenting media responses?

The few that diverged from the mainstream opinion were more sympathetic to the killers and focused on their lives and tribulations. Through this focus, these media responses suggested that the killers thought what they were doing was right and were vulnerable to external factors, such as religious beliefs. These media accounts were also more sympathetic to Mormonism and avoided generalizing the killers' beliefs to all of Mormonism.

How influential was the media in the outcome of the case?

Although the media responded strongly to this case, it did not play a central role in affecting the outcome. The media seemed to reflect the prevailing public opinion, rather than to actively mold the public opinion. In either Ron or Dan Lafferty's case, this public or media opinion did not unduly influence the outcome.

Since both of the Laffertys were convicted, it might seem that the outcome of the case aligned with the majority media opinion. However, during the course of the trial, events occurred that did not agree with the prevailing media opinion. For example, at one point, the Tenth Circuit Court tossed out Ron Lafferty's initial conviction, claiming that the initial finding of his competence to stand trial was not legally sound. The State of Utah and the media were not happy about having to retry Ron Lafferty. And since the identity of the killers was not really in question, their main defense would have been insanity, a defense that both Laffertys, especially Ron, impeded to some extent. As a result, factors relating to the insanity defense were more important to the outcome of the case than the media involvement.

Why did the insanity defense, or diminished capacity, succeed or fail in this case?

The insanity defense was not used due to the strong religious beliefs, what some termed the irrational pride, of Ron and Dan Lafferty. Their psychotic beliefs, to some, their strong religious beliefs, to others, were so strong that the brothers refused to compromise or discredit any of their thoughts or what they called their prophesies.

What do we learn about the insanity defense from this case?

From this case, we learn how extreme religious views, in this instance a form of fundamentalist Mormonism, can or cannot be interpreted as insanity in a court of law. The defense experts argued that Ron Lafferty developed his psychosis when his wife left him and took their children. From this experience, Lafferty allegedly developed schizoaffective and delusional disorders. The defense experts further argued that Lafferty's delusional behaviors and thoughts, such as believing that God was speaking to him directly, or that the angel Moroni was trying to invade his body through his rectum, strongly indicated that he was insane.

The prosecution, on the other hand, argued that Lafferty's seemingly delusional ideas were actually very similar to what he had learned as a child, and that many of his behaviors were consistent with several of the irrational or illogical beliefs that many religious people have. In addition, the prosecution argued that Lafferty did not exhibit any other symptoms of schizophrenia. In the end, the jury was persuaded by the prosecution and found Ron Lafferty guilty.

How accurate is that learning?

This learning is accurate, because it considers both sides of the argument. Depending on the strength of the expert witnesses and the effectiveness of the lawyers in a case, of course, different outcomes may occur.

How valuable is that learning?

This learning is valuable because it shows how the relative scarcity of cases like the Lafferty brothers' means that their case sets a powerful precedent for assessing the insanity of religious fundamentalists, what some term extremists or fanatics, in future cases. Nevertheless, the outcome of such cases can still vary dramatically, depending on the individual makeup of each case.

What other issues were involved in this case?

The pivotal issue in this case was religion and whether overwhelming religious fundamentalism, or extremism, or fanaticism indicates a lack of criminal responsibility. Ron and Dan Lafferty subscribed to their own strange brand of Mormon fundamentalism, and their religion effectively consumed their lives. After converting to his brothers' private sect, Ron Lafferty quit his job and lost his house and his family. Dan Lafferty and the younger Lafferty brothers also abandoned their places as working members of society in order to devote their time toward religious pursuits, such as building the City of Refuge at the base of the Dream Mine. The brothers' commitment to their odd beliefs in spite of detrimental consequences raised the issue of whether they were capable of making rational decisions.

Most disturbing of all, of course, was the fact that they sincerely believed they were communicating with God, who told them to kill four innocent people. Supposing that their faith in this revelation was sincere, it was easy to understand why they felt they had no choice in the murders. Who, after all, was going to disobey the direct order of God? Certainly the insanity defense was a viable option in this case, but in the end it was up to the jury to determine whether the Laffertys' religious commitment destroyed their ability to understand and to control their criminal behavior. The jury determined that both brothers were responsible for their roles in the murders.

How representative of insanity defense cases is this case?

The Lafferty case was in many ways an unusual case and certainly was not representative of insanity defense cases as a whole. Most notable in this case was the fact that the insanity plea was rooted in fanatical religious beliefs, rather than a diagnosable mental impairment. Almost the only trait that the Lafferty case shared with the typical insanity defense case was that the insanity plea was unsuccessful.

What concluding comments could be made concerning the insanity defense itself?

The Lafferty case served as a vivid example of the truth that a defendant can be deemed utterly crazy by societal standards and still have his insanity plea fail. The bottom line is that many people suffer from serious psychological disorders, and the majority of the world subscribes to illogical religious beliefs, yet those who subscribe to those religious beliefs retain the ability to control their behavior and do not commit crimes. Overzealous religious beliefs may lead a person to want to commit a crime, but unless another factor, such as psychosis, deprives him of his ability to understand the crime or to control his behavior, religion alone does not qualify a defendant as insane.

How would you sum up this case in a brief paragraph?

This was the case of zealous fundamentalists in the Church of Jesus Christ of Latter Day Saints, who, through what some would term delusional influence, murdered their brother's wife and child. Ron and Dan Lafferty, former members of the Mormon church and respected members of their Mormon community, gradually became fundamentalist Latter Day Saints, disregarding United States law in the name of their leaders. Extreme in their behavior, the brothers were excommunicated from church membership, and became radical members of the fundamentalist movement, practicing blatant polygamy and statutory rape. Quickly they sought revenge for their excommunication, targeting as victims those who separated them from their former community, including their brother Allen's wife, who had convinced him against joining the fundamentalists, and their infant daughter. In July 1984, they sacrificially murdered Brenda and her baby, failed in locating their further target, then fled to Las Vegas convinced the other murders were not meant to be. Upon their discovery and arrest, they admitted to the murders, yet denied any wrongdoing. Claiming that God had told them to kill these people, they felt that these murders would only expedite God's work. Dan Lafferty, the younger brother, was convicted and despite a request that he be executed was sentenced to consecutive terms of five years to life. Ron Lafferty, also unrepentant and deemed as more the mastermind of the operation, was convicted as well, and was sentenced to die. He chose bullets to the heart from close range. Ron Lafferty still awaits execution.

9

Case Studies

Kenneth Bianchi

In the summer of 1977, Kenneth Bianchi moved to California, from Rochester, New York, to join his cousin Angelo Buono, who was making a living as a car upholsterer but moonlighting as a pimp with brutal tendencies. Bianchi, who had been rejected in applications for jobs with the police departments of Los Angeles and nearby Glendale, was bitter and easily led. He also had a violent temper, but managed to hide it, thus winning a reputation as a charismatic and friendly person.

Arrested over a year later in Bellingham, Washington, for the murder of two young women who had answered an advertisement seeking someone to be at a home when telephones were installed, Bianchi was tied through his fingerprints to the Los Angeles killings. Having moved without his cousin to Washington, Buono was also implicated in the Los Angeles killings.

Bianchi's reputation as a diligent security guard and a considerate family man changed after he had confessed to raping and killing several women, leaving their naked bodies on hillsides around Los Angeles, California. The Los Angeles police deemed the case solved, as they had finally found the so-called Hillside Strangler who had eluded them for so long.

Yet the case took a bizarre turn. Bianchi's confession had been elicited while he was hypnotized. But the confession did not come from Kenneth Bianchi. It came from what the psychologist and the defense claimed was another personality, Steven Walker, who said he had been the killer. The psychologist, hired by the defense, had brought forth this other personality, Steve Walker, who said he had been the killer and that Kenneth Bianchi was unaware of him. Because of what was then termed multiple personality disorder and was subsequently renamed dissociative identity disorder, Bianchi's attorney raised the insanity defense. The prosecution accused Bianchi of malingering, or faking. The insanity defense and psychology themselves were put to the test as the court weighed Bianchi's alleged insanity or malingering.

Bianchi's early years

As a child, Bianchi experienced physical problems: rolling his eyes, exhibiting tics, and falling down. Fearing petit mal seizures, doctors referred him for psychiatric treatment. A Dr. Dowling, who saw him at the DePaul Clinic, described Bianchi at that time as repressed, anxious, and lonely. According to Dr. Dowling, this was partly due to Bianchi's relationship with his mother, who was at times harsh and overbearing. Bianchi, he said, was quite dependent on his mother and would attempt to placate her by hiding his hostility. When Dr. Dowling was later contacted about Bianchi's case, he concluded that Bianchi's condition at age eleven was consistent with a subsequent diagnosis of multiple personality disorder as an adult.

Charges in this case

In the late 1970s, the Los Angeles police were discovering the bodies of murdered and raped women around the city. At first, the victims were prostitutes, raising little concern, but fears ran high after young girls, 12 and 14 years old and non-prostitutes, were murdered. Most of the victims were found in the hills surrounding Los Angeles and often near freeways or ravines, leading the media to name the murderer the Hillside Strangler. The police, however, believed the murderer was not acting alone. In any case, the police admitted that the killer or killers were smart, cunning, and left virtually no leads. The killer also seemed to be familiar with police methods, leading the police to advise the citizenry not to stop on side streets for police officers. All ten Los Angeles victims had been raped and strangled to death.

The chilling campaign of slaughter began on October 16, 1977. The first victim had been Yolanda Washington, a prostitute. She had been strangled. An autopsy revealed she had had sex with two men shortly before she died, but in her line of work, this was neither surprising nor incriminating. In 1977, the murder of a prostitute in Los Angeles was not considered worthy of more than a paragraph in the city's papers. Nevertheless, over the next eight weeks the Hillside Strangler claimed the lives of another nine women in the hills surrounding Los Angeles. Several of the victims, including a twenty year old art student, were not prostitutes, and this began to draw attention to these violent crimes.

The public became enraged when three bodies were found on a rubbish dump on the Sunday morning of November 20, 1977. Two of the victims were school girls, 12 and 14 years old. Suddenly, the Hillside Strangler was making front-page news and causing panic across the city and its suburbs.

After November's killing spree, the pace dropped off. There was another murder in December and then another in February. Bianchi and Buono were becoming nervous. The Los Angeles police had twice questioned Bianchi, and Buono wanted them to split up to reduce the risk of being caught.

In May 1978, Bianchi moved to Bellingham, Washington, to join his girlfriend, Kelli Boyd, and their newborn son. This could have been the end of the Hillside Strangler story, and if Bianchi and Buono had stopped then, they might never have been caught. However, Bianchi had become addicted to killing and when he met an attractive student, Karen Mandic, his compulsion took hold.

Bianchi was then working as a security guard and was responsible for a house in Bellingham. He convinced Mandic and her friend that the house's burglar alarm needed to be taken away for repair and offered them one hundred dollars to housesit for a few hours until it was fixed. They agreed, but Bianchi struck just as he was showing them around the house.

Bianchi attacked Mandic on the stairs leading to the basement and strangled her with a ligature. When he returned, he dispatched her friend with the same method. Bianchi hid the evidence by dumping both bodies in their car.

Mandic's boyfriend informed the police that she had received a job house sitting from a Bellingham security agency. The person at the security agency in charge of that house sitting claimed not to know either woman. Mandic had last been seen driving to the house. Eighteen hours later, their strangled bodies were found in their car on a hillside overlooking Bellingham. There were no fingerprints on the vehicle.

The Bellingham police arrested Bianchi, then twenty-seven years old and a security guard for the security agency. This surprised everyone who knew Bianchi and believed him to be a charming, upstanding person. Dean Brett was appointed as Bianchi's lawyer and was soon surprised by Bianchi's apparent amnesia for parts of his childhood. He turned to psychological experts for help.

Police in Los Angeles learned that Bianchi had lived near some of the Hillside Strangler victims. Kenneth Bianchi had arrived in Los Angeles in September 1977. Meanwhile, investigators in Bellingham found Bianchi's pubic hairs, as well as hairs from the two victims, on a stairwell of the house. The Los Angeles Police Department matched Bianchi's prints to those of some of the Hillside Stranger murders. The police then turned their search to a co-conspirator and focused on Angelo Buono, Bianchi's cousin and seemingly the only person with whom Bianchi associated.

Lawyers in this case

Judge Ronald George, who later became the chief justice of the California Supreme Court, presided over Bianchi's trial. His greatest influence on the trial came when he ruled that Bianchi was not hypnotized and did not suffer from multiple personality disorder. This largely preempted Bianchi's insanity defense and led to his acceptance of a plea bargain and an agreement to testify against his cousin Angelo Buono in order to avoid the death penalty. In making this decision, Judge George relied heavily on the testimony of a psychiatrist hired by the prosecution, Dr. Martin Orne. Judge George was less complimentary about the other psychological experts, one of whom was hired by the defense and the other of whom was hired by the court. He criticized the methods of both of them and called one of them naive.

Dean Brett, the lawyer appointed to defend Bianchi, attempted to mount an insanity defense for Bianchi by researching Bianchi's childhood in order to find evidence to support Bianchi's alleged multiple personality disorder. In response, prosecutor David McEachran recruited Dr. Orne, an expert on hypnosis.

Psychoforensic professionals in this case

Since Bianchi's lawyer, Dean Brett, claimed that Bianchi was insane at the time of the murders, the early stages of the trial centered on psychological testimony. Bianchi himself, it later turned out, had learned a bit about psychology, particularly about multiple personality disorder. He had seen the film *Sybil*, in which Sally Field played a person suffering from multiple personality disorder triggered by childhood abuse. Most of the time Sybil was a pleasant, polite, and shy young woman, but when under pressure, she unleashed another personality, a spiteful, vicious, and manipulative one that would taunt the normal Sybil. Bianchi also had psychology textbooks in his home and he knew of *The Three Faces of Eve*.

As he began talking to Bianchi, Brett initially noticed large gaps in Bianchi's memory. Brett feared that Bianchi might be suffering from amnesia and asked Dr. John Watkins, an expert in the field, to examine him. Dr. Watkins visited Bianchi for an interview, which was recorded on videotape.

Under hypnosis, Kenneth Bianchi revealed an evil persona to Dr. Watkins. His other personality introduced himself as Steve Walker and spoke with anger and pride about his behavior. Walker admitted killing the two Bellingham women and confessed to the other Hillside Strangler murders. Steve Walker ridiculed the normal Kenneth Bianchi and then implicated Bianchi's cousin, Angelo Buono. Furthermore, Walker explained how he and Buono had pretended to be police officers and had made fake badges to support their charade. They found it easy to persuade prostitutes to get in their car, having convinced them they were being taken downtown to be booked for soliciting. However, non-prostitutes were harder to manipulate. Sometimes the pair pretended to ask for directions or feigned working on their car before bundling their victims into the vehicle and driving off.

As the interview progressed, Walker vanished and the mild-mannered Bianchi reappeared. The interview convinced Dr. Watkins that Bianchi was suffering from the classic symptoms of multiple personality disorder.

However, Los Angeles detective Frank Salerno, who had been watching the videotaped interview, remained skeptical. Salerno spotted that Walker had frequently referred to himself as he, rather than I. Convinced Bianchi was faking the condition and with an eye toward preempting an insanity defense, Salerno persuaded the court to dispatch a second expert, Dr. Ralph Allison, to further examine Bianchi. After interviewing Bianchi, Dr. Allison was more convinced than Dr. Watkins, concluding that Bianchi was neither competent to stand trial nor criminally responsible. Allison even appeared frightened by Walker. After much negotiation, the prosecutor recruited a third psychologist, Dr. Martin Orne.

Hired by the prosecution, Dr. Orne postulated that if Bianchi were malingering, he would probably modify the symptoms of his alleged multiple personality disorder if he believed that doing so would help his defense. Before interviewing Bianchi, Orne watched the videotapes of the other professionals interviewing Bianchi. As an expert on hypnosis, Orne devised a series of tests to help determine whether Bianchi was faking a multiple personality. When Orne began one of his interviews and before he began to hypnotize Bianchi, for example, he casually mentioned to Bianchi that people suffering from multiple personality disorder typically have more than two personalities. As Orne expected, Bianchi revealed a third personality during the interview, a meek, almost childish Billy, who claimed not to know Bianchi but called Walker a bad apple.

This solidified Orne's suspicion that Bianchi had been malingering. Moreover, Orne did not even believe that Bianchi had been truly hypnotized, but believed he had faked that also. To support this contention, Orne argued that Bianchi overplayed his role as someone with multiple personalities. For example, when Bianchi returned from hypnosis to the wake state, he had made a great fuss about how his rosary had left his pocket and how his cigarettes had been smoked on the unfiltered end. Bianchi's implication was clearly that Walker had taken the rosary and had smoked in that way. Yet, Orne said, neither Bianchi's girlfriend nor anyone else had ever before seen Bianchi smoke that way. While Orne conceded that it was not unusual for a hypnotized person to be surprised by something like this, he contended that Bianchi's repeated and dramatic pointing out of these discrepancies was indicative of Bianchi's purposefully trying to convince Orne and the other psychological professionals that he was hypnotized and unaware of the Walker persona.

When the trial began, these and other experts took the stand. Dr. Allison, appointed by the court, testified that Bianchi suffered from multiple personality disorder and was legally insane. In addition, Dr. Allison claimed that Bianchi was experiencing leakage. This meant that his main personality, Kenneth Bianchi, was beginning to gain consciousness of Steven Walker's presence.

Dr. Allison's testimony lost some of its strength as he gave his conclusions without explaining his rationale. Moreover, the discovery that he was pursuing a world record for identifying multiple personalities and had planned to write a book on the subject compromised his perceived neutrality. Facing an impending, aggressive cross-examination, Dr. Allison changed his position. After having visited prison, where he was taking up a new job, he claimed that he could not testify regarding Bianchi's condition, because, unlike with a regular patient, he could not be sure that Bianchi was telling him the truth. This further undermined his credibility.

Despite the importance of the expert psychological testimony, non-experts also influenced the outcome of the trial. Tiny Boyles, a bouncer, was one such person. He testified that Bianchi and Buono had run a child pornography ring and had tried to blackmail an attorney. This attorney then hired Boyles to convince Bianchi and Buono not to bother him. Boyles then visited Bianchi and Buono individually and used a blend of diplomacy and brute force to persuade them. Even if this part of Bianchi's past had not in itself been enough to undermine his defense, Bianchi claimed only to remember Boyles having visited Buono, but not Bianchi himself. Orne used this to argue that Bianchi was faking amnesia, as a visit from Boyles would have been difficult to forget.

Another psychologist, Dr. Weingarten, was not an expert in Bianchi's trial, but his name figured prominently, nonetheless, when the court discovered that Bianchi had obtained some of Dr. Weingarten's diplomas and changed the name on them to Bianchi's. Bianchi had then advertised himself as a psychologist and offered a counseling service. When the police searched Bianchi's apartment, they found it filled with psychology textbooks. The prosecution used this to contend that Bianchi was not only motivated, but also knowledgeable enough to fool experts into believing he suffered from multiple personality disorder and amnesia.

If that had not been enough, a final name emerged: John Steven Walker. This was not the Walker of Bianchi's alleged multiple personality disorder which had apparently emerged when Bianchi was young, but rather a real person on whose transcript Bianchi had later removed Walker's name and inserted his own. The court did not accept that Bianchi's alter ego's name of Steve Walker was simply a coincidence, but rather concluded that it was an act to emphasize multiple personality.

Case process

Judge George ruled under California law on Bianchi's competence. Convinced by Dr. Orne's methods and his testimony, Judge George deemed Bianchi legally competent and sane. In addition to rejecting Bianchi's claim of multiple personality disorder, Judge George ruled that Bianchi had not even been hypnotized. This was an important move, because under California law, testimony elicited under hypnosis was not admissible. Such inadmissibility would have made Bianchi unable to testify against Angelo Buono. In response to these rulings, Bianchi accepted a plea bargain and dropped his insanity defense, so his insanity was not put to a legal test before a jury.

In response to Judge George's ruling Bianchi competent and sane, Bianchi abandoned his insanity defense and accepted a plea bargain. The conditions of the plea bargain stipulated that he drop the multiple personality defense, stop claiming insanity, plead guilty, and testify against Angelo Buono, his cousin and accomplice. In return, Bianchi would be spared Washington's death penalty and would receive a life sentence with the possibility of parole in California. Bianchi accepted the deal and confessed in detail to the murders that had petrified women in the greater Los Angeles area in the late 1970s.

Angelo Buono's trial began in 1981 but was problematic. Bianchi's testimony was conflicting and unreliable. Eventually the Attorney General brought in a new prosecution team, and after a new trial in 1982, Buono was finally convicted of nine murders, but was spared the death penalty by the jury inasmuch as Bianchi had been spared the death penalty. Bianchi received life imprisonment as a concession for having testified against his cousin.

Media response and commentators

When the killings began, they attracted little attention, as the murder of prostitutes in Los Angeles was not very newsworthy. However, as the killing spree continued and spread to non-prostitutes and young girls, it garnered widespread media attention and gripped the public in terror as the police remained unable to stop or solve the crimes. The police suspected that the killer or killers might have some background in police methods, so they warned the citizenry through the media not to stop for police officers on side streets. Indeed, Bianchi later confessed that he and Buono had often posed as police officers in order to lure their victims.

After the case, Dr. Margaret Singer, a professor of psychology at the University of California at Berkeley, consulted with Dr. Orne. She did not believe that Bianchi was legally insane, but concluded that he might just be evil. She admitted that Bianchi had psychological problems, including being a sexual psychopath, a diagnosis with which Dr. Orne agreed. However, she maintained that Bianchi knew right from wrong and was able to control himself, rendering him legally sane.

This pointed to a larger issue with the insanity defense. The mere presence of psychological problems in a person did not render a person legally insane if that person still understood the wrongfulness of his actions and had control over those actions, as determined under the legal test used in a given case.

Although not commenting directly on this case, Dr. Michael Welmer developed an online depravity scale for evaluating the evilness of criminals that might be of interest in cases where a heinous crime has committed, as in Bianchi's case. This scale can be found online at: http://www.depravityscale.org.

The insanity defense itself

Although malingering may not figure as prominently in every case as it did in Bianchi's, it remains an issue in every trial where the insanity defense is raised. Forensic psychologists must evaluate defendants who, unlike most patients, are strongly motivated to lie. Thus, forensic psychologists must not only diagnose a defendant's symptoms, but must also determine whether those symptoms are true or fake. In addition, in many states, psychologists are called to testify as to the ultimate issue of legal insanity.

While Bianchi's malingering was eventually detected, his case demonstrated the importance to the justice system of remaining vigilant for malingering, as Bianchi nearly escaped punishment when he fooled several experts.

Brief summary of case

Under alleged hypnosis, Kenneth Bianchi confessed to raping and killing several women. His defense lawyer, Dean Brett, raised the insanity defense, presenting evidence that Bianchi suffered from multiple personality disorder.

Judge Ronald George ruled that Bianchi was not insane, did not suffer from multiple personality disorder, had not been hypnotized, and was competent to stand trial. Bianchi then accepted a plea bargain, dropped the insanity defense, pled guilty, and testified against Angelo Buono, his cousin and accomplice. In return, Bianchi received a life sentence and dodged the death penalty.

Note on sources

This commentary on Kenneth Bianchi's case relied heavily on information found in Frontline video transcripts related to the documentary *Mind of a Murderer*, which can be accessed online:
http://www.pbs.org/wgbh/pages/frontline/programs/transcripts/206.html
http://www.pbs.org/wgbh/pages/frontline/programs/transcripts/207.html

Ted Bundy

Theodore Robert Cowell, also known as Ted Bundy, was born on November 24, 1946. In February 1976, he went on trial in Utah for kidnapping a woman who managed to break free and flee from him. A psychological report on him at that time found no mental illness, no sexual dangerousness. In January 1977 he was released and transferred to Colorado where he was to be tried for murder. He escaped from the Aspen Courthouse library. He traveled to Florida where he murdered a number of women in the Chi Omega sorority house. He represented himself and was sentenced to death. In 1980 in another case, he was also sentenced to death. Despite appeals, he was executed by electric chair on January 24, 1989.

Though a plea of not guilty by reason of insanity was considered in both cases, it ultimately was not used in either trial because of Bundy's wish to be his own lawyer and his rejection of the plea. Further, his original Chi Omega case defense lawyer's strategy was to offer a guilty plea in exchange for a life sentence, rather than to risk a death sentence with a probably unsuccessful insanity plea. While no pleas of incompetency to stand trial or of insanity at the times of the killings arose in the initial trials, those pleas of incompetency and insanity were revisited during Bundy's appeals for a stay of execution.

His early life

Bundy was born out of wedlock to Louise Cowell, and never knew his father. After five years of living with Bundy's grandparents, Louise Cowell married Johnnie Bundy, and they had four children together. There were claims that Bundy was emotionally detached from his stepfather and that he resisted his stepfather's attempts to become close. Bundy, however, claimed that he lived in a stable, loving, Christian home with devoted parents who instilled moral values in him. The family attended church regularly, and there was no fighting. Bundy warned against ascribing any of the blame for his killings on his parents or his upbringing.

Indeed, the facts do seem to corroborate most of Bundy's portrayal of an ordinary, and even healthy, upbringing. However, his last lawyer, Polly Nelson, mentioned that Bundy's aunt recalled a time when Bundy was three and staying at her place. One night, she claimed to have awakened to find Bundy arranging knives to surround the bed with the points aimed at it.

As a youth, Bundy was said to be shy, sensitive, and self-doubting, but later he became more popular in high school. He was characterized as well-mannered and was said to have performed well academically all through college. But there were also accounts of Bundy being teased in junior high school, and of having a reputation for being dishonest through high school and college. He supposedly started petty stealing from school and workplaces, and then later progressed to shoplifting and burglarizing homes.

In one of his final interviews with his last lawyer, Polly Nelson, Bundy confided that he began to exhibit problems as early as age thirteen. But rather than stealing, he said that these problems were sexual in nature. For instance, Bundy said he became increasingly voyeuristic and preoccupied with sex and violence. He claimed that he would run around the woods naked at times. According to Bundy, these problems began when he became acquainted with soft-core pornography at age thirteen, which served as a door to hard-core, violent pornography. He said he would acquire pornographic materials from garbage dumps in his neighborhood, and gradually became addicted to it. Later, he claimed he needed more and more violent pornography. Though he later claimed responsibility for his actions, he stated that pornography had been the fuel that crystallized his sexually violent thoughts and urges.

Most reports of Bundy's early life also referred to Bundy's relationship with a girlfriend, whom he thought of as his first love, as a cause of his eventual problems. The two met in the spring of 1967 at the University of Washington because of their mutual hobby of skiing. But she was less infatuated with him than he with her, and she eventually ended the relationship because of his character flaws, including his dishonesty and lack of direction. Subsequently it was said that Bundy never recovered from the loss of that relationship, that he continued to obsess over her, and that Bundy's future victims bore a striking resemblance to her.

Bundy was never considered mentally ill until he was arrested and received a psychiatric evaluation in 1979. Dr. Emanuel Tanay, who examined him, stated that Bundy suffered from a lifelong personality disorder, which prevented him, for example, from having more than a simply intellectual appreciation of his impending death. He concluded that Bundy exhibited poor impulse control and would make self-sabotaging choices during his trial, as in his decision to relieve himself of his counsel so he could perform as his own counsel, and in his not wanting to plead insanity.

Another psychiatrist, Dr. Dorothy Otnow Lewis, diagnosed Bundy as having a bipolar mood disorder, or manic-depressive illness. The major symptom of this illness was the oscillation of moods between elation or hysteria and depression. Dr. Lewis also spoke of the possibility of his having a multiple personality disorder, which was later renamed dissociative identity disorder.

Dr. Peter Macaluso, who examined Bundy during his 1978 to 1979 stay in the Leon County jail while he was being evaluated for mental competency, prescribed tranquilizers and other psychotropic medication. Dr. Macaluso diagnosed Bundy with acute anxiety neurosis, and prescribed Ativan for Bundy's anxiety and Limbitrol for his agitated depression. After observing increased agitation and depression, he later changed Bundy's prescription to chlorhydrate, a psychoactive sedative. It appeared that Bundy complied and took his medication. However, he was also ingesting smuggled alcohol and Valium.

Charges in this case

In the early morning of January 15, 1978, two weeks after Bundy escaped from a Colorado prison, he attacked four women in the Chi Omega sorority house at the University of Florida in Tallahassee, killing two, and injuring others. Bundy raped, clubbed, and strangled the women in their sleep. He was eventually sentenced to death for two counts of first-degree murder. These would constitute two of three death sentences Bundy would receive in the span of less than a year.

The third sentence was for the murder of twelve year old Kimberly Leach whom he abducted from her junior high school in Lake City, Florida, on February 9, 1978. Her body was found two months later, with semen stains on her underwear. Less than a week after Leach's disappearance, Bundy was arrested in Pensacola, Florida while driving the Volkswagen he had used in attempting unsuccessfully to abduct the woman who subsequently identified him. It was only some time after the arrest that the police realized they had arrested the notorious Ted Bundy.

Lawyers in this case

The chief prosecutor in the Chi Omega sorority murder case was Larry Simpson. Simpson's most convincing pieces of evidence were an eyewitness' identification of Bundy as the man whom she had seen fleeing the scene as she returned home late to the sorority house, and the testimony of a forensic dental expert who identified the bite marks on one corpse as belonging to Bundy. Mike Minerva was appointed as chief defense attorney. Minerva also asked local attorney Robert Haggard to assist him since Haggard was knowledgeable about the Miami court system and its jurors.

Minerva attempted to persuade Bundy to enter a guilty plea to the two Chi Omega murder charges and to the Leach murder charge, and any affiliated charges such as burglary, in return for three consecutive sentences of twenty-five years without parole, or one sentence of seventy-five years without parole. Although Bundy initially seemed to comply with this plan, he later surprised his lawyers entering a request to be relieved of his counsel. Both cases were sent to trial, and Bundy's motion was accepted. Bundy was later granted permission to be co-counsel, and then eventually chief counsel during the Chi Omega trial. Throughout the whole trial, Bundy was fickle with his decisions and often sabotaged his own defense.

Bundy's motion was extremely upsetting to Minerva and the rest of the defense team, who entered a motion for a continuance in order to prepare for a trial they had been expecting to avoid through the plea bargain. Nevertheless, the case moved forward with a psychiatric evaluation and the competency hearing without Minerva's participation. Haggard also later withdrew from the case because of interpersonal conflict with Bundy. In spring 1979, Harvey assumed the role of chief defense attorney in the Chi Omega case.

In June 1979, attorney Brian Hayes was appointed as special counsel to Bundy for the Chi Omega competency hearing ordered by Judge Cowart. Despite diagnoses by two experts, Drs. Cleckley and Tanay, Hayes did not enter a plea for Bundy's incompetency because of his client's insistence on his competence.

Judge Wallace Jopling presided over the Leach case. The prosecutor in the Leach trial was Assistant States Attorney Bob Dekle, who was optimistic about the case's eventual outcome due to eyewitnesses, credit card slips which put Bundy at the scene of the crime, other circumstantial evidence, and especially some physical evidence. For example, Holiday Inn employees identified Bundy as having reserved a room under an alias the day before Leach's disappearance. A handwriting expert confirmed Bundy's signature on the reservation slip. The prosecutor presented the testimony of sixty-five witnesses connecting Bundy to Kimberly Leach on the day of her disappearance. Fiber evidence from Bundy's clothes and van linked him to the crime scene, while fiber evidence from Leach's clothes were found on the clothes Bundy wore that day and inside Bundy's van. Moreover, the lead witness was a school crossing guard who testified that he saw Bundy leading a girl to his white van on the morning of the disappearance.

Julius Africano was the defense attorney appointed to the Leach case. Africano had little hope that Bundy would not be convicted, and thus decided to argue that the state had not proved Bundy's guilt beyond, and to the exclusion of, every reasonable doubt. Africano also believed that a plea of not guilty by reason of insanity was Bundy's best chance at success. No incompetency issue or insanity defense was raised, however, since it had not been used in the Chi Omega trial, which had only taken place six months before. In fact, the ruling of the competency hearing had been intended to apply to both cases.

Polly Nelson and James Coleman, from Wilmer, Cutler, and Pickering, were the pro bono defense attorneys who appealed for a stay of Bundy's execution.

Psychoforensic professionals in this case

Mike Minerva, Bundy's original defense attorney in the Chi Omega case, hired Dr. Emanuel Tanay to advise on the viability of an insanity defense. In April 1979, Dr. Tanay examined written case materials and his preliminary recommendation was that the question of sanity and competency should be explored. Tanay then examined Bundy in person in May 1979. His ultimate conclusion was that

Bundy was a psychopath who had no control over his illness and was not competent to stand trial.

Dr. Hervey Cleckley was Florida's appointed psychiatrist for the competency hearing. Dr. Cleckley stated that although Bundy was sociopathic, another term for psychopathic, he was competent to stand trial. Surprisingly, Dr. Tanay later conceded to Dr. Cleckley, citing Cleckley's expertise in this particular field of psychiatry.

Dr. Charles Mutter and Dr. Umesh Mahtre were the two psychiatrists hired by the state in the appeals cases. Both never personally interviewed Bundy, but made diagnoses based on written documents. Both concluded that Bundy was competent. Dr. Norman was the psychologist hired by the defense to do a psychological evaluation. However, to the surprise of Bundy's lawyers, Dr. Norman testified that Bundy had murdered girls not because of a mental illness, but because of a simple desire to kill.

Despite suspicions of Bundy's mental health, he was never held in a mental facility, but rather treated in prison.

Test of insanity used in the case

All cases, including the appeals, occurred in Florida. In Florida, a defendant was considered incompetent to stand trial if he lacked enough rational and factual understanding to cooperate with his lawyer and to comprehend the charges against him. An evidentiary hearing to determine incompetency was warranted only if there was clear evidence of substantial doubt about whether the defendant met those standards. The burden of proof was high and fell on the defendant.

In terms of the insanity defense, Florida courts used the M'Naghten rule, or the right wrong test. If the defendant was unaware that his actions were wrong due to mental illness, or if the defendant was unaware of what he was doing, or of the nature of his actions, he was considered legally insane.

Diminished capacity was not recognized in Florida courts. The concept of diminished capacity only applied insofar as it affected the defendant's ability to know right from wrong. Moreover, Florida courts did not admit the irresistible impulse test, which classified a defendant as insane as long as he lacked the ability to control his actions, even if he knew his actions were wrong.

In these particular cases, the burden of proof placed on the defendant was difficult to meet. While in the later appeals process there was a fierce and formal argument for Bundy's incompetency and insanity in order to stay his execution or prevent his execution altogether, there was corresponding strong popular opinion against his innocence or clemency, especially because of the horrendous nature of his crimes. And finally, and perhaps most importantly, Bundy himself claimed to be competent and sane.

Case process

The insanity and incompetency issues only became relevant during the appeals to stay Bundy's execution.

When Polly Nelson was appointed to the case, there had been a criminal charge in the Florida state trial court, but the case was still in the direct appeal process. Therefore, Nelson first filed a stay of execution in the Florida Supreme Court which, as expected, was denied. Nelson then filed a stay in the United States Supreme Court, which was quickly and easily granted. Bundy had previously submitted a motion for stay to the U.S. Supreme Court himself, but had been denied with the recommendation that he acquire counsel. The execution was postponed from March 4 to March 29, 1986. Nelson filed a petition to have the U.S. Supreme Court review the last court's decision in the case. The request was in the Chi Omega case alone, and was founded on three claims: one, that Bundy was never given an opportunity to challenge the impartiality of the Florida grand jury before the indictment was given because the indictment hearing had been held in secret due to media attention; two, that the testimony of the principal eyewitness in the Chi Omega trial should have been inadmissible because it was enhanced by hypnosis; and three, that jurors opposed to the death penalty were eliminated during the selection process by the prosecution.

While awaiting the U.S. Supreme Court's decision on whether to review the Chi Omega case, Nelson filed an additional petition for the Leach case due to the possibility that the former petition would be rejected. Nelson's arguments about incompetence in both cases seemed convincing because the judge in the Chi Omega case had likely erred in allowing Bundy to overrule his lawyers' strong opinions about his incompetence. As for the Leach trial, since it had occurred only six months after the first case, it could be assumed that Bundy had remained in the same state of mind. Another promising contention for the defense was the fact that the prosecution's crucial eyewitness who claimed to have seen Leach enter Bundy's van on the day of her disappearance had also been exposed to hypnosis.

An unexpected development occurred on May 22, 1986, when the Florida governor signed a death warrant for Ted Bundy, scheduling his execution for that July 2. Nelson still continued with the appeals process, beginning collateral proceedings at the trial level with the same judge in the Chi Omega trial. Among seventeen claims of pretrial publicity, unreliable bite-mark evidence, incompetent counsel, a sleeping juror, among others, Nelson believed her strongest argument for a stay was Bundy's incompetency. Nevertheless, the judge denied the appeal and his decision was affirmed by the Florida Supreme Court. Nelson then submitted a habeas corpus petition to the U.S. District Court in Ft. Lauderdale which also denied all seventeen claims without a hearing. However, a judge did grant Nelson a certificate of probable cause to appeal to the Eleventh Circuit Court of Appeals in Atlanta.

Meanwhile, between the Chi Omega appeal in the circuit court and the Leach case appeal to the U.S. Supreme Court, Nelson also applied to be Bundy's clemency counsel in order to protect Bundy from a death warrant if all of the other appeals failed. This application was denied as being premature, but was later granted when the Leach case appeal was denied by the U.S. Supreme Court. Nelson then filed a motion to reopen the case, arguing that Bundy should have had a competency hearing before the Leach case trial. The judge denied the motion, stating that Bundy had been one of the most competent lawyers he had ever met. The Florida Supreme Court also denied Nelson's subsequent appeal, as did a district court judge.

A favorable ruling finally arrived on November 18 when the Eleventh Circuit Court granted Ted Bundy a stay of execution. On January 15, 1987, this court not only remanded the Chi Omega case, but also ruled unanimously to remand the Leach case. The court claimed that there was substantial evidence of Bundy's incompetence, and that Dr. Tanay's evaluation of Bundy should have held more weight in the lower court's decision than the defense counsel's failure to raise the issue of competency. Moreover, the circuit court stated that the defendant's insistence on his competency should not be unconditionally accepted for the very reason that the defendant could be incompetent. Although the court also ordered that both the Chi Omega and Leach case competency hearings be consolidated, the cases were later separated due to the different stages of progress in the two cases.

In October 1987, evidentiary hearing was held for Bundy's incompetency claim. Psychological experts and lawyers involved in both of the cases testified, including Dr. Dorothy Otnow Lewis, Dr. Peter Macaluso, Margaret Good, Lynn Thompson, Ed Harvey, and others, while Jim Coleman cross-examined the witnesses for the defense. The ruling was swift. Without even hearing closing arguments, the judge ruled Bundy as the most competent serial killer and a diabolical genius. Thus, the stage was set for an appeal of the Chi Omega case to the U.S. Supreme Court.

As for the Lake City case, in July 1988, the Eleventh Circuit Court denied Bundy's appeal citing Drs. Mutter and Mahtre's testimony and other evidence of Bundy's competence, such as his good academic record or his letters. Though this was not Bundy's last resort, the most promising options had already been attempted. Furthermore, the governor signed Bundy's second death warrant and scheduled it for the following week. Eventually, after more denials, including one from the Florida Supreme Court and the U.S. Supreme Court, Bundy was executed.

Media involvement

The media covered the Ted Bundy case heavily. A poll taken from Orlando residents prior to the Leach trial showed that ninety-eight percent of respondents recognized Bundy's name, a percentage similar to recognition of the current president. Media presence remained constant from the Chi Omega and Leach cases all the way to each of the death warrants, stays, and multiple appeals. In fact, even after his execution there was footage of public celebrations of Bundy's death.

Bundy was portrayed in the media as a charismatic, charming, and highly intelligent ladies' man who was also a diabolical killer. The media contributed to society's fear of Bundy by casting him as a conniving killer who needed to be eliminated for the sake of society. His sensational crimes were emphasized; the media took as much advantage as they could of Bundy's fascinating killing sprees.

The media had a direct influence on the case. For instance, pretrial publicity forced the Chi Omega trial to move from Tallahassee to Miami, Florida. Because of widespread knowledge of Bundy's case among Orlando residents, caused by the heavy media coverage of the case, there was difficulty in finding unbiased jurors. In fact, one of the Leach trial jurors stated the impossibility of not knowing of Ted Bundy. Bundy himself blamed the media's prejudice against him as the reason for the misrepresentation of his guilt during the Chi Omega trial.

The media also had an indirect effect on the case through its influence on public opinion. For instance, Nelson claimed that a judge had denied Bundy's stay of execution because he did not want to be known as the judge who saved Bundy's life. Nelson also claimed that the Eleventh Circuit Court decided to deny Bundy's appeal of the Leach case in July 1988, for political reasons, regardless of logic and the law. Also, NBC aired a TV miniseries about Bundy and his victims during the appeals process, which noticeably inflamed the public against

Bundy. As a result, Nelson, Bundy's lawyer, fought the release of any more case material to NBC after observing the new wave of public pressure for Bundy's execution. Nelson mentioned that it was difficult even for her to continue as Bundy's lawyer after watching the movie and its humanization of Bundy's victims, and that she had to force herself to push dreadful thoughts out of her mind.

Commentators

Many legal commentators faulted the lawyers of the Chi Omega and Leach cases for not having introduced an insanity or incompetency defense at that time. Regardless of whether Bundy was legitimately insane by psychological standards, much of the legal community believed, and probably correctly so, that Bundy could have, and should have, argued both incompetency and insanity in court.

As for psychological commentators, there were conflicting opinions as to whether Bundy was indeed incompetent or insane. Even if many did admit that Bundy exhibited traits of psychopathy, whether Bundy was mentally ill enough to be considered incompetent was another matter.

As for my view, there would never be a definitive answer as to whether Bundy's case was one of true insanity or of a man whose appetite for pornography went awry. Or perhaps Bundy's self-defeating behavior with his lawyers or during trial was not evidence of mental incompetence, but simply unrelenting pride. He was characterized as a sexual sadist who derived his pleasure from possession and then control of women. As his time of execution neared, he increasingly confessed, though in the third person, to his crimes, to necrophilia, to severed heads, to killing thirty women. Regardless of the question of Bundy's insanity, however, I retained confidence in our criminal justice system because of the multiple appeals, and checks and balances available to the defendant. Granted, the question was whether the outcomes of these checks and balances had been predetermined by the judge, the jury, or the public's opinions. Perhaps there existed a time when public opinion against a defendant became so strong that no judge dared to disturb it and the defendant's fate was effectively sealed from the start. If so, then the question was raised whether the courts were truly protected from the whims and opinions of the people; or whether there was there a level of insanity that drove people like Ted Bundy to commit such horrific crimes that such extreme insanity, even if insanity, could not be tolerated, or shown mercy, by society.

The insanity defense itself

Bundy's case demonstrated the difficulty of utilizing the insanity defense when the defendant was unwilling to comply. This situation was ironic because the lawyer had to seriously consider the client's wishes though the client was suspected of being mentally incompetent.

This case also presented the question of the way in which the timing of the defense's introduction of an insanity defense may affect its success. In other words, in Bundy's case the insanity defense was only formally presented in court during the appeals process. Perhaps Bundy would not have received the death penalty had the insanity defense been raised from the beginning, rather than being introduced later when public opinion had already been firmly established against him.

Granted, this case was not representative in that many defendants, unlike Bundy, would be eager to utilize any defense to mitigate their sentence. Not being eager might be an indication of an inability to recognize the need for such a defense, which could be evidence of genuine or true insanity. This case was also not representative because of the extremity and sheer number of Bundy's murders, and therefore the complete lack of mercy that the public had for him. As a result, the insanity defense, regardless of its timing and how well it was argued, might have been doomed to failure.

Brief summary and significance of this case

Ted Bundy was sentenced to death three times without an insanity or incompetency defense. When Bundy finally consented to such a defense and numerous appeals for a stay of execution were made to multiple courts, it seemed the public and the judges had already made their decisions and it might be argued that Bundy's insanity defense was never seriously considered at these later times by the courts. Did anyone ever think Bundy would not be executed?

Notes about sources

The primary source for information about the insanity defense and the incompetency plea in Ted Bundy's case was Polly Nelson's *Defending the devil: My story as Ted Bundy's last lawyer*. Background for more general information about the insanity defense and incompetency came from Wrightsman, Green, Nietzel, and Fortune's *Psychology and the legal system*. Many of the facts about Bundy's childhood, his crimes, and information about the Chi Omega and Leach cases came from Michaud and Aynesworth's *The only living witness,* and from the internet resource crimelibrary.com.

Jeffrey Dahmer

In the summer of 1991, Jeffrey Dahmer was charged with fifteen counts of first degree murder. He admitted to killing these fifteen victims plus two more for which he was not charged. Because of the amount of evidence and Dahmer's confession, his only hope for escaping prison was to mount an insanity defense. However, against the advice of his lawyers, on July 13, 1992, he changed his plea to guilty but insane. The Dahmer trial shocked the public and everyone involved as the facts of the case came out. The most shocking aspect of the case was due not only to the number of victims, but to the bizarre and grotesque way in which Dahmer murdered them and dealt with the corpses, including acts of necrophilia and cannibalism. The case raised questions of whether or not a sane man could commit these acts and whether Dahmer was insane or evil. Ultimately, Dahmer was found guilty on all fifteen charges and was given fifteen life sentences or 957 years in prison.

His early life

Jeffrey Dahmer was born to Lionel and Joyce Dahmer on May 21, 1960. He was a normal and healthy child born into a family that, while no means without problems, loved Jeffrey and wanted a child. The earliest signs of trouble occurred when Dahmer was six years old. He was suffering from a double hernia and needed surgery. His father claimed that after the surgery Jeffrey Dahmer never fully recovered his exuberance. By first grade, Dahmer seemed to have developed a general fear, lack of self-confidence, reluctance to change, and near isolationism. This trend continued through his life and by high school he was considered a loner as well as an alcoholic. His parents' divorce when he was eighteen years old further exacerbated his growing fear of abandonment and arguably became one of the sparks of his thirteen year killing spree. His problems with alcohol continued to develop and resulted in his failing out of college after the first semester and later receiving an early discharge from the Army.

Jeffrey's fascination with dead things was also traced to his early life. His father recalled an incident when he was sweeping under the porch when Dahmer who was just four years old, came across some animal bones. He describes his son's delight and interest in the bones and the sound they made when they clinked together. Throughout his time in school this interest grew and Dahmer began collecting road kill. He experimented with preserving and disposing of the flesh of the animals.

While Dahmer's fascination with dead creatures and problems with isolation and alcohol in his early life were retrospectively very important to his case, these issues were never considered serious enough in his early years to diagnose or treat him for mental illness. The first time Dahmer ever regularly talked to a professional was after his first encounters with the law. Dahmer was charged with two cases of sexual misconduct, the first in 1982 when he exposed himself to a crowd at the Wisconsin State Fair Park, and the second in 1986 when he masturbated in front of two young boys. Then, in 1989, he was charged with second-degree sexual assault for enticing a child for immoral purposes. For this, Dahmer was put for a year into a House of Correction work-release program and put on probation for five years. He was required to meet with a probation officer regularly. Apparently during this time he also was receiving psychological counseling for depression and suicidal thoughts, but his mental-health records were protected from being released to the public.

While some commentators emphasized the imperfections and neglect of his parents, as well as the impact of their divorce, others argued that his family's problems were nothing out of the ordinary and certainly not enough to explain the creation of a serial killer.

Charges in this case

Jeffrey Dahmer was charged with fifteen counts of first degree murder, two counts fewer than the seventeen murders to which he confessed. The first of these murders occurred in June of 1978, soon after he graduated high school. Dahmer picked up Stephen Mark Hicks who was hitchhiking near his hometown in Ohio. Hicks accepted the offer to go to Dahmer's house for some beers, but when he got restless and wanted to leave, Dahmer struck him in the head and strangled him with a barbell. He later disposed of the body, using acid to destroy the flesh and hacking the rest apart with a sledgehammer.

Dahmer did not kill his second victim until more than nine years later, when he claimed to have killed Steven Toumi in September of 1987. At this time Dahmer was living in his grandmother's basement in Wisconsin. He met Toumi at a gay bar and killed him in a hotel. He took the corpse back to his grandmother's house where he reportedly had sex with the corpse and masturbated on it before cutting it apart and throwing it in the garbage.

Dahmer killed twice more while still living at his grandmother's house. Then, he moved into his own place in Milwaukee. By this time he had established certain methods to his crimes. He generally would find his victims at gay bars or bathhouses in the area. He would then entice them back to his house with offers of money to pose for photographs or just drinks and a good time. Once he had them at his place, he would drug them, strangle them, perform sexual acts on the corpse, and dismember and dispose of the body. Sometimes he kept the skull or other body parts as souvenirs of the crime. He painted the skulls so that they looked like props used in science classes. He kept the body parts preserved in jars of formaldehyde or in the freezer. He used acid to melt much of the flesh down into black sludge which he could pour down the drain. Most of his victims were killed in some variant of this standard method.

One of his most unique cases was the murder of Konerak Sinthasomphone, a fourteen year old Laotian boy. Dahmer enticed Sinthasomphone back to his apartment where he made him pose for pictures and gave him a drink laced with a sleeping potion. The drug knocked the boy out at which point Dahmer performed sexual acts on him. Then Dahmer left the apartment to get some more beer. During this time, Sinthasomphone regained consciousness and staggered out of the apartment. Nicole Childress and Sandra Smith found the boy completely naked, dazed, and bleeding from the buttocks. They called 911. When the police arrived, Dahmer claimed that Sinthasomphone was his nineteen year old homosexual lover who had had too much to drink and gotten in a quarrel with him. The police escorted Sinthasomphone, who was too drugged to object, back to Dahmer's apartment where he was then murdered.

It was not until Dahmer had killed seventeen people that he was finally discovered. On July 22, 1991, two police officers saw a black man with handcuffs dangling from his wrist. The man was thirty-two year old Tracy Edwards, who told of his escape from Dahmer's apartment. The police went with Edwards to investigate. One of the officers decided to go to Dahmer's bedroom with him to get the key for the handcuffs because Edwards claimed that Dahmer had also threatened him with a knife in the bedroom. In the apartment the police found much more than a knife. They found the evidence and remains of the murders of young men. They arrested Jeffrey Dahmer immediately.

Lawyers in this case

The key lawyers in the case were District Attorney Michael McCann and Dahmer's defense attorney, Gerald Boyle. Boyle had defended Dahmer in the sexual misconduct case a few years earlier. Jeffrey Dahmer did not take Boyle's advice, but instead entered a plea saying that he was guilty but that he was also insane. Therefore, the only way Boyle could hope to win the case was to mount a successful insanity defense. Boyle's strategy was to try to convince the jury that Dahmer's actions were so bizarre that only someone who was legally insane could have done them. Thus, Boyle purposefully emphasized every unusual and gruesome aspect of the murders. For this purpose, he had ready forty-five witnesses willing to testify on various aspects of Dahmer's bizarre behavior and to argue that he did not understand the nature of his crimes due to the influences of his sexual and mental disorders. In his closing statement, Boyle described his client as a runaway train on a track of madness, picking up steam as he went along.

District Attorney Michael McCann set about to prove that Dahmer was sane and understood his actions. McCann pointed out that Dahmer was able to pass as normal in society, do normal things like fill in his tax forms, and hold down a job. In showing that Dahmer knew what he was doing, McCann appealed to the meticulous detail and planning involved in the murders. In addition, he argued that the murders were not done impulsively or randomly. Dahmer chose his victims carefully, and he was able to put off his actions if he could not find an appropriate victim. He was also able to talk his way out of trouble and to hide his actions from the police for years. Finally, McCann warned the jury that Dahmer was manipulative and tricky. In his closing statement, McCann appealed to the jury not to let Dahmer fool them, as he had fooled so many others along the way.

Judge Laurence C. Gram, Jr. presided over the case.

Psychoforensic professionals in this case

The defense assembled a team of forty-five expert witnesses who were willing to testify about some aspect of Dahmer's bizarre behavior. Among them was the main psychiatrist for the defense, Fred S. Berlin from the Sexual Disorders Clinic at Johns Hopkins Hospital. He had interviewed Dahmer for four hours and had come to the conclusion that Dahmer was a necrophiliac and unquestionably suffered from mental illness. However, during cross-examination, District Attorney Mike McCann got Berlin to admit that Dahmer could control himself when necessary.

Other expert witnesses for the defense included Drs. Wahlstrom and Becker. Psychiatrist Carl M. Wahlstrom argued that some of Dahmer's bizarre behavior, such as his detailed plan to build an altar or temple out of human skulls, revealed a delusional and distorted thought process that lacked a basis in reality. Again, McCann partially undermined the defense witness' testimony, this time by pointing out that Wahlstrom had never testified as an expert in court. Judith V. Becker, a sexual disorder specialist from the University of Arizona, insisted in her testimony that Dahmer was not faking insanity. Like Berlin, she diagnosed him as a necrophiliac, but she stopped short of diagnosing him as psychotic.

The prosecution called two psychiatrists during the course of the trial. The first was Frederick Fosdal who had interviewed Dahmer for more than a hundred hours. Fosdal concluded that Dahmer's disorders were adequate to explain his motivation and behavior in committing the crimes, but he argued that he did not lack the substantial capacity to distinguish right from wrong. The prosecution's second witness, Park Elliott Dietz, was no stranger to testifying as an expert witness in court. Dietz argued that Dahmer knew exactly what he was doing. He acknowledged that Dahmer seemed to be a case of paraphilia as well as a person who had a strong dependence on alcohol. However, he also claimed the Dahmer knew right from wrong and could have stopped himself at any time. Specifically, Dietz pointed to the fact that Dahmer always used condoms when he had sex with a corpse in order to show that his acts were not impulsive. Also, he described how Dahmer would prepare himself the night before a murder to show that the crimes were always deliberate and planned.

The court appointed expert witness was George Palermo. Palermo testified that Jeffrey Dahmer had a serious personality disorder which required medical treatment. However, he claimed that Dahmer did not qualify as either psychotic or as legally insane at the time of the murders.

Test of insanity

The Jeffrey Dahmer trial took place in Wisconsin, where there was no death penalty but there was an insanity defense. The standard in Wisconsin was the ALI, the American Law Institute standard. This law stated that a person could be found not guilty by reason of insanity if he or she was either unable to appreciate the wrongfulness of his or her actions or was unable to conform his or her conduct to the requirements of the law. The burden of proof was on the defense to prove that Jeffrey Dahmer was insane. If Dahmer had been found not guilty by reason of insanity, he would have also borne the burden of proving that he was no longer a danger to himself or society if he wanted to be free from custody.

Case outcome

The trial lasted for twelve days. The jury consisted of eleven white jurors and one black juror. Many people were extremely upset by the jury's racial composition because most of Dahmer's victims were black, and the trial had already caused racial tensions to rise.

The jury deliberated for five hours before returning with a guilty verdict to all fifteen of the first degree murder charges. One factor that influenced sentencing was the lack of a death penalty in Wisconsin. Wisconsin abolished capital punishment in 1853 and was one of thirteen states without it as an option in sentencing. As a result, Dahmer was sentenced to fifteen life terms, or a total of 957 years.

Dahmer reportedly adjusted quite well to prison life. He was initially kept fairly isolated from the other prisoners, largely for his own safety. However, after exhibiting good behavior, he was allowed increased contact with other inmates. He was allowed to eat communal meals and did janitorial work with a couple other inmates. On November 28, 1994, he was paired with two other inmates including Christopher Scarver. Scarver was a black man who was in prison for first-degree murder. He had been diagnosed as a delusional schizophrenic and claimed that he was the son of God. Given the racial issues surrounding Dahmer's trial, pairing the two inmates proved to be unwise. That day Scarver murdered both Dahmer and the other inmate on their team who had killed his wife and blamed it on a black man.

Media involvement

Given the sensational aspects of the Jeffrey Dahmer case, it was not surprising that the media followed the case closely. The courtroom was packed whenever he made an appearance. The constant trial coverage in Milwaukee was seen by some as a step towards helping the community face the horrors and advance the healing of the atrocities of the crime. One aspect of the trial that the media covered in depth was the racial tension that arose surrounding the trial. The majority of Dahmer's victims were members of ethnic minorities, particularly African American, and many people speculated that if Dahmer were black and his victims were white, he would have been caught and stopped much earlier.

The media's coverage of the insanity defense was very negative. They talked about the defense of mental illness as if it were a legal loophole. They focused on the prospect that a cannibal like Dahmer could be let off and released back into the community. The most often cited case was that of John W. Hinckley Jr., who had been found not guilty by reason of insanity for the attempted assassination of President Reagan. The media, however, generally neglected to discuss how the insanity defense actually worked in practice or what was actually likely to happen to a person found not guilty by reason of insanity. Instead, the media coverage presented the insanity defense as both a cause and a symbol of social ills and danger for the community. Such publicized views tended to increase animosity towards the insanity defense as a practice and to create pressure for jurors to vote for conviction.

Commentators

Legal commentators on the Dahmer case said the fact that the insanity defense failed had important implications. Most significantly, commentators claimed that the failure of Dahmer's paraphilia defense would mean that perpetrators of rape or child abuse would have a much more difficult time using their compulsive behaviors as excuses for their crimes. More generally, some commentators called the failure of the insanity defense in this case the death of the insanity defense itself.

Psychological commentators on the Dahmer case argued that his case was not so different from cases of other serial killers. In addition, they argued that the insanity defense was unlikely to be successful for serial killers for three reasons. First, serial killers did not generally suffer from diseases or mental defects that would excuse a person from criminal behavior. Second, bizarre behavior was not enough by itself to prove insanity. Finally, consistent behavior and a sense of control found in most serial killers did not provide support for finding them insane. In addition, the fears of the community and people's desire to find people responsible for their actions created pressure for conviction. Some said that explaining violent behavior by mental illness would reduce the importance and role of restraint in the behavior of those with mental and emotional problems.

The insanity defense itself

One of the central issues raised by the Jeffrey Dahmer case concerned the question of when a person should be considered mad and when he should be considered bad. On the day of his sentencing, Dahmer read his written apology. In it he stated that he had known that he was either sick or evil or both. He said that he now believed that he was sick because the doctors had described his sickness to him.

The tension between evil and sickness has become particularly pronounced in cases like Dahmer's because the crimes committed are so bizarre and horrendous. Many people have difficulty believing that any person who could commit acts of cannibalism, necrophilia, and corpse mutilation could be considered sane. This however raises two questions: can the evidence of the acts themselves be sufficient to infer the mental status of the perpetrator without even examining his or her particular mental status; and can the extreme level of depravity of acts mean that a criminal goes unpunished? Another way of putting these might be: are there certain acts that are so terrible that it is impossible for a human being to be fully responsible for committing them?

This tension between evil and sickness in this case also highlighted two problems with the insanity defense. The first problem was the difficulty that most people, including many jurors, had in understanding and applying the legal definition of insanity when people already have a preconceived notion of what insanity means. It was not uncommon for people to use the terms insane or crazy to describe the acts of serial killers like Dahmer in everyday conversation. However, this did not mean that everyone was using these terms in the legal sense of insanity. The second problem came from the difficulty in evaluating a criminal committing extreme acts. The bounds of responsibility have been impossible to establish scientifically. When considering a person's sanity at the time of a crime, one has little to go on apart from an examination of the person's actions at the time of the crime. In the case of Jeffrey Dahmer, his actions were so unusual and gruesome that some might regard them as an indication that he was not sane. Apart from actions, diagnoses of mental illness are generally considered in cases of the insanity defense, despite the fact that mental illness is not congruent with legal insanity. In extreme cases like Jeffrey Dahmer's, however, some have argued that the fact that he committed the crimes was one of the largest indications of mental illness. Once again, the depravity of the crime and the considerations of mental illness seemed inextricably intertwined. Yet even so, psychological commentators after the Dahmer trial argued that the bizarre or gruesome nature of actions was not enough to qualify a defendant for meeting the legal standards of insanity.

Another major issue in cases of extreme or horrendous crimes is public concern over the implications of the insanity defense. This may be one of the reasons that the insanity defense fails so often, particularly in some of these highly publicized, sensational cases. People seem to have an inherent fear of the possibility that a murderer like Dahmer could be released into society if the insanity defense succeeds. Fear may make people more likely to vote for conviction regardless of their opinions on whether or not the defendant met the legal standards of insanity. In addition, this fear often causes public outcry against the insanity defense in such highly publicized cases. This was certainly true in the Dahmer case and was even more apparent in the Hinckley case when the defense succeeded, even though Hinckley has not been released but has remained incarcerated in a mental institution. Yet the public has also noted that Hinckley has argued successfully for more unsupervised time away from St. Elizabeths Hospital.

Notes about sources

The primary sources of information for this case included www.crimelibrary.com, *The Milwaukee murders, nightmare in apartment 213: The true story* by Don Davis, *Milwaukee massacre: Jeffrey Dahmer and the Milwaukee murders* by Robert J. Dvorchak and Lisa Holewa, and articles from *The National Law Journal*. In addition, I drew information from several articles from around the time of the trial, including Lincoln Caplan's article "Not so nutty: The post-Dahmer insanity defense" from the *New Republic*, Albert Drukteinis' article "Serial murder: The heart of darkness" from the *Psychiatric Annals*, Anne C. Gresham's article "The insanity plea: A futile defense for serial killers" from the *Law & Psychology Review*, and Joan Ullman's article "I carried it too far, that's for sure" from *Psychology Today*.

John duPont

John Eleuthere duPont, born on November 22, 1938 to William duPont, Jr. and Jean Liseter Austin duPont, shot Dave Schultz on January 26, 1996, and was subsequently charged with nine counts, including the third degree murder of Schultz. After duPont was found competent to stand trial following some psychiatric treatment, the defense team entered a plea of not guilty by reason of insanity, as they hoped to use duPont's strange behavior in the years preceding the shooting to show that he was not culpable for Schultz's murder. Ultimately, duPont was found guilty but mentally ill on the count of third degree murder and sentenced to between thirteen and thirty years in prison, during which time he would receive psychiatric treatment. An appeal attempted by duPont was denied.

His early life

A millionaire from birth due to the wealth of his family, John duPont was born into a troubled marriage. He was the youngest of four children by ten years, and before he turned two his parents separated, with their divorce finally granted in February 1941. DuPont's mother was given custody of the boy, and he remained with her at their Pennsylvania estate, Liseter Hall.

John duPont never saw much of his father, who ignored him and his siblings, and due to the age discrepancy between duPont and his brother and sisters, he was often alone during his childhood with his mother. He attended the Haverford School, which was for males only, from kindergarten on. His mother was unable to deny him anything, and never reprimanded him for any action, so he was allowed to do virtually whatever he pleased.

When his mother hired Hubert Cherrie, Sr., a retired police officer, to become her chauffeur, John duPont looked to Cherrie as a father figure, and to Cherrie's son, Hubie, as a brother. Throughout his childhood, and attributable at least in part to his mother's lack of reprimands, duPont tortured animals and his classmates. He happily watched his own dog get electrocuted, often tormented pet rabbits and a pet parrot, and delighted in shooting rats with his only companion, Hubie Cherrie. John duPont did not graduate high school with his class due to his feeble academic performance. After being accepted to and enrolling in the University of Pennsylvania, he dropped out before the end of his first year with hopes of becoming an Olympic swimmer, pouring vast sums of money into the sport. After finally realizing that he was not a very talented swimmer, duPont set his sights on becoming a pentathlete, even building a course on his own estate, made possible in 1965 by the death of his father, who left duPont with hundreds of millions of dollars. However, duPont failed in this attempt as he had failed in swimming, and he replaced his dedication to sports with a dedication towards history and the creation of a museum.

John duPont was considered socially inept, diffident, and detached by those who knew him during his early years. He did not attempt sexual relationships with anyone, male or female, and was simultaneously conceited about his wealth and wary about being taken advantage of by women. As he grew older, people became more aware that he had a dependency on alcohol, as he was often drunk well before lunch.

John duPont began to become increasingly paranoid about his safety, adding guard dogs, guns, and tall steel fences to his estate. He built a shooting range on his property, evolved into a crack shot, and was very generous in allowing police officers to train in his facility free of charge.

On September 24, 1983 duPont married Gale Wenk, who was fifteen years younger than her new husband, but she left the house after half a year and the couple divorced within a year. Wenk claimed in court that duPont had accused her of being a Russian spy and had aimed a gun at her, making threats that he would shoot her.

Having been an enthusiastic wrestler in his childhood, duPont dedicated much of his wealth to the sport in his adult years, pouring millions of dollars into both the United States national team and Villanova University; he also built a state of the art facility on his property, Foxcatcher National Training Center for Olympic athletes. The wrestlers who came to live and train on his estate became like a substitute family for the lonely duPont.

On August 9, 1988, duPont's mother died, and this event could have been what pushed John duPont decisively towards a mental imbalance, though no attempt was made to intervene in his life to seek medical attention for his apparent disorders. Despite the lack of a formal diagnosis, duPont was exhibiting signs of bipolar disorder, which his older brother supposedly suffered from and which can occur in families. John duPont became increasingly paranoid and delusional, insisting that his house was haunted and not safe; he almost always carried a gun with him, and he cut himself severely trying to kill alien insects that he believed were crawling on him. His mood swings were severe, and his actions became very rash as he began to insist that he was the Dalai Lama.

Charge in this case

The victim, David Schultz, was born in California to a middle class family. He met the multimillionaire John duPont in 1986, when the latter gifted five million dollars to build an athletic complex at Villanova University, where Schultz was coaching wrestling. Having begun construction of a gigantic wrestling facility on his estate, Foxcatcher Farm, in Pennsylvania, duPont was able to persuade Schultz with a very high salary to move his family there in order to train and to instruct wrestling for Team Foxcatcher. Throughout his wrestling career, Schultz had established himself as one of the world's elite, winning both national and world championships, as well as Olympic gold. People who saw the two interact agreed that Schultz was the only person who duPont seemed to trust and also the only one who could calm down the delusional man.

On January 26, 1996, duPont drove with his personal bodyguard, Patrick Goodale, to Schultz's house on the estate and shot Schultz three times, two of the bullets hitting the victim in the back and the third in the arm. Schultz, a thirty-six year old husband with two children, had been outside fixing his car. After Nancy Schultz heard a shot and a scream, she ran outside and watched her husband die. After the killing, Goodale jumped out of the car to try to help Schultz and duPont returned to his mansion on the property and held out from the authorities for two days.

Initially, there were three people besides duPont in the house when he barricaded himself inside, but they were all allowed to leave by the evening of the first day of negotiations. During talks with the police, duPont insisted that he would only respond to police if they recognized him as the Dalai Lama. He also claimed that he was a Bulgarian secret agent, Jesus Christ, and the president of the United States. The police denied several requests of duPont's to send into the house people whom duPont knew, such as Goodale and a wrestler on the property. The police did not try to storm the house as they were not sure whether duPont had set traps for them, but after his electricity was turned off by the police, the unarmed duPont was arrested when he left the safety of his mansion in order to repair his broken heater, which the police had refused to fix themselves.

John duPont was initially arraigned on February 1, 1996 on charges of first degree murder, third degree murder, voluntary manslaughter, involuntary manslaughter, criminal homicide, aggravated assault, simple assault, reckless endangerment, and possession of a deadly weapon. At that time, he entered no plea.

Lawyers in this case

The prosecution team included District Attorney Patrick Meehan and Joseph McGettigan. While the prosecution agreed that duPont was not mentally stable, they did not believe that Schultz's murder was directly caused by duPont's delusions, and they attempted to counter any insanity arguments by asserting that duPont was imbalanced but still legally sane, and that he was simply trying to remove the blame from himself by highlighting his eccentricities. The prosecution endeavored to persuade the court that duPont was clearly not insane for, during the time period that the defense held him to be just that, duPont was able take care of his finances and speak with his lawyers on a regular basis.

John duPont's defense team included Richard Sprague, William Lamb, and Taras Wochok, who had managed duPont's divorce. All three were hired by duPont, who had ample means to retain a very good team of lawyers. The defense team attempted at first to prepare a case of self defense, as Schultz had a .22 caliber rifle in his car at the time he was killed. Once they decided on an insanity defense, the defense lawyers argued that duPont was severely mentally ill, as shown by his sustained delusions and disordered thought, and maintained that he was a paranoid schizophrenic. The defense based their statements on duPont's behavior in the years leading up to the murder, including violent outbursts, paranoia, and hallucinations, citing the fact that duPont had become so obsessively fearful that he had secret tunnels and mechanical trees built all over his property. Highlighting the allegedly schizophrenic nature of his personality, the defense team drew attention to duPont's claims that he was, at various times, the Dalai Lama, a member of the Russian aristocracy, and Jesus Christ.

Psychoforensic professionals in this case

Forensic psychiatrists were called in by the defense team as early as two days after duPont's arrest. Robert Sadoff and later Phillip J. Resnick were asked to give duPont a psychiatric evaluation. However, as duPont claimed to be nervous about his prison cell being bugged, the evaluation was done on March 5, 1996, in a prison conference room. The defense then asked for intense neurological tests to be run on duPont's brain, and a six hour session was arranged where various examinations were made by Dr. Robert Barchi.

Both Sadoff and Resnick testified for the defense that duPont was a paranoid schizophrenic who thought that Schultz was involved in some sort of international plot to kill him. While the psychiatric witnesses for the prosecution, most notably Dr. Park Elliott Dietz, agreed that duPont was mentally ill, they asserted that duPont's killing of Schultz was not connected to his mental imbalance.

Test of insanity

John duPont was placed on trial in Pennsylvania, the state in which he killed Dave Schultz. At the time, Pennsylvania used the M'Naghten test of insanity, which was concerned with the defendant's ability to distinguish right from wrong. The defense held the burden of proof of showing that duPont was indeed insane when he shot Schultz three times. While the prosecution in the duPont murder trial was pressing for a conviction on a more severe charge, the jury found the duPont guilty but mentally ill of third degree murder, no doubt influenced by the evidence presented of his diminished capacity resulting from his abnormal mental condition.

Case process

After duPont's initial arraignment, he was held without bond in a Delaware County Jail, separated from the other prisoners, where he refused numerous times to undergo required medical tests. On February 9, 1996, District Justice David Videon rejected the defense's request to postpone duPont's hearing. The defense requested that duPont be allowed to return to his estate to retrieve papers that he claimed to need for his defense. The prosecution vigorously fought such an allowance, and on February 21, 1996, Judge Patricia Jenkins denied the request. The prosecution decided not to seek the death penalty on March 12, 1996. No plea bargain was offered to duPont.

While initially found incompetent to stand trial on September 24, 1996, there was, after treatment and medication in Norristown State Hospital by Drs. John S. O'Brien II and Theodore J. Barry, a second competency hearing in December of 1996. When Judge Patricia Jenkins decided that the medication that duPont had taken had made him capable of understanding the charges against him and the potential consequences of a guilty verdict, she found him competent to stand trial. John duPont was brought to trial in January of 1997, where the jury found him guilty but mentally ill. The defense introduced evidence of duPont's delusional nature in the years leading up to the murder, while the prosecution tried equally hard to show that duPont had been able to function meaningfully in those years and that the murder was not tied to his imbalances.

As a result of his conviction, he was sentenced to between thirteen and thirty years in prison, with psychiatric treatment to be rendered throughout. Although duPont filed for appeal on May 4, 1999, on the grounds that the verdict of guilty but mentally ill violated due process and his imprisonment was cruel and unusual punishment, the Supreme Court denied the appeal on June 29, 1999.

Media involvement

The media was very interested in the duPont murder trial because of the high profile nature of the defendant. The wealth and eccentricity of duPont made for a good news story, and thus there was no shortage of media involvement from the moment the case broke. Since the facts of the case were never called into question, the media accepted duPont as the one who had pulled the trigger and although most admitted that he did indeed have a mental defect, there was overwhelmingly more support for a guilty verdict than for acquittal. The media did not, however, play a very strong role in determining the outcome of the trial. Although the high profile status of the case may have made some jurors wary of acquitting a man who killed another, even if it might have been as a result of a mental defect.

The insanity defense itself

The main issue concerning the insanity defense raised by the trial of John duPont was that of the verdict guilty but mentally ill, and of the potential consequences of such a verdict. Despite the fact that the jury found John duPont mentally ill, he was sentenced to a prison term, not hospitalization. Such an outcome was seen by some as troubling. If the state declared someone both guilty and mentally ill and sent him to prison, as was true in this case, it was essentially saying that locking someone up was more important than treating their mental condition. The coupling of psychiatric treatment with the prison term did not assuage the concern of those who saw the contradiction in that verdict.

Brief summary and significance of this case

John duPont shot and killed his friend David Schultz, who was living and training for wrestling on his estate in Pennsylvania. When duPont went to trial for the murder of Schultz, the issue at hand was not whether or not he pulled the trigger and killed the wrestler. The issue to be decided was how responsible duPont should be for the murder since he clearly had some sort of mental defect. The defense used the insanity defense to try to exculpate duPont from his actions. Despite being initially found incompetent to stand trial and the evidence of years of mental instability, the jury found duPont guilty but mentally ill and he was subsequently sentenced to a prison term of between thirteen and thirty years. Although the insanity defense failed, in that he was not acquitted, the jury was influenced by diminished capacity and found duPont guilty of third, not first, degree murder. The case was significant in that it involved a rich, high profile defendant using the insanity defense for an indisputable act, and that the verdict used the comparatively recent guilty but mentally ill.

Notes about sources

The most helpful source in compiling this case study was Carol Turkington's book, *No hold barred: The strange life of John E. duPont*. The secondary sources for the information regarding John duPont and his trial included the transcript of his appeal and various newspaper articles concerning his arrest and trial. In addition, the website www.pbs.org contained useful information regarding background for the case.

John Wayne Gacy

The date was February 6, 1980, and twelve jurors were about to get a glimpse of the man publicly known as The Killer Clown. They may have expected a large jovial man with a round red nose and snow-white make-up. But when John Wayne Gacy stepped into the Cook County Criminal Courts Building in Chicago, Illinois, nobody was laughing. That's because Gacy, a thirty-eight year old businessman and seemingly upstanding member of society, was charged with thirty-three brutal murders. In the coming weeks, these stunned jurors would face a difficult decision. They would have to decide whether the controversial insanity defense could be used to excuse such heinous acts. Whatever the outcome of the trial, those twelve jurors would make a statement about the scope of the insanity defense to remove culpability.

His early life

By all accounts, John Wayne Gacy enjoyed a normal and relatively uneventful childhood. Part of a nuclear, middle-class family, he was a hard-working and likeable boy. Although he was no social butterfly, Gacy had no trouble making friends in school and was an active member in groups such as the Boy Scouts. With no real indication of mental illness before his savage crimes, one must search hard for some sort of cause for Gacy's alleged psychosis.

Some suggest that Gacy's physical abnormalities could have contributed to his mental instability. At age eleven, he was struck in the head by a swing on the playground. Though not an immediately debilitating injury, the accident caused a blood clot in his brain that was not discovered until he was 16. In addition to the blackouts that resulted from the clot, Gacy suffered from a non-specific heart ailment that would plague him for the rest of his life.

If these physical problems alone could not account for Gacy's mental state, it would make sense to examine his relationship with his parents as a possible factor. John Wayne Gacy, Sr. was a demanding and abusive father. He frequently beat his wife and verbally assaulted his children. Even so, John Wayne Gacy, Jr. admired and loved his father, constantly seeking approval and affection. Some suggest that this unhealthy relationship may have warped Gacy into a psychotic killer. However, even when combined with his physical deficiencies, these factors do not seem to sufficiently account for Gacy's behavior. Gacy never sought treatment for psychosis, nor was treatment ever recommended. If John Wayne Gacy was indeed insane, his insanity was a very private matter.

Charges in the case

As gruesome as a charge of thirty-three counts of first-degree murder sounds, such a charge does not sufficiently capture the barbarity of Gacy's acts. As the lone survivor of Gacy's cruelty, Jeffrey Ringall provided a disturbing account of Gacy's acts. In this, Gacy's first abduction, the heavy-set man drugged his young victim before viciously torturing and raping him for hours. Ringall awoke under a statue in Lincoln Park the next day, alive, but severely battered and bruised. Most of Gacy's later victims would experience similar torment, but they would meet a much more definitive end.

In 1974, after serving one and a half years in prison for having sex with a teenage boy, Gacy opened a contracting business called PMD contractors. Although claiming to hire teenage boys for the sake of low costs, Gacy proceeded to use PMD contractors as a source for innocent victims. Jonny Butkovich, Michael Bonnin, and Gregory Godzik were just a few of the boys who worked for Gacy and mysteriously disappeared in 1976. It would not be until December of 1978, when police dug up Gacy's property, that the mystery of their disappearance would be solved.

On December 22, 1978, John Wayne Gacy confessed to police that he killed over thirty people and buried most of the remains on his property. When police searched Gacy's house, they found twenty-nine bodies buried there, most beneath the crawl space under the floorboards. In addition, four bodies were found floating in nearby rivers. Gacy explained that he disposed of several in rivers because he had run out of room on his property. After two months of investigation, the state finally charged Gacy with thirty-three counts of murder.

Lawyers in the case

The prosecution threw everything they could at the jury to ensure that John Wayne Gacy would be put away for a long time. They called over sixty witnesses to the stand, ranging from psychological professionals to relatives of the victims. The first witness, the father of Gacy's victim John Butkovich, was one of many who took the stand in order to tug on the jury's heartstrings. Some broke down in tears, while other simply recounted their final goodbyes with the victims. Though these witnesses provided little substantial information, they were weapons in a clear strategy to convince the jury that such malice should be punished, regardless of Gacy's mental state.

In addition to these sentimental witnesses, the prosecution also called friends and co-workers of Gacy, who attested to his mood swings and improper behavior. The prosecution wanted to paint Gacy as a normal man who simply did not care how his behavior affected others. The prosecution also accounted for the possibility that the defense would have strong psychological evidence that proved Gacy insane. They called several psychologists who testified that Gacy must have been sane during the murders, primarily citing the lengths to which Gacy went to keep his acts a secret. They also brought up Gacy's public life and his continued competence as a member of society during his murderous period.

Once the prosecution had rested its case, Gacy's attorney, Robert Motta, began to construct a defense around Gacy's mental state. To the surprise of many, the first witness called by the defense was Jeffrey Ringall, his first victim. The defense used Ringall to show that Gacy seemed to have no control over his urges. Ringall's description of his abduction painted Gacy as crazed and frenzied, a depiction that Gacy's attorneys thought would exhibit his mental instability.

Further bolstering the defense's claim of insanity were Gacy's mother and sister, who recounted in detail the abuse he suffered at the hands of his father. In addition, the defense called to the stand several of his friends who testified about the generosity and kindness he exhibited on a regular basis. The defense hoped that the jury would notice the juxtaposition of Gacy's two lives and concede that such a man must be insane.

The defense also called a variety of medical experts who all had concluded that Gacy's behavior exhibited elements of abnormal psychology. Thomas Eliseo, a psychologist who interviewed him before the trial, claimed that he had borderline schizophrenia, which would have prevented him from understanding the true magnitude of his acts. Though the other expert witnesses primarily supported this diagnosis, some suggested that Gacy might have suffered from multiple personality disorder or antisocial behavior. But all agreed that he must not have fully comprehended the extremity of his crimes.

Psychoforensic professionals in the case

In 1968, John Wayne Gacy was accused of engaging in sodomy with a young male. Before his trial, the judge ordered Gacy to be evaluated for psychological competence. The psychiatrist who examined him determined that he was mentally competent to stand trial, but suffered from antisocial personality disorder and would not benefit from any known medical treatment. It would be twelve years before Gacy again received psychiatric attention, but by that point, it was too late.

Before his trial, the defense had psychologist Thomas Eliseo interview their client. Eliseo found that Gacy suffered from borderline schizophrenia, a disorder that allegedly impaired his ability to understand the magnitude of his crimes. A variety of other psychological experts for the defense offered similar diagnoses, all agreeing that he did not comprehend the gravity of his actions. Although the prosecution attempted to nullify the his insanity plea simply by displaying the heinousness of his crimes, they also called forth several experts that testified that Gacy was in fact sane during the murders.

Gacy's first psychological treatment actually began as he prepared for his trial. His psychiatrist, Dr. Helen Morrison, testified briefly for the defense, concurring with Dr. Eliseo's assertion that he could not control himself during the crimes. Morrison went a step further, however, claiming that Gacy had a split personality and that his alter-ego, Jack Hanley, came out when he was angry and was responsible for the murders. Morrison's multiple personality claims were all but dismissed by the court and by observers of the trial. Most believed that it was all an act by Gacy to prevent a conviction. And considering the fact that Morrison was alone in her assertions, such critics might have a case. However, Dr. Morrison did treat Gacy for fourteen years until his death in 1994, and she continues to stand by her convictions to this day.

Interestingly, upon his death, a pathologist, along with Dr. Helen Morrison, removed Gacy's brain for analysis. Despite the various claims by psychologists about Gacy's insanity, his brain was found to have no abnormalities.

Case process

The trial of John Wayne Gacy lasted just over a month. Each side fought with vigor for five weeks, calling over one hundred witnesses to the stand. They waited for only two hours before the jury returned and pronounced Gacy guilty as charged. On March 13, 1980, John Wayne Gacy was sentenced to death. He was soon after transferred to the Menard Correctional Center in Illinois where he spent fourteen years as his various appeals played out in court. After his last appeal failed, Gacy was sent to the Statesville Penitentiary near Joliet. It was here that he enjoyed his final meal and, just after midnight on May 10, 1994, Gacy met his end by way of lethal injection. The Killer Clown's final words were "Kiss my ass."

Test of insanity

As shown in the case of John Wayne Gacy, being absolved of guilt by the courts for reasons of insanity was no easy task in the state of Illinois. According to the Illinois Criminal Code of 1961, Article 3, Section 2, when an affirmative insanity plea was presented, the burden of proof fell to the defendant to show his insanity at the time of the crime. In Illinois, according to Section 2 of Article 6, this meant that he lacked at the time of the crime substantial capacity to appreciate the criminality of his conduct as a result of mental disease or mental defect. If the defendant failed to prove his insanity at the time of the criminal act(s), the jury might find him guilty but mentally ill. This meant that the defendant suffered from a significant mental disorder which impaired his judgment, but not to the extent that it prohibited him from comprehending the wrongfulness of his behavior.

John Wayne Gacy tried to show that he was insane enough to not understand the magnitude of his criminal acts. At this task, his defense team failed, and Gacy was found guilty with no caveats.

Media and commentators

The public response to Gacy's trial was reasonably straightforward. The media portrayed him as a sick and twisted individual, bolstering this persona with the moniker, The Killer Clown. However, even while painting Gacy as a clearly abnormal individual, commentators on the case seemed appalled at the prospect of his presenting an insanity plea. Some critics called for his lawyers' heads, while others questioned the morality of the insanity defense in general. But all was for naught when the judge handed down a death sentence to The Killer Clown.

Effect on insanity defense

The trial of John Wayne Gacy had a profound effect on contemporary views of the insanity defense. Although Gacy's deplorable acts were well beyond the range of normal behavior, the acts themselves did not justify an insanity plea. The defense failed to show the pervasiveness of his psychosis, independent of his crimes. Thus, one could not escape culpability merely for committing an insane act.

Also, the trial of John Wayne Gacy set an important precedent regarding the scope of the insanity defense to excuse truly heinous crimes. By convicting Gacy of first-degree murder, the jury in the case showed that extreme crimes deserve to be punished in full, regardless of the defendant's mental capacity. A verdict of not guilty by reason of insanity would have opened the doors of the insanity plea to crimes of any severity.

Note about sources

The primary sources used for this paper were found on the internet. The website crimelibrary.com offered a fairly comprehensive oversight of the case, while CourtTV.com filled in some of the gaps left in the story as a whole. In order to find more detail about the Gacy case, I scanned through several books, including T. Cahill's *Buried Dreams: Inside the Mind of a Serial Killer*, and C.L. Linedecker's book, *The Man Who Killed Boys*. In order to find information about Gacy after the trial, I read Charles Nemo's article, "Johnny, We Hardly Knew Ye!" Finally, I found information concerning regional insanity definitions at Law.com.

Andrew Goldstein

Andrew Goldstein, thirty, was accused of second-degree murder in January 1999, for fatally pushing Kendra Webdale, thirty-two, into an oncoming subway train. Goldstein's lawyers entered a plea of not guilty by reason of insanity because the defendant had been suffering from severe schizophrenia for eleven years. Goldstein's first trial, occurring in November 1999, ended in mistrial, as the jury was deadlocked. A second jury convicted him of second-degree murder in March

2000. Goldstein was sentenced to twenty-five years to life in prison by Judge Carol Berkman in May 2000. Most recently, Goldstein attempted an appeal, but the original judgment was affirmed on November 30, 2004.

His early life

Although no one actually knew the relationship between Goldstein and his family, the prosecution and defense painted contrasting pictures of the defendant's early life. Goldstein's parents Barbara and Edmund Goldstein divorced when he was eight years old. The defendant also had two brothers, Douglas and Richard Goldstein. Surprisingly, the family of Andrew Goldstein remained absent from the trial and refused to even speak to an expert psychiatrist working with the defense. This raised questions about the nature of the relationship within the family. The prosecution argued that Goldstein suffered severe abuse from his parents, which helped to spark the attack on Webdale. Goldstein alleged that his father regularly beat him and his mother before his parents divorced, and then beat him again in 1998 because he believed the defendant was giving his medication to his father's dogs. The defense instead said the family was so frustrated from dealing with a dysfunctional state mental health system that they had to give up.

Goldstein was an above-average student and varsity tennis player who graduated from the Bronx High School of Science, one of the leading public schools in New York City, in 1987. He spent a year at the State University of New York at Stony Brook where he also performed well. However, in 1989, he had his first psychotic breakdown, during which he pushed his mother against the wall, and was diagnosed with schizophrenia. Goldstein was forced to drop out of school, and he moved in permanently with his mother. During this time, he repeatedly confronted her violently and threatened to kill her. Later, he was hospitalized in the state Creedmoor Psychiatric Center, and his medical records indicated extensive delusions.

In 1992, he moved to Delaware to live with his father. There, he tried to re-enroll in college. He took classes at a local community college, but he failed nearly all of them. After a few months, he went back to New York to live again with his mother. Within weeks, she was forced to call an ambulance after Goldstein stood catatonically for several hours. She also reported his bizarre and potentially violent behavior. After he was released from the hospital, his mother was too frightened to take him back.

At this point, Goldstein began to live wherever he could find a space, and his parents gave him money sporadically over the next few years. There was one brief visit to his father, but overall very little contact. Starting in 1997, his downward slide accelerated. He walked into hospitals five times and was sent out each time, always in less than a week. He was given medication, but he only took it part of the time. Although Goldstein thought that his family had disowned him, records show that his mother had attempted to get him more help before the killing. She asked that he be admitted to Creedmoor for long-term care after he was treated at North General Hospital in Manhattan from November 24 to December 15, 1998, which was just two weeks before the attack in the subway. Goldstein's mother's pleas were ignored, and Goldstein was released back to the streets.

Charges in this case

On January 3, 1999, Kendra Webdale, a thirty-two year old aspiring writer who had moved to New York City from Buffalo, was waiting for the N train on the twenty-third street platform. Andrew Goldstein, a diagnosed schizophrenic, was at the platform as well and, according to witnesses, was pacing erratically and acting bizarrely. Goldstein walked up behind Webdale, a complete stranger to him, and, as the train came into the station, grabbed her and shoved her onto the track. She was crushed to death by the oncoming subway. After the act, Goldstein waited at the station and made no effort to escape. When the police arrived, he was taken to the thirteenth precinct where he confessed to his crime.

Lawyers in this case

Though Andrew Goldstein had been diagnosed several times as schizophrenic, he was deemed competent to stand trial for second-degree murder in April 1999. In New York, the threshold for competency was purposely very low so that the largest number of people could stand trial. Judge Carol Berkman presided over the trial at the Manhattan Supreme Court.

The prosecution was led by Assistant District Attorney William Greenbaum, who argued that Goldstein should be held responsible despite his illness. The prosecutor's theory of the attack was that Goldstein was filled with rage at being continually rejected by women and attacked Webdale out of frustration. He further argued that this anger towards women stemmed also from his tumultuous relationship with his mother. And he emphasized the idea that Goldstein acted with intent and even calculation by utilizing the fact that the defendant attacked Webdale on his mother's birthday.

The defense was led by attorneys Harvey Fishbein and Jack Hoffinger, who were hired by the defendant's father. They countered that Goldstein was not responsible by reason of mental disease and that he was incapable of rational thought at the time of the attack. According to the defense, the defendant had suffered from schizophrenia for eleven years and his chronic disease had taken away his capacity to control his actions. Fishbein said that Goldstein did not intend or want to attack Webdale; he just could not help it.

The prosecution built upon the evidence that Goldstein had studied and planned his crime. The prosecutor said that the timing of the attack was too exact. It was neither too early nor too late: he attacked at just the point when she had no chance to save herself. The prosecutor argued that Goldstein acted rationally. His reason for killing Webdale was his rage against women. This anger was only intensified by the fact the just moments before the attack, another woman, Dawn Lorenzino, had rejected him.

While the prosecution brought in witnesses at the scene to testify, the defense mainly used psychological experts to emphasize its point that Andrew Goldstein's mental illness was what led him to attack Kendra Webdale. In an unusual manner, the defense rested its case with a videotaped confession in which Goldstein admitted to committing the killing. The defendant's lawyers thought that Goldstein's manner on the tape was so odd that it would help his plea of not guilty by reason of insanity. The confession had been taped twelve hours after the murder and was shown earlier in the trial by the prosecution. In the tape, Goldstein laid blame for the fatal push on a type of seizure that he had suffered many times in the past. He said that he felt like something was entering his body and that he was filled with an uncontrollable desire to shove, kick, or punch. His demeanor was odd and his affect flat as he repeatedly lost his train of thought and appeared to have difficulty concentrating.

Psychoforensic professionals in this case

Dr. Spencer Eth, director of psychiatry at St. Vincent's Hospital and Medical Center in Manhattan, testified for the defense. His testimony supported the defense plea of not guilty by reason of insanity. He clearly stated that Andrew Goldstein had long suffered from schizophrenia, a severe and persistent neurobiological brain disorder that profoundly disrupts normal cognitive, perceptual, and emotional functioning. The defense lawyer led Dr. Eth through a history of

Goldstein's illness. The psychiatrist also maintained that Goldstein was unable to get the treatment he needed and wanted from the mental health system. Further, Dr. Eth denounced the prosecution's theory that Mr. Goldstein was motivated by anger towards women.

During the testimony, the prosecutor raised frequent objections, and the judge sustained most of them. However, when the prosecutor cross-examined Eth, he focused on small details rather relentlessly. The defense lawyer's objections were mostly overruled. Unfortunately, the defense lawyer was prevented from asking questions that would illuminate important facts about Goldstein's illness. Even more significant, the prosecutor was allowed to propose unsupported theories about the defendant's thought process, and the jury only received half of the story.

Wilfred G. van Gorp, an associate professor of psychology at Cornell University, also testified for the defense. He testified about the confession tape and how it showed Goldstein's suffering. Van Gorp stated that the defendant displayed a slowed ability to think, an inability to understand what details are important, an emotionless demeanor, and an inability to concentrate. Professor van Gorp testified that he believed Goldstein was legally insane at the time of the attack and suffered from a severe form of schizophrenia. He stated that the effect of the disease was displayed in tests of intellect he had given to the defendant. Goldstein's IQ had apparently dropped from one hundred twenty-two when he was a child to ninety-four in 1999.

During the cross-examination, the prosecutor asked van Gorp about unconfirmed, second-hand accounts of Goldstein's behavior. The defense lawyers objected but Justice Berkman allowed the questions to continue. The lawyers argued that bringing up these uncorroborated accounts was an attempt to denigrate the defendant.

Psychologist William Barr testified that results from basic psychological tests taken by the defendant suggest that he may have suffered from attention deficit disorder and not schizophrenia. At the trial, Professor Barr testified that he had never heard of a person suffering from a psychotic attack that only lasted a few minutes as Mr. Goldstein claimed. The expert witness said that schizophrenic individuals might have episodes that last for several days or even up to a week. Upon cross-examination, Professor Barr admitted that he had not read Mr. Goldstein's ten-year medical record which listed repeated diagnoses of schizophrenia from several doctors. Professor Barr then admitted that without reading the record, he could not make a reliable diagnosis for what mental illness the defendant suffered from.

Test of insanity

The case was tried in the Manhattan Supreme Court in New York. New York used the American Law Institute test of insanity which stated that a defendant was not criminally responsible if he lacked the capacity to understand the criminality of his conduct or to conform his conduct to the law as a result of a mental disease or defect at the time of the crime. The burden of proof was on the defendant to show that he was not criminally responsible by reason of mental disease or defect.

A diminished capacity plea differed from a plea of not guilty by reason of insanity. While the insanity defense was an affirmative defense to the crime which would find the defendant not culpable, diminished capacity would result in the defendant's being convicted of a lesser offense. The New York Penal Code defined second-degree murder as causing the death of a person with intent to cause the death of a person. However, second-degree manslaughter was defined as causing the death of a person recklessly. The diminished capacity plea assumed some people to be incapable of possessing the mental state required to commit a certain crime because of mental illness or impairment.

Case process

The first trial of Andrew Goldstein began October 1999, and ended up in mistrial in November 1999. During the trial, several key witnesses besides the experts provided testimony. One of these witnesses was Dawn Lorenzino, who testified for the prosecution. Moments before the attack, Lorenzino, who was tall and blonde like the victim, allegedly saw Goldstein pacing erratically on the platform. When he stopped to look at her, she questioned what he was doing and he moved away. She said that he then turned his attention to Webdale and asked her what time it was. When she told him it was five o'clock, he resumed his pacing and then stood still with his back to the wall opposite Webdale. Lorenzino testified that when the train came into the station, Goldstein shoved Webdale with such force that she flew over the track.

Upon cross-examination, defense lawyers suggested that Lorenzino never actually spoke to Goldstein. They proposed that she may have invented that part of her story to support the prosecution's theory that Goldstein was motivated by rejection and not an uncontrollable urge caused by his schizophrenia.

Another witness, Jacques Louis, the man who drove the train and initially confronted Goldstein after the incident, testified that after the attack, Goldstein was very calm and that the defendant told him that he was a mental patient who needed a doctor. Louis and the police who arrived at the scene saw that Goldstein's demeanor was flat and unaffected, symptomatic of schizophrenia. Raymond Loughlin, the first officer at the scene, testified that when he arrived, Goldstein was just sitting on the platform, staring straight ahead and devoid of expression.

The prosecution also brought nurse Nury Nelson to the stand. Nelson had treated Goldstein for a sprained ankle at Jamaica Hospital in Queens the day before the attack. The nurse testified that she only realized that Goldstein was a psychiatric patient when she asked him if he was taking any medication. He told her that he was taking two anti-psychotic medications. Upon cross-examination, Nelson revealed that although Goldstein claimed to be taking the medication, he had not shown any side effects of the drugs, which might have included some drooling and having some difficulty speaking.

During the trial, Justice Berkman seemed to favor the prosecution. During expert testimony, she frequently allowed the prosecutor to ask questions about unsubstantiated evidence and also ruled in favor of the prosecution's objections to certain testimony that could help the defense's case. The defense felt it did not have the chance to present all of the evidence that it wanted to and had to combat unconfirmed second-hand accounts that were provided as evidence.

When it came time for deliberation, the jury found itself hopelessly deadlocked at ten votes to convict the defendant and two to acquit by reason of insanity. It was later found that one of the jurors who had opposed the conviction had recently been prosecuted by the Manhattan district attorney's office. That juror, Octavio Ramos, was convicted of harassment and resisting arrest three weeks before he became a juror, a fact that most likely would have disqualified him for serving. However, neither the judge nor the prosecution had asked Ramos if he had been convicted of any crimes.

The other hold-out juror was a former social worker who had previously worked with mentally ill clients. The majority of the jurors favored conviction because they feared that if Goldstein were sent to a mental hospital instead of jail, he would quickly be released. Rather than calmly weighing the evidence, the jury, according to reports, spent five days yelling at one another. In the end, no decision could be reached, and a mistrial was declared.

The second trial in March 2000, resulted in the conviction of Andrew Goldstein of second-degree murder, which carried a penalty of twenty-five years to life. Jurors for the retrial stated that they believed Goldstein had a mental illness, but were convinced that he knew what he was doing when he pushed Webdale into the subway. In May 2000, Justice Carol Berkman sentenced Mr. Goldstein to twenty-five years to life in prison. This severe sentence was most likely in response to the public outcry for justice in this case.

Media involvement

The media played a key role in this case from the beginning. Because Goldstein's attack became so publicized, the use of the insanity defense appeared doomed at the outset to fail. Numerous articles about the tragedy were published in *The New York Times* and other newspapers and magazines. Most of these pieces focused on the victim and her family while presenting Goldstein as a dangerous, psychotic criminal. The case made television headlines as well. On December 20, 1999, *Dateline NBC* aired a report on the killing. Although the program noted that Goldstein had slipped through the cracks of the system, reporters are clearly unsympathetic toward him. The lack of facilities and case managers was made apparent, but little was said beyond that. Instead, the audience was forced to relive the murder from Webdale's perspective and *Dateline* emphasized its interview with Kendra Webdale's family. In contrast, Goldstein was portrayed in the company of his police escort, which further alienated him from the rest of the audience.

The media became even more involved when the Webdale family pushed for new legislation regarding mentally ill patients. In August 1999, Governor George Pataki introduced Kendra's Law which was designed to protect the public and individuals living with mental illness by ensuring that potentially dangerous mentally ill outpatients were safely and effectively treated. The legislation authorized courts to issue orders that would require mentally ill persons, who were unlikely to survive safely in the community without supervision, to accept medications and other needed mental health services. The media coverage of the passing of the law further added to the sympathies given to the Webdale family at the expense of Goldstein.

Commentators

Although legal commentators were divided on whether or not they felt the insanity defense should be used in such a high profile case, since it was rarely successful, they were more concerned with how the trials themselves progressed. Goldstein's mistrial was a blow to the court system. The fact that neither the prosecutor nor the judge had asked one of the jurors if he had been convicted of any crimes displayed negligence. The judge's favoring the prosecution also raised suspicions. Commentators argued whether these trials were actually fair or if an abuse of power was occurring within the courtroom.

Most psychological commentators who knew of the case and the medical facts were infuriated by the outcome of the trials. They considered the judicial system to be faulty in the Goldstein verdict. Many commentators claimed that the majority of the medical facts were ignored by the jury and obstructed by the prosecution and the judge. Some considered Goldstein to be just as much the victim in the crime as Kendra Webdale. The mental health system had failed him by not giving him the treatment he needed, and in turn, this tragedy occurred.

Media commentators reflected the feelings of the general public on the case. Most considered Goldstein to be an imminent danger and wanted to see him brought up on murder charges. Nearly all sympathized completely with the Webdale family, for Kendra Webdale was a young, attractive woman who came from a loving family. If something like this could happen to her, no one was safe. The public outcry for justice only increased after the mistrial, as many thought Goldstein could fail through the cracks of the judicial system as well.

The insanity defense itself

From the Goldstein case, we are reminded once again that the insanity defense rarely works in high-profile murder cases, even if the defendant has had a long history of mental illness. This case was similar to the Tortorici case in that both defendants suffered from schizophrenia and that fact was largely ignored by the jury and the public. Often in cases such as this, the judge and prosecution will seem to take extra measures in order to sway the jury to convict the defendant. The judge might prevent certain testimony from the defense that would help the defendant's case or might ignore objections made by the defense about a prosecutor's questions.

This case reiterated the idea that laws may not always protect those that they are aimed at protecting and that the public still knows very little about mental illness. The idea of the insanity defense includes an effort to provide individuals who commit acts which are otherwise crimes but who are not criminally responsible because of their mental illness with treatment rather than prison time. However, the public often sees the insanity defense as the defendant's attempt to escape punishment. Many times jurors are not even told that if the defendant is found not guilty by reason of insanity, he would be just as confined in a mental facility as he would be in prison. Unfortunately, many ill defendants end up in prison despite the fact that they may not have been responsible for their actions.

The Goldstein case was actually fairly representative of other murder cases in which the defendant used the insanity defense. Though many schizophrenic individuals have attempted to use the insanity defense, but it has rarely been successful. In most trials, especially murder trials, the insanity defense has failed because the burden of proof was on the defense. This combined with the public's skepticism about the insanity defense and mental illness made it a difficult case to argue.

Brief summary and significance

Andrew Goldstein, a severely schizophrenic individual who had been in and out of several mental facilities in New York, pushed Kendra Webdale in front of a subway in January 1999, killing her instantly. During the trial of October 1999, the defense attempted to use the insanity defense for Goldstein, arguing that he had been suffering from delusions at the time of the attack and that the mental health system had failed him. The prosecution countered by proposing that although Goldstein might have been mentally ill, he displayed a motive in attacking Webdale and his actions showed evidence of premeditation and planning, or at least of forethought. Several witnesses and psychological experts testified during the trial presenting differing accounts of the situation and the defendant's illness. The jurors returned from deliberation deadlocked, and a mistrial was declared. A second trial was held in March 2000, and Goldstein was found guilty of second-degree murder and sentenced by Justice Berkman to twenty-five years to life in prison. In this case, the media and the public played a large role in the outcome of the case. Because of the media attention that the case received, it was nearly impossible for the insanity defense to succeed. Furthermore, the family of Kendra Webdale pushed for new legislation which would force the mentally ill to take medication. This combined with the public's lack of knowledge about the nature of mental illness worked against the defense in this case.

Notes about sources

Most of the information on the Andrew Goldstein case was drawn from newspaper, magazine, and journal articles. Many of my sources came from *The New York Times* and various mental health organizations. In addition, I consulted the official report for the Goldstein appellate case.

William Bergen Greene

William Bergen Greene, born in 1954, spent most of his adult life in prison on various charges of burglary and sexual assault, but he became a notable criminal only after he molested his therapist in 1994. The therapist, identified only by the initials M.S., had diagnosed Greene with dissociative identity disorder, formerly known as multiple personality disorder, a psychological illness in which two or more separate identities take turns controlling one body. When Greene found himself facing charges of kidnapping and indecent liberties, both he and his victim, M.S., blamed the incident on one of Greene's alter personalities, a three- or four-year-old child named Tyrone. Because Greene's mental illness allegedly precluded him from controlling his behavior and because Tyrone's young age prevented him from understanding the wrongfulness of his conduct, Greene pleaded not guilty by reason of insanity. The original trial judge, however, barred Greene's insanity defense because he did not find dissociative identity disorder to be a universally accepted mental illness. The jury returned a verdict of guilty on both counts, and Greene was sentenced to life in prison. An appeals court overturned the conviction on the grounds that Greene should have been permitted to present his insanity defense, and Greene was given a new trial. Even with the help of expert psychological testimony, including that of his victim, Greene was again convicted. As of November 2004, he remained in prison serving a life term and awaiting trial in another case, a 1979 rape-murder in which he was implicated by DNA evidence and faced the possibility of the death penalty.

His early life

William Greene was subjected to severe physical, emotional, and sexual abuse from a very early age. At the age of eight, he became a ward of the state and spent the rest of his youth in a number of foster homes and public institutions, where he continued to experience abuse. In one particularly brutal incident, at the age of twelve he was gang raped by three older boys. During these years he began to abuse a number of drugs. At seventeen, he escaped from his facility but soon found himself in prison after being convicted of grand theft auto. A string of subsequent convictions followed, mostly for sexual crimes, which ensured that Greene spent little time outside prison before returning again. Following a 1988 conviction, he enrolled in a sex offender treatment program at the prison, where psychotherapist M.S. diagnosed him with depression and dissociative identity disorder. Through hypnosis, twenty-four different alter personalities were eventually manifested, including identities of both genders, varying ages, and even non-human species, as Auto the robot and Smokey the dragon. Not all of the prison's therapists agreed with the diagnosis: one written report hypothesized that Greene was malingering dissociative identity disorder and plotting a strategy to victimize M.S. in the future. M.S. treated Greene for dissociative identity disorder in prison, and, following his 1992 release, he voluntarily continued to receive twice-weekly treatment from M.S. At that time Greene appeared to be adapting well. He maintained employment, he had a number of friends, and he carried on a normal romantic relationship. By February 1994, however, Greene's condition had begun to deteriorate, and M.S. worried that he would commit suicide, so she began to speak with him on the phone daily and visited him at home on several occasions.

Charges in this case

On April 29, 1994, M.S. received a particularly distressed phone call from Greene and decided to visit his apartment to investigate his condition. Greene behaved very strangely, speaking very slowly, crying, and referring to himself as we. After she ascertained that he was under the influence of cocaine, M.S. got up to leave, but he stopped her. During a struggle, M.S. tripped and fell, and her shirt tore open in Greene's hands. From the floor, she begged him to stop, but he managed to remove her bra and began to molest her. After a moment his demeanor changed, and he helped her to the bathroom to wash up. He then changed his mind and sat her in a chair in the bathroom and spent the next two hours touching her breasts with his hands and mouth, stopping several times to go to the sink and inject a substance, presumably cocaine, into his arm. M.S. described his behavior as that of a child. He would periodically place his head on her shoulder and cry. At one point, he pulled down his pants and began to massage his penis, but he never achieved an erection or attempted to rape M.S. Suddenly his appearance changed. He straightened his posture and told M.S. she could leave, but as she attempted to go, he changed his mind again and bound and gagged her in the bedroom and fled the apartment in her car. M.S. was soon able to escape her bonds and called the police from a hospital across the street. Greene was quickly apprehended and charged with kidnapping and indecent liberties.

Lawyers in this case

Greene pleaded not guilty by reason of insanity prior to his trial, and the presiding Judge Thorpe held a hearing to determine the admissibility of testimony concerning dissociative identity disorder. After the judge decided that the proffered testimony could not be used to establish insanity, prosecutor Seth Fine moved to exclude any mention of dissociative identity disorder during the trial, which the judge granted. Thus, the prosecution presented a straight-forward case to establish that Greene was responsible for the crime. Defense attorney David Koch was barred from even mentioning dissociative identity disorder. Koch was assisted by Greene, who insisted on participating in his own defense as one of his alter personalities claimed to hold a law degree. Faced with the straight-forward question of whether Greene had attacked M.S., the jury convicted Greene on both counts.

Co-counsel Koch and Greene appealed the verdict to the Washington Court of Appeals in 1998 on the grounds that Greene had been unduly denied the opportunity to present an insanity defense. Prosecutor Fine objected by arguing that dissociative identity disorder was not a generally accepted illness and that even if it were, dissociative identity disorder testimony was not relevant to Greene's particular case. Both sides maintained these stances throughout the subsequent appeals process. During the retrial, the defense was permitted to present its insanity defense based on dissociative identity disorder, while the prosecution argued that Greene was malingering dissociative identity disorder to avoid punishment. Koch remained Greene's counsel during the 1998 appeal to the Washington Court of Appeals and the 1999 appeal to the Supreme Court of Washington, but by the time of his 2002 appeal to the U.S. Ninth Circuit Court, Greene had dropped Koch to become sole counsel in his own case. During the retrial, public defenders Teresa Conlan and Marybeth Dingledy represented Greene, while deputy prosecutor Paul Stern presented the state's case.

Psychoforensic professionals in this case

William Greene first received psychological treatment in 1989 in a program for sex offenders while in prison. M.S., a psychotherapist and a registered nurse specializing in mental health, was one of the prison therapists treating Greene, and she was the first to diagnose him with depression and dissociative identity disorder, although some of her colleagues disagreed with the diagnosis. While using hypnotherapy to treat Greene's depression, M.S. realized he had multiple identities. Under further hypnosis, she eventually discovered twenty-four different complete personalities and fifteen fragmentary personalities. As she began to treat him for dissociative identity disorder, some of his alters began to regress in age, suggesting to her a pattern toward eventual integration of the various personalities. After Greene was released from prison, he continued to voluntarily receive twice-weekly treatment from M.S. During the trial, M.S. wanted to testify for Greene because she recognized which of Greene's personalities were in control during the attack. In the original case, she was not allowed to mention dissociative identity disorder but did testify as a witness. In the retrial, she was permitted to testify for Greene regarding his illness. According to M.S., it was several of his alters, rather than Greene that had attacked her. She said that Greene had used cocaine that day which had inhibited his ability to control the personalities. Auto the robot held her down, but most of the assault was allegedly perpetrated by the three- or four-year-old Tyrone. At one point, alter Sam briefly appeared, and the therapist claimed that this personality would have saved her if he had maintained his presence. M.S. said Greene himself did not participate in the assault and did not even learn of the incident until days later.

At the pre-trial hearing to determine whether dissociative identity testimony would be admitted, the defense presented its expert, Dr. Robert B. Olsen, who testified that dissociative identity disorder was generally accepted among psychological experts. While Dr. Olsen considered the alter personality Tyrone to be sane, he stated that he could not testify for the sanity of Greene because, due to the number of different personalities, he did not know who Greene really was. The prosecution's expert, Dr. Gregg J. Gagliardi did not disagree that dissociative identity disorder was generally accepted. The doctor, however, argued that Greene's dissociative identity disorder diagnosis should not be used as grounds for an insanity defense because it was impossible to evaluate the sanity of each personality and because it was unclear when each personality was in control of the body or knew what was happening.

Dr. Olsen had been hired as an expert for the defense at Greene's original 1995 trial, but he later testified as an expert for the prosecution at Greene's 2003 retrial. Olsen testified that in the years since the first trial he had learned more about dissociative identity disorder and that, when he reexamined Greene, he decided that Greene appeared to be malingering. Psychologist Richard Packard was the second expert testifying for the prosecution. Packard testified that he did not believe Greene had dissociative identity disorder but instead suffered from antisocial personality disorder and paraphilia. According to Packard, Greene was capable of faking dissociative identity disorder and knew what he was doing during the attack. During cross-examination, Packard admitted that he was not sure whether dissociative identity disorder was a legitimate disorder at all. Although not an expert, Greene's former cellmate, Eric Fleischmann, also testified for the prosecution regarding dissociative identity disorder. Fleischmann claimed that he himself had tried to fake dissociative identity disorder but was unsuccessful, whereas Greene had supposedly bragged to his cellmate that he was able to get away with it.

Dr. Marlene Steinberg, vice-president of the International Society for the Study of Dissociation and author of a book on dissociative identity disorder, testified for the defense at the retrial. She believed that dissociative identity disorder was a product of childhood sexual abuse and testified that Greene fit the profile of a typical dissociative identity disorder patient.

Test of insanity

This case proceeded in Washington State, where the insanity standard was the M'Naghten test, which required that the defendant either did not understand his actions or did not know that his behavior was wrong. The burden of proof of insanity lay with the defense. With an insanity plea, the jury had the option of returning a guilty verdict or a not guilty by reason of insanity verdict. A not guilty by reason of insanity defendant could be sentenced to a mental institution or to an out-patient program, but psychological treatment was not mandatory. Expert testimony regarding the insanity defense had to meet the Frye standard, meaning that the relevant mental disorder had achieved general acceptance in the academic community and that the disorder could be evaluated by a universal, accepted standard. Expert testimony could also be challenged under ER 702, which required that the witness qualify as an expert and that the specialized testimony be necessary for understanding the issues in the case.

Case process

In William Greene's first trial, he was denied the opportunity to present an insanity defense because the judge determined that dissociative identity disorder was not generally accepted in the psychological community. The jury convicted Greene on both counts of kidnapping and indecent liberties, and he was sentenced to life in prison under Washington's three-strikes law, as this conviction represented his third felony. The defense appealed the verdict in 1998 to the Washington Court of Appeals on the grounds that Greene was unduly denied his right to an insanity defense. The court found that dissociative identity disorder was an accepted disorder and, thus, Greene should have been permitted an insanity defense. The guilty verdict was overturned, and a new trial was ordered. The prosecution appealed this decision in 1999 to the Supreme Court of Washington, which agreed that dissociative identity disorder was a legitimate illness, but decided that dissociative identity disorder testimony was not admissible in Greene's particular case because no sufficient legal standard existed to evaluate the insanity of dissociative identity disorder defendants. Thus, Greene's original conviction was reinstated. The defense appealed to the U.S. Supreme Court in 2000, which declined to take the case. The defense then appealed to the U.S. District Court, which held that Greene should have been permitted his dissociative identity disorder defense. The prosecution appealed this decision to the Ninth U.S. Circuit Court of Appeals in 2002, where the District Court's decision was upheld and the case was remanded for a new trial. At the retrial, Greene was permitted to plead not guilty by reason of insanity and to present expert witnesses, including M.S., who testified for the defense. According to defense attorney Dingledy, six of Greene's personalities appeared during the trial. The admission of dissociative identity disorder testimony, however, did not change the outcome of the month-long trial. After deliberating for five hours, the jury convicted Greene once again of kidnapping and indecent liberties, reinstating his mandatory life sentence in prison. While Greene was serving time in prison, the police declared that he was a suspect in the 1979 rape murder of Sylvia Durante in Seattle, which was committed before Greene's first assault conviction. After nearly twenty-three years without a suspect, the police had matched Greene's DNA with semen found at the crime scene. As of 2004, Greene was awaiting trial and possibly facing the death penalty in that case. It was unclear whether he would employ an insanity defense.

Media involvement

The national media paid little attention to this case, but Washington area newspapers provided moderate coverage of the case from the time that Greene was first charged in 1994 through 2004, when Greene sat in prison awaiting trial in another case. In 1998, NBC's *Dateline* aired a program investigating the case. The media coverage almost exclusively sided against Greene by expressing skepticism of his dissociative identity disorder claim. Its limited coverage prevented the media from exercising any appreciable influence in the outcome of this case.

Commentators

Some legal commentators criticized the Washington Supreme Court for failing to establish a legal standard for evaluating the sanity of dissociative identity disorder defendants in the Greene case. The court held that dissociative identity disorder testimony was inadmissible in this case because no legal standard existed to evaluate the sanity of those suffering from multiple personalities. Rather than establish such a standard, the court stated that it first required more scientific evidence regarding the relationship between dissociative identity disorder and insanity. Some commentators disagreed with the ruling, arguing that enough scientific evidence existed to form a legal standard and that Greene should have been permitted to present dissociative identity disorder expert testimony.

The insanity defense itself

The Greene case illustrated the fact that juries rarely acquitted defendants by reason of insanity. An unusual aspect of Greene's case was that his victim actually testified for the defense, claiming that Greene had no control and no knowledge of the crime while it was happening. Nonetheless, the jury still found Greene responsible for the crime. Because the insanity defense rarely succeeded in trials, it was not terribly surprising that Greene's plea also failed. Yet, if even the victim argued for a not guilty by reason of insanity verdict and the jury still convicted the defendant, this case raised the question of where the insanity defense could have worked.

The central issue in this case concerned the admissibility of expert testimony on dissociative identity disorder in respect to two specific issues, its acceptability as a mental disorder and its applicability to insanity. While it was far from being a universally accepted disorder in the Diagnostic and Statistical Manual of Mental Disorders, DSM-IV-TR, it did not claim significantly lower levels of acceptance than most other disorders. Thus, it was considered to be a generally accepted illness among the psychological and legal communities.

The second issue posed a more serious problem for the admissibility of testimony by expert witnesses. Psychological experts had not established an effective standard for determining whether a suspected dissociative identity disorder patient was malingering. In criminal cases, where the defendant may have had a strong incentive to fake a mental illness, the difficulty in assessing malingering posed a serious problem for the courts. Even in cases where it was unanimously accepted that the defendant suffered from this disorder, the courts faced the nearly impossible task of determining which personality or personalities were responsible for the crime. This problem was compounded by the difficulty of determining which personalities may or may not have been aware of the crime. Assessing the sanity of each of the responsible personalities posed yet another problem. In Greene's case, the alter who allegedly committed the assault was a three- or four-year-old child, who, by virtue of his age, was legally not responsible. For a defendant with dissociative identity disorder, at least one of the personalities committed a crime, and assuming that he or she was sane and criminally responsible, that personality deserved punishment. The concern, however, then shifted to the other, innocent personalities and raised the question: was it fair that they had to share in the punishment of the guilty person who happened to inhabit the same body?

Brief summary and significance of this case

After being charged with kidnapping and sexually assaulting his therapist, William Greene pleaded not guilty by reason of insanity, blaming the crime on several of his alter personalities. Both Greene and his victim who was his therapist claimed that he suffered from dissociative identity disorder, formerly known as multiple personality disorder, and, because it was argued that Greene himself did not commit or even know of the crime, his victim and his defense concluded that he was not criminally responsible. In the original trial the judge barred Greene from even mentioning dissociative identity disorder because it was not considered a generally accepted disorder, and the jury returned two guilty verdicts. After a series of appeals, Greene was granted a new trial in which he was allowed to present his insanity plea and expert testimony on the disorder. After this retrial, he was again convicted and sentenced to life in prison. Despite the fact that Greene's victim testified for the defense, his insanity plea failed because the jury did not believe that Greene was suffering from dissociative identity disorder.

Note about sources

The information for this case was obtained from published court opinions; newspaper articles in *The Seattle Times*, *Seattle Post-Intelligencer*, and the Associated Press; and the article "One crime, many convicted: Dissociative identity disorder and the exclusion of expert testimony in State v. Greene" by Mary E. Crego, published in the *Washington Law Review*.

Patty Hearst

Her early life

Patricia Campbell Hearst was born February 20, 1954, in San Francisco, California. She was the third of five daughters born to Randolph A. Hearst and Catherine Hearst. Her grandfather was the publishing icon William Randolph Hearst, who pioneered tabloid journalism, or what used to be referred to as yellow journalism, and, at his peak, he owned twenty-eight major newspapers and eighteen magazines, along with several radio stations and movie companies. As a result of her family's success, Hearst, who was called Patty by those close to her, lived a very sheltered and affluent lifestyle. She grew up in the San Francisco area, attended Catholic schools throughout her childhood, graduated from high school a year early, and earned the award as best student her freshman year at Menlo College. She was a model child and student, whose only act of defiance throughout her childhood and early adulthood was when she went against her parent's wishes and moved in with a man who had been her tutor in high school. Otherwise, she was extremely conservative. In a time of liberalism, Patty Hearst often talked about her distaste for hippies and the dirty conditions in which they lived, and she even broke up with her first serious boyfriend because he smoked marijuana.

After her freshman year at Menlo College, Hearst followed her boyfriend, Steven Weed, to the University of California at Berkeley, where he was teaching. She enrolled as a sophomore at Berkeley, and in the fall of 1973 she moved in with Weed, and the two became engaged, with plans to marry in the summer of 1974. She was only nineteen years old at the time.

Charges in this case

On February 4, 1974, Patty Hearst and Steven Weed were at home in their apartment when a group of two black men and a white woman broke into the apartment, violently attacked Weed, and kidnapped Patty at gunpoint. The kidnappers identified themselves as the Symbionese Liberation Army. The Symbionese Liberation Army was a group famous for its liberal views and extreme tactics. The group was led by escaped convict Donald DeFreeze, known as General Field Marshal Cinque Mtume. His leadership was modeled after that of Charles Manson. DeFreeze required complete submission and worship from his followers, and he constantly preached to them his goals of starting a revolution among the underprivileged by sabotaging people with status and money. The group originally kidnapped Patty Hearst to negotiate the release of some of their followers who were in prison for murder. When the authorities refused these conditions, the Symbionese Liberation Army requested that Randolph Hearst and the Hearst Foundation give two million dollars to feed California's poor. Even though the Hearsts obeyed, Patty Hearst was not released, and when the Symbionese Liberation Army requested an additional four million dollars in funds, the Hearsts declared that they would set the money aside but would only make it available to the poor when their daughter was released. After this, bargaining between the Army and the Hearsts ceased, and the family feared that their daughter was most likely already dead.

Immediately following her kidnapping, DeFreeze kept Hearst locked in a closet for fifty-seven days. Hearst later claimed that she was subject to physical and sexual abuse by a number of gang members. Hearst also reported that during this time she was continuously told that she was at risk of dying and that nobody was trying to rescue her, that she was fed propaganda about oppression and the Army's valiant efforts, and she was forced to record messages that criticized her family and the lifestyle in which she had been raised. A number of these recordings were released to the Hearst family throughout the weeks after her kidnapping. The Hearsts believed that she was being forced to record the things she said, but then they received a photo in which Hearst was holding a rifle in her arms and standing next to a painting of the Symbionese Liberation Army's symbol, a seven-headed serpent. She recorded that she now had a new name, Tania, a name taken from the girlfriend of Cuban revolutionary Che Guevera, and that she had joined the Symbionese Liberation Army and their efforts.

Further evidence of Patty Hearst's strange assimilation to the Symbionese Liberation Army came a few weeks later, on the morning of April 15, 1974, in the form of a surveillance videotape. The tape caught four white women and a black man robbing the Hibernia Bank in the Sunset district of San Francisco. When police reviewed the tape later, they were able to make out the face of Patty Hearst among the armed robbers. The five criminals had been able to steal ten thousand dollars, wound two bystanders, and flee the scene in a car in under four minutes. The Hearst family was shocked to hear of the police's discovery, but they were even more shocked when the police received another recording from their daughter less than forty-eight hours after the robbery in which Hearst angrily explained that the Symbionese Liberation Army had robbed the bank, that she had been part of the robbery and was in no way coerced into her actions, and the fact that anyone believed that she was brainwashed was beyond belief.

There was further evidence that led authorities to believe that Hearst was not being coerced into her actions. A month after the bank robbery, on May 16, Hearst took part in another heist. She was getaway driver while two members of the Symbionese Liberation Army held up a sporting goods store. Hearst was left alone in the car for the entire time that her kidnappers were in the store, and yet she made no attempt to try to escape or even seek out help. When her two accomplices were apprehended in the store, Hearst aided in their escape by firing a round of warning shots into the building, some of which barely missed the store's employee. Hearst and her two comrades all escaped by stealing a series of cars. Throughout this chaotic scene, all witnesses claimed that they felt that Hearst had not shown any signs of being either scared or coerced.

The next day, May 17, 1974, the Los Angeles police found members of the Symbionese Liberation Army living in an East 54 Street home. The police issued eighteen requests to surrender to the Army but all were ignored, and the police eventually began their attack with tear gas. The house lit on fire after being hit with multiple rounds of gunfire, three Army members were shot as they tried to escape the house, two died of carbon monoxide poisoning in the house, and DeFreeze, the leader of the group, shot himself in the head. Many Americans feared that Patty Hearst would be found in the rubble. However she watched the whole scene on a TV, along with millions of other TV viewers across the country, from the safety of a hotel room where she and two fellow Symbionese Liberation Army members were hiding.

Hearst and these two remaining members became fugitives and traveled across the country throughout the summer of 1974. The FBI was finally able to catch her when she returned to the west coast in September. She was arrested on September 18, 1975, in San Francisco, and she showed signs of defiance throughout the ordeal, smiling for news cameras and declaring herself an urban guerrilla. Hearst was charged with armed bank robbery and use of a firearm in the commission of a felony. She would be brought to trial in the San Francisco federal court.

Lawyers in this case

The case was highly publicized, and it was labeled the trial of the century by most Americans. The Hearst family hired F. Lee Bailey, a renowned trial attorney. His previous successful cases included Sam Sheppard's acquittal, an arranged deal for Albert DeSalvo the Boston Strangler, and a successful defense of Captain Ernest Medina in his trial for the 1968 My Lai massacre in Vietnam. In accepting the case, Bailey sought a great deal of media attention, and intended to personally benefit from the trial by claiming in his original contract book rights to the content of Hearst's trial. The judge presiding over the case was Oliver Carter, who also sought out media attention when he granted interviews to *Time* and *The New York Times* prior to the trial. The prosecutor was James Browning, the U. S. Attorney for Northern California. Browning had not tried a case in seven years.

Psychoforensic professionals in this case

Patty Hearst's trial began on February 4, 1976, which was exactly two years to the day after she had been originally kidnapped by the Symbionese Liberation Army. Her defense lay in the idea that she had been brainwashed throughout the ordeal, and therefore was not in control of her actions at the time of the crimes. The defense brought in medical and psychiatric experts to listen to Hearst describe the Symbionese Liberation Army's physical and sexual abuse, their threats, and their complete devotion to the group's ideologies. Using these harsh conditions as grounds for brainwashing, the witnesses attempted to display evidence of Hearst's mental deterioration. Psychologist Margaret Singer explained that her IQ had dropped since her abduction, and Dr. Louis Jolyon said that Hearst had been in a continuous state of extreme physical stress.

The defense also brought in several experts in mind control, including Dr. William Sargent, Dr. Martin Orne, and Dr. Robert Jay Lifton. Each expert argued that Hearst had been brainwashed into following the Symbionese Liberation Army, its political ideals, and its extreme actions, thus identifying with her aggressors. However, jurors later explained that they found the experts' details to be inconsistent and that the experts failed to show how their individual research applied to Hearst's situation.

Dr. Lifton explained the process of personality transformation through brainwashing in the greatest depth. He related Hearst's situation to that of prisoners in Communist China in the 1950s who were brainwashed into following communist principles. Lifton further explained that in times of extreme social or environmental change, people exposed to new ideas or environments could change their belief systems. With enough external pressure, these personal changes could be extreme. Lifton tried to apply typical methods of brainwashing to Hearst's case, including total control of communication, continual references to ideologies, creation of an illusion of a higher purpose or a sacred blessing for the group's cause, and use of other shaming and guilt-producing tactics. He concluded that Defreeze and the radical group had used all of these tactics on Hearst, according to her account of what had happened to her during her first few months of captivity. Dr. Lifton tried to explain that these procedures had worked for armies and governments for years, which was why they were continually used, and why they also proved successful on Hearst.

Drs. Conway and Seigelman added to Lifton's argument, claiming that Hearst's belief systems were meticulously destroyed by Defreeze and his group. As a result, she then was forced to identify with the ideologies of her captors, thus rebuilding her belief systems to the point where she underwent a dramatic personality change. Conway and Seigelman analyzed her behavior a year after her arrest and they found that she showed behavioral patterns similar to those of a cult victim. Hearst laughed and cried at inappropriate points in conversations, claimed that she had barely any memories of the time she spent locked in a closet at the beginning of her captivity, had severe mood swings, and displayed extensive anxiety. In the opinions of Drs. Conway and Seigelman, her avoidance and repression of her time with the Symbionese Liberation Army were signs of the extreme trauma she had faced, which they argued meant that she could not, under this trauma, have formed true criminal intent, an understanding of what she was doing, and that what she was doing was wrong.

The prosecution called one expert to counter the arguments of the three defense witnesses, Dr. Joel Fort, who offered his opinion that Hearst was a willing participant in all of the crimes and was simply an aimless young girl looking for a cause. Though it was argued that Dr. Fort did not appear to have any credential to testify in court, or any significant evidence to back up his opinions, Judge Carter would not allow the defense to challenge his appearance in court.

Case process

In total, the trial lasted thirty-nine days, and on March 20, the jury returned a verdict of guilty after twelve hours of deliberation. The jury claimed that they had found the brainwashing defense confusing and had a hard time applying the experts' research to Hearst's situation. The unsympathetic media had continually portrayed her as an undeserving rebellious rich girl and many Americans had trouble understanding how a wealthy, educated person could have fallen into the terrorist actions of the Symbionese Liberation Army. The brainwashing theory did not fully explain this extreme personality shift for most people. Additionally, many people felt that the politically-charged atmosphere in America at the time of the trial had contributed to Hearst's guilty verdict and harsh sentencing. In a time of revolutions and uprisings, especially within younger generations, more conservative Americans resented the left-wing actions of young activist groups.

Patty Hearst had been a perfect example of the rebellious young person looking for a cause, while creating irreparable damage in the process. As a result of all of these factors, Hearst received the maximum penalty and was sentenced to twenty-five years for the robbery, plus ten for the firearms charge.

After Judge Carter, who had presided over the case, died, a judicial review shortened Hearst's sentence to a total of seven years. Hearst's defense requested an appeal to the Supreme Court, but the request was declined. She began to serve her time at the Federal Correctional Institute in Pleasanton, California in 1977. Patty Hearst had been behind bars nearly two years when President Jimmy Carter commuted her sentence in early 1979. After her release, Hearst married her bodyguard and began to lead a normal life with her husband and children. She avoided all media attention until 1982, when she released her autobiography, explaining that not all of the details had been released during the trial, and she wanted people to hear her whole side of the story.

In June 1999, after twenty-four years on the run, Hearst's former Symbionese Liberation Army colleague, who had been using the pseudonym Sara Jane Olson, was finally arrested in St. Paul, Minnesota, where she was living in a wealthy neighborhood with her husband and her daughter, volunteering at church, reading to the blind in her free time, and participating in a gun-control advocacy group. Olson was charged as Kathleen Ann Soliah who had been indicted in absentia for terrorist activities with the Symbionese Liberation Army during Hearst's trial. Because Hearst had written in detail about Soliah's illegal activities in her autobiography, Hearst was considered a key witness in the trial and was forced to revisit her history with the Symbionese Liberation Army in front of the public eye once again, testifying for the prosecution. In January 2001, just before the trial began, President Bill Clinton issued Hearst a full pardon before he left office, thus expunging the crimes from her record. Soliah felt that this gave Hearst, who could now appear in court as an innocent victim, more credibility on the witness stand and protested her appearance. However, Patty Hearst testified in court, and at the end of the trial Soliah was found guilty and sentenced to twenty years to life for her prior actions.

Notes about sources

The most important source for this case study was the Crime Library article on the case of Patty Hearst, which can be found at this website: http://www.crimelibrary.com/terrorists_spies/terrorists/hearst/1.html. Additional information was found in the CNN profile of Patty Hearst, which can be found at this website: http://www-cgi.cnn.com/CNN/Programs/people/shows/hearst/profile.html. For more extensive sources, see Patty Hearst's autobiography, entitled *Patty Hearst: Her own story*, and *Rescuing Patty Hearst: Growing up sane in a decade gone mad* written by Virginia Holman. For a visual source, see the film version of Hearst's autobiography, which is entitled *Patty Hearst* and was released in 1988 by director Paul Schrader.

John Hinckley, Jr.

On March 30, 1981, John Hinckley, Jr. stunned the nation as he attempted to assassinate President Reagan in a desperate effort to impress the actress Jodie Foster. The shots wounded three other people, including press secretary James Brady, who suffered a grave injury. Hinckley's defense lawyers quickly issued a plea of not guilty by reason of insanity, citing his delusional motivation for the shooting and his psychological background. The burden of proof rested on the prosecution, as they brought in expert witnesses to try to prove that Hinckley was sane at the time of the crime. Ultimately, the jury found Hinckley not guilty by reason of insanity. The verdict outraged the country, and spurred states and Congress to revise and amend their own insanity defense legislation.

Hinckley was committed to a federal mental hospital, St. Elizabeths Hospital, in Washington, D.C, where he has continued to receive treatment.

His early life

John Hinckley, Jr. was part of a stable family of two older siblings and loving, but unaffectionate, parents. Though less social than his siblings, he was never considered a loner, and those close to him described him as a happy boy. It was during his teenage years that he began to withdraw from both social and athletic activities. He became lethargic, often remaining in his room, listening to or playing music for hours. He ceased to participate in the activities characteristic of boys his age. Those around him assumed that he was merely another introverted teenager experiencing a phase of teenage angst. But angst may have turned to pathological behavior during his high school years.

After graduating from high school and attempting college at Texas Tech, Hinckley quit and decided to try to succeed as a songwriter in California. While there, he became obsessed with the movie *Taxi Driver*. The film, inspired by the life of an aspiring assassin, starred Robert DeNiro and Jodie Foster. Hinckley's obsession with *Taxi Driver* was quickly transferred to the movie's beautiful young star, Jodie Foster.

The events that occurred in the months preceding the attempted assassination provided possible explanations for the rapid deterioration of Hinckley's already feeble mental state. Hinckley had begun spending much of his time at Yale University in New Haven, Connecticut, where Jodie Foster attended school, in order to transform his *Taxi Driver* fantasy into reality. He wrote numerous love letters and poems to her, tried to deliver presents to her, and had two phone conversations with her, in which she politely, but firmly, declined his advances. Hinckley later wrote about how this rejection completed his disillusionment with life.

Even in his despair, Hinckley refused to accept reality and continued to imagine ways in which he could win the actress' heart. Identifying strongly with *Taxi Driver* character Travis Bickle, who attempted to kill the president in the film, Hinckley began to stalk President Carter and later President Reagan. He sent an anonymous letter to the FBI claiming there was a plot to kidnap Jodie Foster, and began amassing guns.

Hinckley moved back home, and his parents urged him to seek psychiatric help. From October 1980 to March 1981, he saw a Dr. Hopper for a dozen sessions, roughly once every two weeks. Dr. Hopper used biofeedback techniques, and also prescribed antidepressants and tranquilizers, such as Valium. Though no precise information was available about Hinckley's compliance with the treatment, it seemed that Hinckley cooperated to a fair degree, attending his therapy sessions and taking the prescribed medication.

Less than a week before he tried to kill the president, his desperate situation was made worse when his parents, following Dr. Hopper's tough love advice, kicked their son out of the house. Dr. Hopper thought that Hinckley was a standard case of underdevelopment, and that his parents allowed him to depend on them too much. Hinckley later said that he intended to travel to New Haven to commit suicide in front of Jodie Foster or to kill her and then himself, but he first made a stop in Washington, D.C. On March 30, he awoke at his hotel and noticed that the president's schedule appeared in the morning paper. He decided he would make a final attempt to prove his importance to the world and to Foster.

Charges in this case

Hinckley waited outside as the newly inaugurated president made a speech to a labor convention at the Washington Hilton Hotel. At 2:35 p.m. on March 30,

1981, as the president exited the building walking toward his limousine accompanied by Secret Service members, Hinckley took aim and in three seconds fired an entire round of six shots before being tackled to the ground. The first shot struck press secretary Jim Brady in the head directly above the left eye. He fared worst of all from the attack; the bullet piercing his brain and leaving him permanently paralyzed. The second shot hit police officer Thomas Delahanty in the back. The fourth hit Secret Service agent Timothy McCarthy in the stomach as he jumped in front of the president. The final bullet caught Reagan in the chest. All four victims survived.

Hinckley was immediately tackled, overpowered, and arrested. Police found several pictures of Jodie Foster in his wallet, as well as a card with the Second Amendment right to bear arms inscribed on it. The victims were taken to the hospital. Reagan underwent a successful operation, and all victims were expected to live.

Hinckley was charged with a total of 13 crimes.

Lawyers in this case

During the initial stage, the senior attorney for the defense was Vincent Fuller. Since many eyewitnesses observed Hinckley's assassination attempt and video footage existed to prove his involvement, the insanity defense was the only option for Fuller. He quickly had Hinckley transferred from a federal detention center in Maine to a federal penitentiary in North Carolina for psychiatric evaluations. The three psychologists hired by the defense thought Hinckley was legally insane at the time of the crime. Fuller strategically tried to depict Hinckley as a deranged, lonely individual. By the end of his closing argument, he reportedly had Hinckley in tears.

Roger Adelman, who served as the government's senior prosecutor during the trial, also had three government hired psychologists who proclaimed that Hinckley was sane at the time of the crime. Adelman and his team of experts tried to depict Hinckley as a man who suffered from minor personality disorders that were not enough to qualify as mental diseases or defects. He emphasized the severity of Hinckley's actions.

Most recently, Hinckley has hired a new team of lawyers who have been trying to negotiate certain privileges and freedoms from his confinement in St. Elizabeths Hospital.

Psychoforensic professionals in this case

The government and defense each had a large team of psychological professionals. Dr. Park Elliott Dietz headed the government's team, while Dr. William Carpenter, Dr. John Hopper, and Dr. David Bear were important expert psychological witnesses for the defense. Dr. Dietz, a psychiatrist, led extensive investigations concerning Hinckley before the trial even began. Many of his investigative approaches were unconventional and fairly new at the time, such as examining the physical evidence, perusing books that might have had an effect on Hinckley, interviewing witnesses who had had interactions with Hinckley, and visiting the crime scene. When Dr. Dietz visited Hinckley's home, he found firing range targets that indicated that Hinckley was only accurate at close ranges.

Dr. Dietz, along with the other government psychiatrists, diagnosed Hinckley with three types of personality disorders: narcissistic, schizoid, and mixed. These disorders allegedly also had passive-aggressive and borderline elements, along with a dysthymic disorder characterized by constant sadness.

Dr. Dietz testified in Hinckley's trial that, despite his mental problems, Hinckley knew his actions were wrong and was therefore criminally responsible. To support this assertion, Dietz described how Hinckley was aware of the Secret Service's supervision, or lack thereof; how Hinckley based, in part, his decision to fire on whether the public was watching him, indicating that he knew what he was about to do was wrong; how Hinckley had selected the deadliest bullets, called Devastators; and how Hinckley had told him that he had succeeded in his objective to impress Jodie Foster on the day of the assassination attempt.

Dr. William Carpenter became the key witness for the defense and argued that Hinckley's schizophrenia began during his lonely teenage years. His condition made him lose his sense of self, which made him susceptible to identifying with characters of movies or books.

Dr. Bear was a psychiatrist who had little experience with court testimony but appeared quite knowledgeable. Dr. Bear watched *Taxi Driver* in order obtain a better understanding of how Hinckley identified with the mentally ill protagonist. He also took a CAT scan of Hinckley's brain, believing it could aid in a diagnosis of schizophrenia. Dr. Bear concluded that Hinckley had been psychotic on March 30. He believed that Hinckley suffered from schizophrenia and clinical depression and that he could not be faking his symptoms because he did not claim to have hallucinations as many people who fake would try to do. Hinckley's major symptoms included a lack of appropriate emotional response and other similar symptoms. Furthermore, Dr. Bear identified on the CAT scan of

Hinckley's brain that the defendant had widened sulci, the folds and ridges on the surface of the brain. These widened sulci were more common in individuals with schizophrenia than in the normal population. He also concluded that Hinckley had a smaller than normal sized brain.

Dr. Hopper was also called as a witness by the defense to testify about his previous treatment of Hinckley, including errors he had made in his diagnosis and treatment. He was therefore not appointed or hired as a medical expert witness for the court case itself.

Other psychological professionals who became involved in the case included Dr. Ernst Prelinger, a Yale psychologist, and Thomas Goldman, a psychiatrist, both of whom testified for the defense that Hinckley was insane. Dr. Sally Johnson, the psychiatrist who had first seen him, testified for the prosecution that although Hinckley might have been suffering from mental disorders, they did not qualify him for legal insanity. She believed that his motive for the crime was to garner publicity.

Test of insanity

This test in the case followed the American Law Institute rule which stated that a person was not responsible for otherwise criminal conduct if his mental disease or defect caused him to lack substantial capacity to appreciate that his conduct was criminal or if he did appreciate it to conform his conduct to the law. Among the problems with the standard were the fact that substantial capacity was difficult to evaluate, to qualify and measure, and that the jury had to try to gauge the extent to which the actor appreciated the wrongfulness of his conduct. Further, a mental disease or defect could be broadly or narrowly viewed. The various ambiguities were later attacked by commentators who sought insanity defense reforms.

Case process

In this case, the burden of proof in relation to the insanity defense rested on the prosecution, and they had to prove that Hinckley was sane. In addition, during the trial the judge ruled that a CAT scan could be used as evidence by the defense. This was the first time CAT scans were included in a trial in relation to insanity.

During the trial, the defense and prosecution called forward their respective experts. The defense also called Hinckley's father to testify that he had pushed his son over the edge and had contributed to his broken mind by kicking him out of the house.

The jurors deliberated for over three days before they came back with the not guilty by reason of insanity verdict. The jurors commented that the prosecution had not adequately proven that Hinckley was sane in response to the defense's arguments that he was insane. In addition, after the trial two jurors claimed that they did not really feel that Hinckley was insane, but they simply went along with the vote because the trial was driving them insane.

Hinckley was committed to St. Elizabeths Hospital. The initial commitment to the mental hospital was mandatory based on the not guilty by reason of insanity verdict statute. There, Hinckley was initially restricted from telephone use, engaging in media interviews, and free roaming of the grounds. Slowly, and after several evaluations, Hinckley began to regain some of his freedoms. By 1987, the hospital supported his request to leave for a short Easter visit with his family. He had entered into a seemingly healthy relationship with another patient, Leslie deVeau, and no longer needed his anti-psychotic medications they said. However, this request required court approval, since he was not going to be monitored by hospital staff. During a court-ordered search, officials found fifty-seven hidden photos of Jodie Foster in Hinckley's room. St. Elizabeths Hospital subsequently retracted its request for Hinckley's release from restrictions. In 1988, the hospital requested that Hinckley participate in a supervised tour of the city. This time the Secret Service found that Hinckley had attempted to order a nude sketch of Jodie Foster. Once again the hospital withdrew its request. That same year he tried to communicate with Charles Manson.

In 1992 and 1996, Hinckley requested twelve-hour unsupervised visits with his family. The hospital and court-appointed psychologists rejected his request. By 1999, Hinckley was allowed supervised visits outside the hospital. In 2000, Hinckley was allowed unsupervised furloughs. A month later this privilege was revoked when guards found a book about Foster in his room. In December 2003, U.S. District Judge Paul L. Friedman granted Hinckley permission to take six unsupervised day trips with his parents, but with several restrictions. If Hinckley were to prove himself on these preliminary trips, the court might then grant him the privilege of taking overnight trips within the fifty-mile radius of D.C. Although no hospital staff would accompany Hinckley on these outings, he would still be followed by the Secret Service, which had continued to monitor him since the assassination attempt.

Media involvement and commentators

Due to the high-profile nature of the crime, every major news channel and newspaper covered the Hinckley trial. The videotapes of the assassination attempt were made public and were played repeatedly for the entire American public to view. After the verdict, the media reflected the public outrage that pushed for reforms.

Legal commentators and political commentators alike were outraged by the case. Similarly, in a poll eighty-three percent of the American population was unhappy with the verdict. While some legal commentators pushed for the abolition of the insanity defense, many psychological commentators encouraged reform of the insanity defense. Almost all agreed that there needed to be some changes in the state of the insanity defense.

The insanity defense itself

The Hinckley case had a monumental effect on the insanity defense. Within weeks after the controversial verdict, bills designed to narrow the insanity defense inundated Congress. By 1985, only three years after Hinckley's acquittal, Congress and half of the states had instituted restrictive reforms to the insanity defense, including limiting the test for determining insanity, shifting the burden of proof to the defense, limiting expert witness testimony, introducing a new verdict of guilty but mentally ill, and even suggesting abolishing the insanity defense.

The Insanity Defense Reform Act of 1984 clarified some of the ambiguous terminology of the Model Penal Code's American Law Institute test which was used in the Hinckley case. Essentially, the act shifted the focus of the insanity defense from some concern with volitional elements to a sole focus on the cognitive aspect of whether defendants understood the nature, or wrongfulness of their crime.

In the Hinckley case, the burden of proof rested on the prosecution. The prosecution had to prove that Hinckley was sane. Commentators criticized by saying that such a task was impossible. As a result, two-thirds of all states shifted the burden of proof to the defense, making it the responsibility of the defendant to convince the jury of his insanity.

The large role played by expert psychiatric testimony in the Hinckley case gave rise to pressures to limit the influence of experts in such cases. In most cases, psychological experts largely agreed on the defendants' mental disorder, but diverged on the ultimate issue of sanity or insanity. As a result, in 1984, Congress limited expert witnesses from testifying on ultimate issues.

One quarter of all states introduced a new verdict of guilty but mentally ill. Meant as an alternative to not guilty by reason of insanity or even a replacement for it, jurors subsequently faced four choices: guilty, not guilty, not guilty by reason of mental illness or guilty but mentally ill. The guilty but mentally ill verdict ensured conviction and a criminal sentence, yet recognized the need for treatment. After conviction, the defendant was to be evaluated by a psychological professional. If the defendant were deemed mentally ill, he would be sent to a mental hospital for treatment. Then, only after the defendant had been found mentally fit would he be sent to prison to serve the remainder of his sentence. Mental illness, of course, in all these instances, remained defined by the states and impacted their civil commitment statutes. Those statutes varied from one state to another.

Some states abolished the insanity defense altogether. They continued to permit evidence concerning the defendant's mental disorder, but its use was limited to disproving mens rea, that a defendant lacked the specific guilty mind required for the crime.

Brief summary

John Hinckley was found not guilty by reason of insanity after he attempted to assassinate President Reagan. The verdict outraged the American public. While justice may not have been served in the Hinckley trial, the controversy it sparked led to needed insanity defense reforms. Congress and states made changes to shift the burden of proof to the prosecution, to reform the rule for determining insanity, to introduce the new verdict of guilty but mentally ill, to limit the use of psychiatric testimony, and in some states, even to abolish the insanity defense altogether.

Notes about sources

The primary sources for information about John Hinckley, Jr. included www.crimelibary.com, www.courttv.com, *The trial of John W. Hinckley Jr.: A case study in the insanity defense* by Richard Bonnie, John Jeffries and Peter Low, and *The insanity defense and the trial of John W. Hinckley, Jr.* by Lincoln Kaplan.

In addition, I drew information from www.cnn.com, http://jurist.law.pitt.edu/famoustrials/hinckley.php, and www.law.umkc.edu

Michael A. Jones

Michael A. Jones was born on March 5, 1955. As of November 2004, he was a second-year bachelor's degree student at the University of the District of Columbia, majoring in journalism. At the time, he was also on the payroll for the District of Columbia Department of Mental Health, and had sat on a committee contributing to the design of two mental hospitals to be built in the next few years.

As a twenty year old resident of Washington, D.C., he was arrested for attempted shoplifting, a crime with a maximum sentence of one year. Jones had a history of mental illness and drug abuse, though no adult criminal record. The day after his arrest, he was arraigned and sent to the District of Columbia jail to await a pretrial court-ordered competency hearing. After a four and a half month long stint in jail, he was committed to St. Elizabeths Hospital, the federal government's first mental hospital. While there, a hospital psychologist wrote in a report that Jones suffered from paranoid schizophrenia, and that Jones' attempted shoplifting was caused by his mental disorder. The defense and prosecution agreed on a stipulation of facts based upon the psychologist's report. On March 12, 1976, almost six months after he was arrested, Jones' court-appointed attorney, who had a heavy caseload, entered on Jones' behalf a plea of not guilty by reason of insanity. The prosecution did not contest the plea, and Jones was acquitted due to insanity. He was then committed to St. Elizabeths Hospital as a dangerously ill individual.

While Jones was in St. Elizabeths, the hospital's acting superintendent, a psychiatrist named Roger Peele, wrote that Jones was still suffering from paranoid type schizophrenia and was on medication. He continued by stating that Jones required further hospitalization and that he posed a threat to himself and to others. A hearing required by D.C. law to take place fifty days after an individual was committed to a mental institution after a not guilty by reason of insanity acquittal occurred on May 25, 1976. At the hearing, a psychologist from St. Elizabeths testified that Jones continued to suffer from paranoid schizophrenia and that his continued illness indicated that he still posed a threat to himself and to others. Jones' attorney, more concerned with securing for his client a transfer to a less restrictive wing of the hospital, did little to challenge the testimony, presenting no evidence and conducting only a brief cross-examination. The judge ruled that Jones should be returned to St. Elizabeths.

On February 22, 1977, Jones had been hospitalized for more than the year that he would have had to serve had he been convicted of the crime. His attorney argued in Superior Court that Jones should therefore be released. The request was rejected, and Jones' attorney appealed to the District of Columbia Court of Appeals. In three hearings, the Appellate Court affirmed, then reversed, and finally affirmed the Superior Court decision, with the final Appellate Court decision coming in 1981. Jones' attorney appealed again, this time to the U.S. Supreme Court.

On June 29, 1983, the Supreme Court ruled in *Jones v. United States* that when someone has been found not guilty by reason of insanity, the government is constitutionally permitted to confine that person to a mental institution until he becomes sane or ceases to pose a danger to himself or society. Jones remained institutionalized for another twenty-two years, until August 20, 2004, when the U.S. Attorney's Office finally agreed to his release contingent upon his good behavior and continued mental health.

His early life

Michael Jones grew up in a very large family in Washington, D.C. He was one of thirteen children, six boys and seven girls. The second oldest son, he was raised with his siblings by his mother and stepfather. Recent telephone interviews with him, his brother, and his later, from 1981, public defense counsel provided significant information for this case study. Jones said he was introduced to drugs at a very young age. He said he began using when he snorted heroin at the age of eight, and that his uncle provided the drugs to him. By the age of thirteen, he had made friends with older teenagers, and with their encouragement, he was regularly using heroin intravenously. Jones said that he first experienced mental problems at age fourteen or fifteen, when he suffered a nervous breakdown. He said he heard voices, a condition that remained with him for years, which encouraged him to act aggressively. At the age of sixteen, he tried cocaine for the first time and overdosed. After the overdose, he spent time rehabilitating at the Oak Hill Youth Detention Center, in Washington, D.C. He bounced around juvenile detention centers due to several drug related run-ins with the law, but he did not commit any crimes that went on his adult criminal record until the attempted shoplifting incident.

Jones' thirty-three year old brother, Rasul El-Amin, said their family had gone through ups and downs, and that Jones' experiences with drugs and the law had taught El-Amin and set an example of behavior to avoid. Still, he said that the family remained tight-knit, with all thirteen siblings corresponding on a somewhat weekly basis. El-Amin expressed pride in his older brother and how far he had come in recovering from his illness and reintegrating into society.

Charges in this case

On September 19, 1975, Jones entered a Hecht's department store in northwest Washington, D.C. Jones said he took a coat off a rack and waited in line at a cash register, though he did not have the money needed to buy the coat. He was arrested for attempted petty larceny, a crime that carried a maximum prison sentence of one year. Though he said he believed he was wrongly arrested and had not done anything wrong, he also said he accepted full responsibility for his actions, and that he understood the wrongfulness of stealing. Jones was arraigned the following day and committed to St. Elizabeths Hospital for exhibiting bizarre behavior, though four and a half months passed before space opened up for him at the hospital. He remained in jail in the interim.

Lawyers in this case

Jones said that at his stipulated not guilty by reason of insanity hearing, his court-appointed attorney treated him poorly, loudly telling him to shut up and using a racial slur in the courtroom to refer to him. Harry Fulton, chief of the D.C. Public Defender Service's Mental Health Division and counsel for Jones since 1981, said he believed that the court-appointed attorney was not very conscientious in Jones' case because the attorney was most interested in shedding his large caseload as efficiently as possible. The defense and the prosecution agreed to the stipulated facts contained in the assessment of Jones' condition made at St. Elizabeths. Jones' lawyer waived the right to a trial by jury and Jones pleaded not guilty by reason of insanity. The prosecution did not challenge the plea. According to Jones' account, the judge had called up Jones' aunt and mother to ask whether either of them would claim custody of Jones, and neither would. The judge also asked the attorney whether he would be willing to take Jones, but the attorney would hear nothing of it.

Seven weeks later, at the legally required hearing to review Jones' mental status, Jones had a different attorney. This lawyer made little effort to win release for Jones, instead focusing on obtaining transfer for his client to a less restrictive wing of the hospital.

In later appeals to the U.S. Court of Appeals and the U.S. Supreme Court, attorneys from the D.C. Public Defender Service represented Jones.

Psychoforensic professionals in this case

After his arraignment, Jones spent four and a half months in prison awaiting a pretrial competency hearing, and then he was moved to St. Elizabeths Hospital when bed space opened up. After a month there, in March 1976, a staff psychologist reported to the court that Jones suffered from paranoid schizophrenia, and that Jones' attempted shoplifting was caused by his mental disorder. The report also stated that Jones was competent to stand trial, but that he had the symptoms of severe mental illness, including hearing non-existent voices, and that he should remain hospitalized. This was the first time that a psychological professional became involved in the case.

Jones was found not guilty by reason of insanity and committed to the forensic division of St. Elizabeths. In late April, Roger Peele, the hospital's acting superintendent, wrote that Jones was still suffering from paranoid type schizophrenia and was on medication. He continued by stating that Jones required further hospitalization and that he would pose a threat to himself and to others if he were released. At a hearing on May 25, 1976, the court sent Jones back to St. Elizabeths after a psychologist from the hospital testified that Jones continued to suffer from paranoid schizophrenia and that his continued illness meant that he remained a threat to himself and to others.

In June 1977, the St. Elizabeths staff recommended conditional release of Jones, allowing him daytime and overnight visits into the community. He was granted this release, and admitted into the less restrictive civil division of the hospital. Due to disruptive behavior, though, he lost his conditional release and was sent back to the forensic division. At several other points during the next twenty-three years, Jones was granted outpatient status, but these attempts were unsuccessful. When asked why the outpatient treatment did not work, Jones said he was not behaving and that he was not prepared for the treatment.

In June 2000, St. Elizabeths had granted Jones outpatient status. Jones said the staff at the group care home in which he lived had treated him poorly, locking him out of the house during inclement weather.

At St. Elizabeths, Jones was involved with a writing program. Later, as an outpatient, Jones earned his high school equivalency diploma and began to pursue a bachelor's degree in journalism from the University of the District of Columbia. In mid-August 2004, after Jones successfully held down a job as a dispatcher for a security company for two months while on outpatient status, he was deemed fit for release into society.

Test of insanity

At the time, in Washington, D.C., the law required that no person be acquitted by reason of insanity unless that person's insanity was established by a preponderance of the evidence.

Case process

At Jones' arraignment, a judge ruled that Jones' competence to stand trial should be assessed, and so he spent time in jail and then at St. Elizabeths. At Jones' stipulated not guilty by reason of insanity hearing, the judge ruled that he was competent to stand trial and not guilty by reason of insanity. He committed Jones to St. Elizabeths. Seven weeks later, at the requisite hearing to review Jones' mental status, the judge ruled that Jones was mentally ill and that he posed a danger to himself and others. Another six months later, at a subsequent hearing, Jones' counsel argued that his client should receive unconditional release because he had been detained for longer than the maximum prison sentence he could have received had he been convicted. No government attorney appeared at this hearing, so the judge ordered a further hearing for a few months later. At that hearing, Jones' lawyer argued that his client should either be released unconditionally or recommitted under the standards for civil commitment, which required a jury trial and proof by clear and convincing evidence of the defendant's mental illness and dangerousness. In other words, Jones' attorney argued that Jones should be released unless the government assumed the burden of proving that Jones should remain hospitalized. The Superior Court rejected the arguments made on behalf of Jones.

On appeal to the District of Columbia Court of Appeals, the court ruled that if Jones had originally been committed legally, the maximum hypothetical prison sentence bore no relationship to his hospital confinement since the hospitalization was not punitive, and therefore should not be an issue. The case was again appealed to the Appeals Court, with Jones' attorney this time arguing that the release hearing procedure was in fact punitive, since those found not guilty by reason of insanity, those who were criminally committed, were afforded fewer legal protections than those who were civilly committed. On this second appeal, the court agreed with Jones' lawyer, and also rejected the notion that a not guilty by reason of insanity acquittee's mental illness and dangerousness at the time of the offense was sufficient evidence of the potential for future dangerousness, and that it therefore created a presumption of continued insanity. The government then appealed to the Appeals Court to view the case a third time, this time in an en banc rehearing. In this third appeal, the previous decisions were vacated and the court ruled in a six to three decision that there was no reason to find the release hearing procedure punitive.

The case was then appealed to the U.S. Supreme Court. In a five to four decision, the Supreme Court upheld the Appeals Court's final ruling.

By entering into a stipulation of facts at Jones' original trial, the prosecution and defense essentially agreed to abide by whatever assessment the staff psychologist at St. Elizabeths Hospital made.

Media involvement

There was no media coverage of the case until it went to the U.S. Supreme Court, and even then, the coverage was minimal.

Commentators

Few people not involved with Jones' case have commented on it. A handful of law review articles included some brief analysis of the Supreme Court case. One professor from New York Law School wrote that the Supreme Court's decision in *Jones v. United States* illustrated its distaste for and discrimination against the insane, and that it was wrong to draw the conclusion that Jones was dangerous simply because he had committed a crime. Other commentators echoed this sentiment.

Several commentators observed that John Hinckley, Jr. was acquitted for the shooting of President Reagan and others mere months before Jones' case went to the Supreme Court, and that both Jones' and Hinckley's offenses were committed in Washington, D.C. One commentator wrote that the *Jones* decision reflected the Supreme Court's unwillingness to contravene the public's displeasure with the insanity defense in the wake of Hinckley, and that it was a baldly political ruling.

Harry Fulton, chief of the D.C. Public Defender Service's Mental Health Division and counsel for Jones since 1981, termed it unconscionable to use the insanity defense for misdemeanors, and that the defense should be used only for major crimes. He said he thought that Jones' original counsel was a poor attorney who showed little regard for Jones' fate. If a defendant could receive a short prison sentence for a minor crime, Fulton said, then an insanity defense should not be used.

Jones himself said that while he wished he were not detained for nearly three decades, he did believe he needed mental treatment. He said that if the Supreme Court had ruled in his favor, he would not have been mentally ready to reintegrate into society.

The insanity defense itself

Perhaps the most prominent feature of Jones' case was how the insanity defense might be a tool that misdemeanor defendants should not use. One study found that because of the potentially long periods of incarceration for not guilty by reason of insanity acquittees, the insanity defense has in some states effectively ceased to be an option. And some attorneys have deemed an insanity plea for minor crimes as constituting attorney malpractice. The authors of the study observed that the effective elimination of the insanity defense for misdemeanor defendants had an undesirable impact. Mentally ill individuals would opt for prison time, and therefore would not receive helpful or necessary treatment. The study recommended the use of a practice already adopted in some states, placing a limit on the period of detention for those found not guilty by reason of insanity for misdemeanors. This policy would be likely to revive the insanity defense as an option for such people.

Another interesting feature of the case was how the criminal justice system's adversarial nature resulted in overlooking what was best for the actual people affected by the decision. The Supreme Court overlooked the undesirable possibility that their ruling would result in a young man being locked up for nearly three decades. Fulton's view of the insanity defense overlooked the fact that Jones might not have received treatment that he himself said he needed if his original attorney had not employed the insanity defense. It has become very easy to look at Jones' case in the abstract without considering Michael A. Jones as a human being.

Summary

Jones was charged with attempted shoplifting, which carried a maximum prison sentence of one year. His attorney launched a successful insanity defense. As a result, Jones spent nearly three decades incarcerated. Thus, one can say that the insanity defense backfired in Jones' case. His case went all the way to the Supreme Court, which ruled that it was constitutionally permitted to detain an insanity acquittee for longer than the prison sentence he would have served if he had been found guilty.

Notes about sources

My main sources were interviews conducted over the telephone in November 2004 with Michael Jones, Harry Fulton, and Rasul El-Amin; the decisions in the Appellate Court cases and the Supreme Court cases, all called *Jones v. United States*, from 1978 to 1983; and a 2002 Virginia State Crime Commission report entitled *SJR 381: not guilty by reason of insanity: a bill referral study*.

Additional sources included the Washington, D.C. code on the insanity defense; *Jones v. United States*: Automatic commitment of individuals found not guilty by reason of insanity, by Louise Dovre; The consequences of the insanity defense: Proposals to reform post-acquittal commitment laws, by James Ellis; 'For the misdemeanor outlaw': The impact of the ADA on the institutionalization of criminal defendants with mental disabilities, by Michael Perlin; and Lack of 'flair' kept Dr. Peele from top job at St. Elizabeths, by Timothy Robinson.

Ted Kaczynski

On April 3, 1996, Ted Kaczynski, known as the Unabomber (Universities and Airlines Bomber) to a terrified nation, was arrested on the property of his small cabin in Lincoln, Montana. For the previous eighteen years, Kaczynski had put fear in the hearts of anyone opening a mail package for he had rigged explosives to mail parcels and unidentified objects in parking lots. Operating out of his remote shack and living the simplistic life of a recluse, Kaczynski had become zealously opposed to the advancement of technology and the effects that advancement had on society, and had acted out against those promoters of technology and science, both educators and for profit operators.

After his arrest, Kaczynski refused to undergo a psychiatric evaluation and pled guilty and even requested self-representation in the case, only to eventually accept a plea bargain following a guilty plea. Kaczynski's reluctance to attempt a defense of not guilty by reason of insanity stemmed from his firm belief in a manifesto he created linking the downfall of society with technology and science. If he were deemed insane, he felt that his work would not be taken seriously. In effect, Kaczynski used his trial as a stage to promote his beliefs. On May 4, 1998, after reaching the plea bargain, the Unabomber was sentenced to four consecutive life terms without parole.

Most recently, Kaczynski has been attempting to appeal his sentence from his jail cell in Florence, Colorado. He has claimed that his constitutional rights were abridged when a judge failed to allow him to fire his counsel and represent himself. Though his appeal was denied in April 2002, he has remained convinced his view will prevail.

His early life

Theodore Kaczynski was born on May 22, 1942, and was raised in the suburbs of Chicago, Illinois. His family was lower-middle class, and his mother Wanda and father Richard were hardworking and strict in raising young Teddy. He had a close attachment to his mother from a young age. According to her, this derived from his being sick at a young age and his resultant dependence upon her care. Kaczynski was bright but not sociable, and his trouble fitting in socially increased when he skipped a grade at a young age. Later in life, Kaczynski claimed he was verbally abused by his parents, told ways he should act and present himself, and lectured not to embarrass the family. He claimed this abuse was partly responsible for his lack of personal relationships in life, and wholly responsible for his estrangement from his family.

Kaczynski enrolled at Harvard at the age of sixteen and again thrived in most of his academic pursuits while struggling socially. According to Alston Chase in his book *Harvard and the Unabomber: The Education of an American Terrorist*, it was during those four years that Kaczynski developed a psychotic personality. After Harvard, Kaczynski obtained his masters degree from the University of Michigan by age twenty-five, and then taught at the University of California, Berkeley, from 1967 to 1969. By 1971, he had become disillusioned with teaching and had decided to live off the land, attempting to purchase land in Canada before settling in Lincoln, Montana. His father committed suicide in 1990.

Kaczynski's mental health had never been questioned while he was a student or teacher. He was quiet and awkward, yet these attributes never led to enough suspicion to deem him unstable or psychotic. At Harvard he took part in a psychological study under the developer of the Thematic Apperception Test, Henry Murray, that tested students' mental toughness and durability. An introvert, Kaczynski failed to maintain any kind of relationship with a woman. While at Michigan, this sexual frustration culminated in his pondering a sex-change operation, only to leave the doctor's office in embarrassment before talking to anyone. He retreated from society searching for a life alone as did one of his favorite writers, Henry David Thoreau.

Charges in this case

Kaczynski began his life of solitude in 1971, in Montana. He had originally attempted to purchase land in Canada with his brother David, but his application was turned down by the government. With his family's help he purchased land in Lincoln, Montana, where he constructed a small cabin outfitted with a stove, bed and chair, and filled with his books and manuscripts. Kaczynski spent time taking care of his garden, cooking, and reading his favorite authors including Thoreau, and playwright Eugene O'Neill, an artist who he felt condemned material living and the advent of technology. He also kept up to date on current events and began reading up on bombs and their construction and composition. After years of study and experimentation, Kaczynski began writing his manifesto, a thirty five thousand word strongly opinionated piece denouncing technology and the advancement of science as the downfall of society and mankind. To get his message out to the rest of America, Kaczynski decided to use explosives. Beginning in 1978 with a mail bomb that detonated on a United Airlines flight, and continuing until his arrest, the Unabomber used package bombs from Sacramento to New Haven to proclaim his manifesto.

Always an intellectual, Kaczynski used hidden messages within his packages, becoming an artist of sorts over time. The bomber always used wood, whether as the container or in a message as a reference to the environment, and signed his notes FC, a reference to a make believe group that he used to conceal his true identity. Kaczynski focused his wrath on university professors, owners of technologically related enterprises, and leaders of anti-environmental groups. His techniques included leaving a bomb on a university campus or in a store parking lot, or simply mailing the package to his target's house with the return address of the target's colleague or friend.

Kaczynski honed his bomb making craft over time and his creations became more and more potent. He filled his small explosives with glass, nails and other sharp objects, and the bombs maimed and incapacitated many of his victims, while killing a computer store owner in Sacramento and a company president in New Jersey. He remained anonymous throughout his actions, sometimes ceasing his mailings for years before resuming. He worked many times from outdated government records he accessed from the internet or the library, often times addressing a package to someone at the wrong location. He had no personal connection to his victims except that he considered that their business or profession went against his own beliefs.

After remaining anonymous in his cabin for almost twenty years, Kaczynski brought himself to the attention of the FBI, treasury representatives, and the United States postal service when he sent a letter, from the F.C., to *The New York* and *Los Angeles Times* newspapers. In his letter he demanded that his manifesto be published for the nation to read, and if he were refused, he threatened that the UNABomber would take out a plane leaving the Los Angeles airport. The newspapers somewhat reluctantly published the writing. Kaczynski's brother David read the manifesto and was sure it was written by his brother. After wondering whether he should turn in his brother, he contacted the authorities after getting from them a pledge that they would not seek the death penalty. With David Kaczynski's input, FBI agents were able to identify the style of writing as that of Ted Kaczynski, and they descended upon his cabin. Upon entering, they discovered all the evidence they needed, including the makings of bombs, copies of the manifesto, and journals in both Spanish and English describing his atrocious acts.

Lawyers in this case

The prosecution team in this case feared Kaczynski would try to avoid the charges by pleading not guilty by reason of insanity. The defense realized the abundance of evidence against them and prioritized saving Kaczynski from the death penalty. In November of 1997, the defense concentrated on eliminating damaging evidence claiming that the evidence from the cabin should be thrown out due to a faulty search warrant. This claim was thrown out by the judge, and on January 5, 1998, Kaczynski requested a new defense team, a request that the judge accepted on the condition that Kaczynski agree to be evaluated. Diagnosed by a psychiatrist, Dr. Sally Johnson, as a paranoid schizophrenic, Kaczynski was deemed competent to stand trial and to defend himself. Not long after this decision, a plea bargain was reached between Kaczynski and the prosecution team stating that he would plead guilty and avoid the death penalty, an agreement that his brother David had sought when he informed the authorities of his suspicions about the writer of the published manifesto.

Psychoforensic professionals in this case

Kaczynski finally came to an agreement with the judge that he receive a psychological evaluation if he wanted self-representation in January of 1998. Kaczynski had originally requested a celebrity defense team, but then decided to represent himself. He was evaluated by Dr. Sally Johnson in a prison facility, and she found him to be a paranoid schizophrenic at the time. Despite his mental state, she concluded that he was fit to stand trial and to represent himself. No treatment was instituted at the time, and when Kaczynski was sentenced at the end of his trial, he was placed in solitary confinement in a Colorado super maximum prison facility.

Case process

The case proceeded in a town near Lincoln, Montana, creating a media frenzy there. The defense of not guilty by reason of insanity appeared to be a possibility for Kaczynski, but he did not wish to use it as he feared it would discredit his manifesto. While the evidence gathered within the cabin was questioned because of issues about the legitimacy of the search warrant, this claim was eventually dismissed by the judge. Kaczynski had refused a psychological evaluation, but when on January 5, 1998, he requested a new defense team, the judge agreed on the condition that Kaczynski be evaluated. Evaluated by Dr. Sally Johnson he was diagnosed as suffering from paranoid schizophrenia. He was, however, deemed competent to stand trial and to defend himself. Though the evaluation of Kaczynski had found him to be mentally ill, he reached a plea bargain with the prosecution, avoiding the death penalty in exchange for four consecutive life sentences with no option to appeal. Psychological material did not change the case in any way, as Kaczynski's evaluation did not factor into the eventual outcome.

Most of the testimony related to the case was from victims and relatives of victims, describing the horrible nature of their injuries, both physical and emotional. Many of these people provided extremely emotional accounts, calling for the most serious punishment for Kaczynski with no compassion for a killer with so little remorse. The jury had little influence on the case, as a plea bargain was eventually reached.

Media involvement

The media reaction was one of great interest because Kaczynski had been a fugitive for almost twenty years, was well educated, and had caused such terrible suffering and death. CBS News broke the story, covering Kaczynski's arrest with aerial shots above his cabin in Montana. The media interest was huge throughout the proceedings, as newspaper and television representatives alike packed the small Montana courthouse leaving little room for any spectators. The case drew national attention both for the severity of Kaczynski's actions as well as for the added buzz surrounding the bomber's intellectual status as a Harvard graduate and former professor.

Following Kaczynski's attempt to manipulate newspaper sources to spread his gospel, the media had extra incentive in portraying him as a crazed lunatic. Other than possibly influencing the speed with which Kaczynski was apprehended and in turn the procurement of a search warrant, and serving as an stimulus for Kaczynski's rants, the media did not influence the case.

The insanity defense itself

The insanity defense was not used in this case and therefore not much can be learned in this instance about its use. The defense was viewed as a crutch by the prosecution team, and as an escape clause by the defense team, but due to the defendant's wishes, it was never utilized. We can infer from this case that the not guilty by reason of insanity plea might make the difference between life and death for some criminals, and might be an extremely important factor in determining the outcome of some cases. Yet much can be learned from this case about its non-use. In fact, the most important lesson we can learn from this case is that individuals who want to spread a message or promote a cause object strongly to any suggestion that their message or cause was the product of mental illness. They view using the insanity defense as a way to diminish, if not destroy, their message or cause. But other psychoforensic professionals and commentators, who consider that particular message or cause to be the product of mental illness, view their refusal of the insanity defense to be itself a product of mental illness. As in this case, the legal system deferred to the defendant's desire for autonomy and authenticity, however ill judged others may have considered that to be.

Notes about sources

The most helpful sources for information about Ted Kaczynski included Alston Chase's *Harvard and the Unabomber: The Education of an American Terrorist*, and the CrimeLibrary website.

Hedda Nussbaum

Joel Steinberg was an attorney in Manhattan who made a good living. Hedda Nussbaum, Steinberg's long time lover, also had a good career. She was a teacher who had made the transition to a successful career as a writer and editor at Random House books, where she received the highest salary in the company's history. The couple had two children, a six year old and a sixteen month old. They lived in a comfortable Greenwich Village apartment. Though to most Joel and Hedda had a normal near perfect life it was in reality far from idyllic.

Elizabeth, the couple's eldest child, was never legally adopted, but rather was acquired illegally by Joel Steinberg through his job as an attorney. For years Steinberg had been physically and emotionally abusive to Nussbaum and their children. Both Steinberg and Nussbaum were heavy drug abusers, using cocaine on a nearly daily basis. Though the couple's dark side had remained largely a secret for many years, the truth of their relationship was exposed to the world on November 2, 1987. Early that morning police and emergency medical service personnel responded to a phone call placed by Nussbaum requesting assistance for her six year old daughter. What the police found was a dark and dingy apartment without a single working light occupied by a filthy infant lying in his own urine and feces, a woman beaten beyond recognition, and an unconscious six-year-old girl. The young girl, Elizabeth Steinberg, known as Lisa, never emerged from her coma. Her father would soon be indicted for second degree murder, first-degree manslaughter, and endangering the welfare of a child. The case soon drew the attention of the entire nation, but not because of the horrific nature of the crime. The murder of Lisa Steinberg would shock the nation because Hedda Nussbaum, after testifying against Joel, was never charged with a crime. She went free, leading the media to train its spotlight on the issue of culpability.

What happened the night before the police found Lisa Steinberg has remained uncertain. Much of what is known was culled from the statements of Nussbaum, but Steinberg himself has always been cryptic and contradictory when describing the incident. According to Nussbaum, the night proceeded as follows: Steinberg was going out to dinner that evening and was changing in the bedroom. Nussbaum was irritated by Lisa's incessant questioning of whether or not she would be going with her father and told her to ask Steinberg herself. Nussbaum then went to the bathroom. At approximately six in the evening, Steinberg walked into the bathroom with Lisa lying limp in his arms. Nussbaum tried to perform first aid on her for the next hour, but was unsuccessful in her attempts at reviving her. Steinberg was ready to leave for dinner by seven. Nussbaum asked him about Lisa and he said that he would help her after he got back. While Steinberg was out, Nussbaum rearranged his files in order to keep busy, all the while believing that Steinberg would revive Lisa when he returned. After Steinberg returned, the two freebased cocaine until four the next morning. During their drug use, Steinberg allegedly said to Nussbaum that he knocked out Lisa the previous evening. For the next few hours, Steinberg searched medical books looking for information that would help his daughter. At roughly six thirty in the morning, Lisa stopped breathing. Steinberg tried CPR but was unsuccessful in reviving his daughter. He finally relented and asked Nussbaum to call 911. They were both arrested after the police arrived.

Hedda Nussbaum has since toured the country speaking about battered woman syndrome. She wrote a book on domestic abuse and appeared on many shows speaking about the topic, including *Larry King Live* and *Oprah* in addition to selling her story, pretrial, to *People Magazine* for upwards of $25, 000. She also wrote a children's book that has yet to be published. Nussbaum was often met with protest at her engagements by those who feel she played a role in the death of Lisa and should have been prosecuted.

Her early life

The arguments for Hedda Nussbaum not being prosecuted for her part in the death of Elizabeth Steinberg were extensive and could often be quite convincing. If one delved into Nussbaum's past looking for evidence of psychological abnormalities that would have made her susceptible to a man such as Steinberg much evidence presented itself. From a young age Nussbaum always felt that she lived in the shadow of her older sister. Her mother made her dress like her sister and she often remanded her into her sister's care. Nussbaum shared everything with her sister. She had no friends by herself; she only shared friends with her sister. As a result, her friends were never really her friends; they were merely friends of her sister with whom she would associate. Consequently, Nussbaum never felt she existed by herself as she once commented. Because of this, she often took on the traits of her sister that she felt were desirable. Nussbaum did not have a personality of her own. A one true Nussbaum did not exist, there were many Nussbaums as she would assimilate into her surroundings.

One of Nussbaum's few close relationships as a child was with her elderly grandmother. Unfortunately, at a young age her grandmother was taken away to an insane asylum. When she returned she spent all of her time in her room and never really associated with Nussbaum again. According to Hedda Nussbaum this loss had a long lasting effect on her, causing her to constantly fear abandonment. After such a loss she was determined to never be alone again. Alas, much of her childhood was marked by a deep sense of loneliness. It was not until college that she made a few friends of her own, and these relationships were marked by clinginess.

Hedda Nussbaum was well aware of her psychological problems long before the tragic death of her daughter. Before she even met Joel Steinberg she was involved in various forms at therapy. In fact, until she met Steinberg, Nussbaum was attending therapy sessions three times a week in order to help her work out various issues she felt prevented her from being a truly happy and healthy person. The very therapy that could have saved her was stopped soon after she met Steinberg. After a long series of unsuccessful relationships, most of which were broken off by the man, Steinberg was a dream come true to her. He was a successful, attractive, single New Yorker, quite the rarity. Yet there he was, and he seemed genuinely interested in her.

Naturally, Steinberg was not abusive at first. During the early stages their relationship was normal, almost idyllic. The next phase of their relationship, often referred to as the tension-building phase of an abusive relationship, was marked by increased criticism and some minor verbal abuse. Only after Nussbaum had become attached to Steinberg did he dare to take their relationship to the next level, the acute battering stage. After the first incident of abuse Steinberg apologized profusely and promised to never do it again. This marked the contrite phase in what is often known as the cycle of violence. Steinberg's acts of repentance pleased Nussbaum and led her to restore her bonds with him. The abuse naturally continued, however, perpetuating the cycle of violence. But by this time Nussbaum was already attached to Steinberg and due to her deeply instilled fear of loneliness she did not want to, or perhaps she could not, leave him. Her tendency to lose those close to her and to change her personality to match those around her were both found at the center of her destructive relationship with Steinberg. She was afraid to lose him and would do anything, or put up with anything, to stay with him. Meanwhile she was losing what little of her individuality remained, melding with Steinberg's dominant personality, as she had done during her life. This was by and large the argument that was made for the case that Hedda Nussbaum was not mentally well enough to do anything to stop Steinberg. It essentially claimed that she was under Steinberg's power to a degree which debilitated her both mentally and physically. Nussbaum's irrational claims about Steinberg supported this assertion. The claims included beliefs that Steinberg had supernatural powers such as extra-sensory perception and the ability to heal, a belief that allegedly played a pivotal role in Nussbaum's decision not to call an ambulance immediately when she saw that Lisa was unconscious. These beliefs were clearly characteristic of a person who was mentally unwell.

One could make other minor arguments that Nussbaum's mental faculties were compromised. Nussbaum's attitudes and views changed significantly during her relationship with Steinberg, and some have contended that the changes showed that the relationship altered her mentally. Some pointed to Nussbaum's changed view of children as an example. An ex-boyfriend of Nussbaum's said she often expressed affection for children, and that she loved spending time with her sister's children. He maintained that Nussbaum was caring towards children in general and was very concerned with their well-being. This made her inaction in the face of the horror perpetrated by Steinberg all the more suggestive of some underlying and perhaps incapacitating mental issues.

Though one could argue fairly convincingly that Nussbaum had a troubled childhood that caused psychological problems which predisposed her to become involved in a debilitating cycle of abuse, an equally good case could be made that Nussbaum had a normal upbringing and was quite capable of preventing Lisa's death. For example, if Steinberg's abuse so debilitated her that she could not recognize the true damage of her lover's abuse until nearly a year after Lisa Steinberg's death, important questions arise. Why, and how, was she able to give her own attorney Barry Scheck extensive information about Steinberg nearly a year before she claimed to be cured of her brain washing? Did Nussbaum merely use abuse and temporary insanity as an excuse to avoid prosecution in exchange for being a witness against Steinberg? Or did the district attorney see that it would be difficult to prosecute Steinberg without Nussbaum's testimony and therefore use abuse and insanity as cover for getting Nussbaum to turn state's evidence? Those who believed that Nussbaum should have been held partially responsible for the death of her daughter argued that she did not fit the standard victim pattern. She was never overtly abused as a child, her family was still intact, and she had a fairly successful career. Nussbaum may have had her share of difficulties in life, but nothing so severe that it should excuse her reprehensible inaction in the face of her daughter's imminent death.

After Nussbaum began to attend college, she started to establish friendships of her own, independently of her sister. One of her best friends was involved with Nussbaum for many years and could offer numerous insights into Nussbaum's state of mind. To begin with, her friend often said that despite what Nussbaum actually thought, she and not her sister served as the favored daughter of their parents. This discrepancy between Nussbaum's beliefs and reality could be explained by numerous psychological phenomena. Perhaps the key to understanding Nussbaum's feelings was what is commonly referred to as the better than average phenomenon, in which most people tend to perceive themselves as superior to most others and thus deserving of more attention than their inferiors. It was likely that Nussbaum felt this way about herself, and due to the actor observer bias she perhaps saw herself as receiving less attention than was true, while simultaneously seeing her sister as receiving more attention that she did in actuality.

Another insight into Nussbaum's personality that her friend disclosed was that by and large Nussbaum was self-centered. One of the many instances which were indicative of Nussbaum's narcissism took place during a vacation in Puerto Rico. The two were out driving one day when they became involved in a car accident. Nussbaum had minor injuries, but her friend suffered some major injuries that required her to stay in the hospital long after Nussbaum had been released. One would expect that Nussbaum would at the very least visit her friend in the hospital. She, however, instead continued her vacation by going out on dates and partying. Not once did Nussbaum ever visit her in the hospital. Considering that she was one of Nussbaum's few truly close friends Nussbaum's behavior was quite peculiar. Upon close analysis of Nussbaum's conduct it became clear that the issue at hand was not one of active aggression or hostile action, but rather of passive inaction towards someone else in favor of self-gratification. Nussbaum's slight of her friend, and many other instances of inaction that were documented throughout her life, could thus have been a precursor to the inaction that ultimately led to the death of Lisa Steinberg.

One of the points raised by supporters of the decision not to prosecute Nussbaum was that she had been seeking intensive therapy for many years before meeting Steinberg, which was clearly indicative of a person who was mentally unwell. This contention had many flaws. The first and greatest was that during the time period of the 1960s and 1970s in which Nussbaum came into adulthood, the whole country was being swept up into somewhat of a revolution. Though sexual liberation was one of the staples of this era, there was also a focus on mental well-being and an enormous surge in people seeking therapy. Thus, Nussbaum attending therapy sessions upwards of three times a week was not that unusual. Additionally, therapy was a very broad category and encompassed many forms both of treatment and of pseudo psychological nonsense that are no longer seen as legitimate. One form of the therapy that Nussbaum received involved her seeking treatment from doctors who traced her problems to alpha waves. Nussbaum took these forms of treatment seriously, as was illustrated by her diary in which she described herself as being divided into four entities: the Devil, the Primal Ooze, the fourteen-year-old girl, and the loving, caring Hedda Nussbaum. Thus, it could be argued that Nussbaum was not a person with deep issues and concerns about loneliness and abandonment who hoped to better herself through serious work with a therapist, but rather was a self obsessed young woman who was merely swept up in the cultural revolution that was upon her.

Much evidence could also be presented against Nussbaum being a helpless victim incapable of caring for herself, much less a child. Throughout much of her relationship with Steinberg, Nussbaum maintained a high level position with Random House books. Her job was fairly demanding, yet she managed to keep up with its workload with very few problems. This was not indicative of someone who could not function enough to call for help if a child were lying unconscious on the floor. Her high level job also offered further evidence against her fitting the typical battered spouse profile. Most female victims of domestic abuse who become stuck in the so-called cycle of violence do not have any system of support other than their abuser. Nussbaum, on the other hand, had a high level position that brought with it a great deal of prestige. Additionally, though Nussbaum was thought unable to care for her children, she maintained a meticulous fish tank within her apartment. The aquarium that Nussbaum kept was in such perfect condition that it caught the eye of those entering the apartment to help her daughter. It stood as a symbol of what could have been, if only Nussbaum had stepped in and cared for her children as well as she had her fish.

The arguments thus far consisted primarily of nullifying the theory that Nussbaum was incapable of protecting Lisa, but have not offered a substantial reason for why a fairly normal woman would act in such a way towards her children. One potential answer to this question, cocaine, offered a fairly simple yet multifaceted argument. Not only had Nussbaum and Steinberg been regular users of the drug for a number of months, but in a key disclosure, Nussbaum admitted that they had freebased cocaine the day of Lisa's death.

Cocaine has many effects. It may cause the user to be more aggressive and violent, and make them take more risks than they normally would, and large amounts of the drug may cause indolence. All of these effects were seen as in some way being partially responsible for Nussbaum's behavior towards her children. Her lack of action in the face of the abuse being perpetrated against her children was clearly very risky behavior as she was basically gambling with her daughter's life. Similarly, lack of action, even the simple act of making a phone call on her daughter's behalf, was indicative of the deep indolence that sometimes sets in with heavy cocaine use. Finally, by being a passive accomplice in the abuse against her children, Nussbaum was in many ways acting violently towards them. When one factored into the equation that Nussbaum was fairly self-centered to begin with, the addition of cocaine made her conduct understandable, but still far from excusable.

Charges in this case

What makes this case so interesting is that no charges were filed against Hedda Nussbaum. This was an instance when diminished capacity was established outside of the courtroom and no formal insanity defense was ever raised. In the end, there was no clear answer as to whether Nussbaum should or should not have been criminally prosecuted for her role in the death of Elizabeth Steinberg. Fairly convincing arguments were made for both sides, but as with all cases of this nature there were adherents to both possibly correct, though opposing, answers. If one wanted to see Nussbaum as capable of stopping Steinberg and chose to look for supporting information by examining her life through such a lens, then one would obviously find much information to support that argument. But the opposite was true as well. As with most arguments, analysis of evidence was not done objectively. It was always filtered through the lens of one's views. Consequently, the truth was not in the arguments for one side or the other, but likely somewhere in between the two. What caused this case to be so controversial was that Nussbaum's lack of legal responsibility was not established in the courtroom, but rather between attorneys.

Lawyers in this case

Because Nussbaum was never actually charged with a crime, there was no attorney prosecuting her. Instead, District Attorney Robert M. Morgenthau had the power to decide whether or not Nussbaum should go to trial. Nussbaum's defense attorney, who she obtained nearly immediately following her arrest, was Barry Scheck. Scheck had been known for taking on high profile cases pro bono, as he did with Nussbaum. He later went on to join O.J. Simpson's so-called dream team of defense attorneys.

Psychoforensic professionals in this case

District Attorney Morgenthau's decision not to prosecute Nussbaum was allegedly influenced by the numerous and extreme forms of abuse that were documented against Hedda Nussbaum. She suffered broken bones, burns, severe bruises, and many other injuries at the hands of Steinberg and eventually had to quit her job due to her physical condition. Towards the end of their relationship Nussbaum became so subservient to Steinberg that she asked his permission before eating or going to the bathroom. Despite all of this, Nussbaum still cared about Steinberg. She believed he was extremely intelligent and that he possessed supernatural powers, such as the ability to heal. She would even refer to Steinberg as God. Though Morgenthau argued that these were the reasons that he chose not to prosecute Nussbaum, because she was paralyzed by terror and pain and thus unable to help save Lisa Steinberg, many felt that his real motive was to gain a witness to ensure the prosecution of Stenberg.

In order to have Nussbaum evaluated officially, Morgenthau had her sent to Four Winds Mental Hospital nearly a year before the trial against Steinberg had begun. During the time she was treated she was never interviewed by someone on behalf of the Morgenthau in order determine whether she was competent to stand trial or whether she could be judged legally insane. During this time, Nussbaum refused to admit to hospital staff what Steinberg had done, despite confessing the day after her daughter's death to her attorney Barry Scheck the abuse both she and her daughter had endured. Consequently, the reasons for her being at the mental hospital, mainly for believing that Steinberg had magical powers and had done no wrong, were highly questionable considering her admission to her defense attorney implicating Steinberg, which occurred nearly a full year before she spoke to the district attorney.

Test of insanity

Again, what made this case so interesting was that no official test on insanity was applied to Nussbaum. In fact, as discussed, she never received an official mental health evaluation in order to help Morgenthau make his decision. Consequently, the real test of insanity that was applied to Nussbaum was something that no one but Morgenthau and Scheck knew.

Case process

Following the arrest of Joel Steinberg and Hedda Nussbaum the media flooded the public with horrific stories of the abuse that Lisa had endured. Pictures of a young smiling Lisa appeared on newspapers across the country, fueling the nation's disgust and hostility towards Steinberg and Nussbaum. Though anger towards Steinberg was nearly universal, many felt that Nussbaum should not be prosecuted, as she was also a victim. On October 26, 1988, one day after the trial against Steinberg began, District Attorney Robert Morgenthau decided that Hedda Nussbaum would not be prosecuted for her role in the death of her daughter. Nussbaum would, however, serve as the star witness against her lover.

At the end of the Steinberg's trial, after eight days of deliberation, the jury reached a verdict. A nation that had been intently awaiting a decision watched as Steinberg was found not guilty of second-degree murder but guilty of manslaughter. He was sentenced to eight and a third to twenty-five years in prison and was released in June 30, 2004, with some time off for good behavior. Though the punishment of Steinberg had neared its end, many questions in this case still remained. Many, such as Lisa Steinberg's birth mother Michele Launders, were appalled that Steinberg was not convicted of second-degree murder. But what concerned them most was not that Steinberg was treated too leniently, but that Hedda Nussbaum had, in essence, escaped all responsibility in the death of her daughter. Though few would argue that Nussbaum was the victim of many extreme forms of abuse, questions abounded as to whether abuse was enough of a reason to excuse Nussbaum's role in her daughter's death.

Joel Steinberg was released on parole, which would continue until 2012, and was forbidden to contact Nussbaum until that date. After his release he was offered a job for New York Confidential, a salacious cable show that dealt gossip, scandals, and crime. He was an intern making $250 a week, but spokesmen for the show said that he might be promoted to a reporter if his work were worthy. The show's interest in Steinberg, once again according to a spokesman for the show, was that he had an interesting perspective and knew many criminals in and outside of prison.

Media involvement

Though the trial against Joel Stenberg and the case against Hedda Nussbaum officially took place within in the courtroom, many argued that Steinberg was prosecuted and Nussbaum was exonerated in the media. As mentioned, as soon as Steinberg and Nussbaum were arrested, the abuse against Lisa Steinberg exploded into a media circus. This continued through Steinberg's trial, which was one of the first trials in which cameras were allowed in the courtroom. Capitalizing upon this was Nussbaum's attorney Barry Scheck. Scheck nearly single handedly converted national outrage against the crimes against Lisa Steinberg into outrage at the abuse against Nussbaum. Many felt that Scheck controlled the whole trial by putting public pressure on Morgenthau to exempt Nussbaum from culpability. Whether Morgenthau's decision was influenced by pressure from battered women groups, a need for Nussbaum to testify against her husband, or a genuine belief that Nussbaum was not responsible for Lisa Steinberg's death was something that could never be known for sure.

Another controversial way the Scheck utilized the media and the public was by recruiting battered women groups and feminist groups, most notably Steps to End Family Violence, and by putting pressure on Nussbaum to testify against Steinberg. His motivation for this was fairly easy to deduce: Nussbaum would be much more likely to go free if she were to turn on Steinberg. Despite Nussbaum's confessing Steinberg's crimes to Scheck, however, she at first refused to testify against him, not out of fear but out of what she considered love. She did not want to send Steinberg to prison. It was only many months later after numerous talks with Scheck and with women's organizations that Nussbaum changed her mind.

Meanwhile, Scheck's rallying to get the public on Nussbaum's side had another effect. It made Steinberg one of the most vilified men in the country. Even if one argued that Nussbaum was capable of helping her daughter, this did not take away any culpability from Steinberg. As a result, in addition to helping his own client, Scheck was essentially helping the prosecution build a case against Steinberg. Consequently, when Scheck approached the prosecutors, he had the upper hand. The prosecution could prosecute both Nussbaum and Steinberg and arguably walk away without a single conviction, as it would merely be a case of speculation, or they could let Nussbaum go free in exchange for testimony against the man who was nearly universally regarded as a monster. Considering Steinberg's poor reputation and the numerous stories in the media, such as his doing lines of cocaine in court when defending his clients, the prosecution no doubt felt a strong need to secure a conviction.

In addition to the notably murky communication between Scheck and the prosecution, both sides were also involved intimately with the press. In addition to Scheck's close connections to the media, the prosecution also had many private interactions with the press that further blurred ethical lines. This was a trial that was not only fought in the court, but behind closed doors with various dealings involving Scheck, Morgenthau, and the press.

Though this portrayal of the trial was generally agreed upon as fairly accurate, some large questions remained. One of these questions asked why if Morgenthau always intended to let Nussbaum go or to ask her to testify against Steinberg did he have her arrested in the first place. The answer to this seemed fairly simple. Morgenthau may have at first intended to prosecute them both, or, even if he did not, he soon realized that Nussbaum was not willing to cooperate in testifying against Steinberg. By charging her with murder, however, he put a great deal of pressure on Nussbaum to testify. This leverage eventually helped him secure a conviction against Steinberg. Yet the irony of this was that in the end Morgenthau did not truly succeed in securing the maximum sentence against Steinberg as he failed to charge Steinberg with the many forms of sexual abuse against Lisa Steinberg that were discovered during an autopsy. Though Nussbaum testified against Steinberg, citing many forms of abuse, she failed to draw attention to the fact that Lisa Steinberg had also been sexually abused since the age of two. This glaring omission suggested that in the end Nussbaum gave Morgenthau just enough information to save herself without testifying against Steinberg to the extent she could have. In turn, this implied that Nussbaum might still have harbored feelings of love towards Steinberg and that her turning on him was not so much a result of a personal epiphany as it was an extraordinary amount of pressure from Scheck, the media, Morgenthau, and the public.

Commentators

Legal and social commentators joined in the media circus and many were interviewed for shows like *20/20, 60 Minutes,* and *48 Hours*. The most common set up on these shows was to have four commentators: two legal and two social. One legal commentator and one social commentator would typically argue that Nussbaum should have been prosecuted and the other two commentators would claim that she should not have been prosecuted. A debate usually ensued.

The insanity defense itself

In the end, the case of Joel Steinberg and Hedda Nussbaum was an example of how some cases dealing with the insanity defense or diminished capacity could be a travesty of justice. This was a case marked by lies, back-room dealings, and a constant attempt to manipulate the public. Nussbaum's sanity was never truly in question. She was not charged because of legal politics, rather than her diminished capacity as a result of years of abuse. Perhaps the best argument supporting this assertion was the case of Frances McMillian. McMillian was a poor black woman who, along with her nine children, endured horrific abuse from her husband. Their family was discovered during a fire in their home and she was charged with endangering the welfare of her children. Upon arrest she sought treatment from the same facilities that treated Nussbaum and the very same organizations that jumped to Nussbaum's defense. She was unsuccessful on both counts and the prosecution did not drop the charges against her, despite being the victim of abuse arguably more severe than that suffered by Nussbaum.

Significance of this case

The question of the validity of the abuse excuse has been hotly debated in recent years, in cases ranging from the Menendez brothers to Lorena Bobbitt. Some of these cases brought in issues of competency to stand trial and used insanity, especially temporary insanity, as a defense. Other cases simply offered abuse as somewhat of rationalization, hoping to garner sympathy from jurors. A typical case might involve a woman in an abusive relationship with a husband or boyfriend. She might have endured years of abuse before one day killing her tormenter. Though this might have been done in self-defense, in other instances the battered woman might kill the man in his sleep or during another moment when she was not in immediate danger. In such cases, when the woman went to trial her attorney likely painted her as the victim and her significant other as the criminal. This strategy could be effective. Lorena Bobbitt was basically found not guilty by reason of insanity. But it often backfired, causing jurors to be more likely to blame the defendant. The backfiring of the abuse defense occurred because of a psychological heuristic that makes people want to believe in a just world. This heuristic caused people to process the world in a way that made it seem fair. Consequently, when jurors heard of the abuse that the defendant endured, instead of feeling sympathy, they might see the defendant as an inherently bad person who must have deserved their harsh treatment.

Hedda Nussbaum's circumstances were, in many respects, similar to most battered spouse cases, but there were some key differences. In many cases in which abuse was a justification, the woman usually struck back against her attacker. Nussbaum, however, never retaliated against Steinberg. In fact, it was likely that she never actively harmed either her husband or daughter physically. Her crime, if any, was a passive one. It was not that she did anything to harm her daughter. She merely did not do anything to protect her. Another significant difference was that the case against Nussbaum never went to trial. Though an attorney might utilize a defense that incorporated the citation of numerous instances of abuse during a trial, the case against Nussbaum never actually went to court. The official reason for this was perhaps best explained by prosecutor John McCusker, whose personal investigation proved to his satisfaction that Nussbaum was so incapacitated on the night of Lisa Steinberg's death that she could not have stopped Joel Steinberg, and that she therefore was not criminally responsible.

Consequently, some would say that in this instance, the abuse defense was extremely effective, as a jury never had the opportunity to decide Nussbaum's guilt or innocence. As a result, many argued that at the very least Nussbaum should have been prosecuted, giving a jury the chance to determine her guilt or innocence.

Whether or not Hedda Nussbaum was capable of interceding on behalf of her children was likely a question that no one, not even Nussbaum herself, had a clear answer to. My personal feelings are somewhat mixed. Though Nussbaum was not abused as a child and according to most did not fit the standard template for domestic abuse victims, I think it might have been possible that she was so mentally incapacitated that she could not help her daughter even if she wanted to, as it would have entailed taking a stand against Steinberg, her abuser. But I have had a difficult time understanding how Nussbaum had gotten to a point in her life in which she was that susceptible to a figure such as Steinberg. It has seemed to me that her upbringing was fairly standard, and not all lonely teenagers become involved in abusive relationships that lead to murder. Though she may have had some psychological problems, I doubt many would have predicted her involvement in such a horrific chain of events. Though she was severely abused by Steinberg, I feel that she was partially responsible for Lisa Steinberg's death. Perhaps she could not have stopped Steinberg, but she could have, and should have, called an ambulance immediately.

The additional element of drug use is a large factor in my mind. She made a conscious decision to ingest the drug, and though cocaine may have been a reason for her impaired judgment, it was not an excuse. The case of Joel Steinberg and Hedda Nussbaum was fascinating because even if one believed that the district attorney let Nussbaum go solely in exchange for her testimony, a question remained: If Nussbaum were prosecuted in addition to Steinberg how would the case against Steinberg have been affected? Perhaps she would still have testified against Steinberg in a similar fashion in order to push the blame away from herself, but she may not have testified as vehemently against Steinberg for one reason or another. Though jurors have denied that Nussbaum's testimony was important in their decision, one wonders if the verdict would have been different without the emotional testimony of Steinberg's battered spouse. In my mind, ideally, Nussbaum would have been prosecuted without adversely affecting the severity of Steinberg's sentence. Nussbaum's sentence should have been, in my opinion, less than Steinberg's, yet still more than just a proverbial slap on the wrist.

Though I have felt that Nussbaum should have been punished, that is not to say that I consider the battered woman syndrome a myth or that the abuse excuse has always been a pretext rather than at times a legitimate justification for one's action. In certain instances, a person who has been repeatedly abused may become temporarily insane and kill their abuser. In such cases, evidence of extensive abuse as a precursor to the defendant's actions would be vital information and should definitely have an effect on the verdict. Insanity is at times a genuine defense. But in this case, attorneys did not rely on psychological testimony to determine the mental state of Nussbaum. They simply used her past abuse as an excuse to let her go free.

In some way or another, everyone is a product of his past. Murderers, rapists, bank robbers, nearly every type of criminal can point to some aspect of their past that could offer some justification for their actions. A murderer in his mid-thirties who kills an innocent woman should not be excused because he may have had an abusive mother. Similarly, though I feel a certain degree of empathy towards a woman who fell into a cycle of victimization at a young age, her involvement in an abusive relationship should not necessarily excuse her actions if she committed a crime. Though it may not be fair, as the family one is born into may largely determine much of a person's life, at a certain point one must take responsibility for one's actions. Hedda Nussbaum found herself in an awful situation, and she was in many respects be a victim. But the true victim was Elizabeth Steinberg, and the fact that Nussbaum could have prevented her death ought to have led to her prosecution.

Summary

Hedda Nussbaum's daughter, Elizabeth, was found dead after suffering abuse. Joel Steinberg, Nussbaum's lover and the girl's father, was arrested for the death. Both Nussbaum and Steinberg had been using drugs immediately before Elizabeth's death, and neither requested medical help for their daughter after she had become unconscious. Nussbaum claimed that Steinberg had abused her, and that she believed Steinberg would be able to save Elizabeth, which led Nussbaum not to summon medical assistance. Nussbaum was never charged with any crime, which was probably part of a deal to get her to help secure a conviction of Steinberg.

Note on sources

Much of my information on the background of this case was drawn from *Crime Library*. Additionally, articles in *The New York Times, USA Today,* and *The New*

York Post proved invaluable. Transcripts from *Larry King Live* and *20/20* helped me understand the media's involvement in this case.

Andrea Yates

Andrea Pia Yates was born Andrea Pia Kennedy in Houston, Texas on July 2, 1964. Almost thirty seven years later, on June 20, 2001, Yates committed infanticide, drowning all five of her children in the family bath tub. She was arrested and charged with capital murder in the cases of three of her five children. Andrea Yates was eligible for the death penalty due to the number and young age of her victims. At first Yates possessed the fervent belief that she deserved punishment and that her death was the only way to end Satan's control over her, refusing the idea of pleading not guilty. Nevertheless, on August 8, a medicated Yates accepted her lawyers' advice and entered a plea of not guilty by reason of insanity due to her long standing history of postpartum depression and psychosis. The defense argued that she was suffering from a violent psychotic episode at the time she committed the killings. The prosecution countered by arguing that although Yates was mentally ill, she still knew the difference between right and wrong at the time of the offense and therefore could not be considered legally insane. On March 12, 2002, the jury returned a verdict of guilty on all counts after deliberating for only three hours. The same jury sentenced Yates to life in prison forgoing the death penalty. Andrea Yates has resided at the Mountain View Unit, a state psychiatric prison in eastern Texas. She will be eligible for parole in 2041 at the age of seventy seven.

On January 6, 2005, a Texas appeals court overturned her convictions on the grounds that the prosecution psychiatrist had lied to the jury and the prosecutor in summing up the case had featured that testimony. The appellate court said that that testimony and summation might have unduly influenced the jury to convict her of murder. Her attorney responded by saying that he would not seek her release from the prison psychiatric unit as she remained mentally ill and in need of treatment. The prosecution said it planned to appeal the decision. Meanwhile, Andrea Yates had only been tried for the murders of three of her children. Beyond the attempt to appeal the appellate decision on the grounds that the errors were minimal and could not have influenced the jury, the prosecution had other options. If the prosecution failed to overturn the appellate decision, they could retry her for the murders of her three children. Further, they could try her for the murders of her other two children and could seek her civil commitment as dangerous by reason of mental illness. In response to the appellate decision, her attorney acknowledged that there was no way that Andrea Yates would be freed into society.

Her early life

Andrea Yates grew up the youngest of five children in a middle class, non-practicing Catholic family in Houston, Texas. She was very close to her father, a demanding man who often expected perfection from his daughter. In high school, Yates was described as a helpful, shy, athletic, and intelligent teenager. She was an avid runner and swimmer and the valedictorian of her class. She attended the University of Texas, studying to become a nurse. She did not date until the age of twenty-three, and when she was twenty five she met her future husband, Rusty Yates, in their shared apartment complex. The couple married in 1993. She soon began to adopt her new husband's religious and old fashioned values of family life. They decided that they wanted a traditional family, in which the man was the breadwinner and the woman a full time stay at home mom. Rusty Yates was employed as a National Aeronautics and Space Administration engineer, and Andrea Yates gave up her nursing career to become a housewife. They both indicated that they hoped for as many children as God gave them. Andrea Yates ended up giving birth to five children, four boys and one girl, all named after figures in the Bible: Noah in 1994, John in 1995, Paul in 1997, Luke in 1999, and Mary in 2000.

This religious and traditional life style accounted for many of her first signs of problems. As her children were born, Yates began to seek total perfection in her role as homemaker and mother, reading countless self-help books on the best methods to raise children. She never met her own high expectations as a mother, constantly feeling as if she were failing her children. With each successive birth, her many responsibilities increased. Because she was solely responsible for raising the children, she soon became overwhelmed with the demands of the tough job. Her husband was later accused by Yates' relatives of never helping with the children, never even changing one diaper. Their cramped living quarters added to her distress. Although the family had enough money for a more appropriately sized home for their rapidly growing family, Rusty Yates decided to move into a trailer and eventually into a bus in order to live the more austere life that God would approve.

Although Andrea Yates was stressed and unhappy with this life, she never complained believing that questioning her husband's decisions was a sin. Throughout their marriage, her religious fanaticism increased dramatically, eventually even surpassing that of her husband's. When Rusty Yates introduced his wife to the radical religious preacher and self proclaimed prophet, Michael Woroniecki, her religious zeal was greatly strengthened. Although both Yates were influenced by Woroniecki's teachings, she became obsessed with them, accepting even his most extremist views. Woronieki and his wife preached that all women were derived from Eve and were therefore sinners. In order for women to overcome their witch nature, they had to be subservient to their husbands and raise their children in strict accordance with idealistic and biblical notions of family. A mother who failed to meet these lofty expectations was considered the worst type of sinner, dooming herself and her children to hell. The Woronieckis also denounced Catholicism, the religion Andrea Yates' family had grown up with. In frequent correspondences, Mrs. Rachel Woroniecki emphasized the sinful nature of Andrea Yates' soul as a woman, bad mother, and Catholic, calling her evil and wicked. Her guilt mounted as she desperately tried to adhere to their views. She took on heavy responsibilities, such as home schooling her children according to Christian text and caring for her father who became sick with Alzheimer's Disease. Although her pressures were building, she never voiced her overwhelming feelings of anxiety, guilt, and sadness.

Yates was not formally labeled mentally ill until after the birth of her fourth child, but her psychological troubles began much earlier. These problems went unnoticed because the observable signs were subtle, and she kept her intrusive thoughts a secret. For example, she began having violent visual and auditory hallucinations after Noah, her first child, was born and she discontinued once enjoyed activities such as running and swimming when she became pregnant with John, her second. When Paul, her third, came along, Yates' outer demeanor changed more significantly, as she became increasingly reclusive, isolating herself from friends and family. Her deeply disturbed mental illness did not begin to surface until her fourth son, Luke, was born.

Four months later, on June 16, 1999, Yates completely broke down. Her husband returned from work to find her shaking uncontrollably and chewing on her own flesh. She made her first suicide attempt by overdosing on sleeping pills. He took her to the Methodist Hospital psychiatric unit, where she was first diagnosed with major depressive disorder and proscribed the antidepressant Zoloft for her anxiety and overwhelming thoughts. She was released after one week of evasive and unresponsive behavior. She said she wanted to sleep forever. Her outpatient psychiatrist was Dr. Starbranch. After she returned home, she refused to take her medication and her mental state deteriorated further. She began to self mutilate, scratching herself so severely that she left sores. She neglected her four children, sometimes refusing to feed them. Her delusions intensified, believing that the television characters were talking to her and that there were video cameras in the walls. She also heard voices and had violent visions involving a knife.

One month after her first suicide attempt, she tried again by putting a knife to her throat and begging her husband to let her end her life. She was checked into the hospital again, where she remained in a catatonic state until an injection of the anti-psychotic drug, Haldol, led to an improvement in her condition. She admitted to visions of hurting someone and her fear as to what the visions might mean. She also vaguely associated her overwhelming stress to her children. After showing signs of slight improvement, she was again released to outpatient care, but this time with a Haldol prescription. The Yates' situation became more optimistic when Rusty Yates moved his family to a Clear Lake home. Andrea Yates took up once enjoyed activities again, slowly began socializing, and began to interact with her children. Although not yet one hundred percent, Yates became pregnant again, disregarding the doctors' warnings that another child could be detrimental to her fragile state. When her father died just a few months after her fifth child, Mary, was born in November 2000, her condition took a turn for the worst. She stopped functioning and returned to her old destructive habits, such as self mutilating, and refusing food and drink. Further, she was now frantically reading the Bible. In the final days before the fatal incident, Andrea Yates was being constantly shuffled back and forth between her home and the doctor's office. Her status shifted to and from near catatonia and the most basic level of functioning. She could no longer take care of the children, and her doctor, Muhammud Saeed, advised that she should be supervised at all times. Rusty Yates' mother came in order to look after her and the children when he was at work.

Yates had begun professional treatment after her first suicide attempt in June 1999. She was hospitalized and diagnosed with major depressive disorder on numerous occasions at such facilities as the Methodist Hospital psychiatric unit and the Devereux Texas Treatment Network. A dizzying number of mental health professionals, from social workers to group therapists to psychologists, met with her during her periods of hospitalization and as a part of her outpatient care. Her primary care psychiatrist was constantly changing. As a result, she never received anything resembling consistent treatment. Her medication was altered every time she was assigned a new physician, resulting in a myriad of different prescriptions for antidepressant, antipsychotic, sedative drugs, including Zoloft, Zyprexa, Haldol, Ativan, Risperdol, Effexor, and many more. Haldol, an antipsychotic prescribed after her second suicide attempt, was the only drug that had a beneficial effect on her state. Unfortunately, her later psychiatrists failed to continue her on Haldol, claiming that they did not recognize any evidence of psychotic features in her. Many blamed the mental health system for Andrea Yates' crime, suggesting that her doctors let her slip through the cracks. Dr. Muhammud Saeed, for example, her psychiatrist just prior to the incident, received scanty medical records, took vague, sloppy, and incomplete notes, and released her with the advice to think positive thoughts.

Although her treatment was far from ideal, some of the blame for its failure lay with the patient herself. Yates was difficult to treat through therapy or medication. When speaking to her therapists, she constantly altered her story and the amount of information she was willing to divulge. At times and to some specialists she would open up, admitting to suicidal thoughts, delusions, and violent ideations. Other times she denied such thoughts and evaded questions altogether. She was also resistant to taking the medications she was prescribed, often flushing the pills down the toilet. She claimed that she refused the medication in order to breastfeed or to get pregnant, but many believed she feared the Woroniecki's disapproval as well. Yates discontinued Haldol as she had all the other drugs. It was impossible to speculate as to whether other medications would have been helpful as well because she never gave them a chance to take effect.

A noncompliant patient coupled with inadequate communication among her treatment team meant there was never really any hope for a positive treatment outcome for Andrea Yates.

Charges in this case

Andrea Yates' mental state was unstable in the days prior to the fatal incident. She had been recently discharged from the hospital and was considered functioning when she was able to eat or bathe herself. Her husband continued to worry about her behavior and brought her back to consult with her latest psychiatrist, Dr. Saeed. In early June, Dr. Saeed took her off antipsychotic medication and claimed that she did not need either Haldol or electroconvulsive shock therapy. He prescribed the antidepressant Effexor, but cut back on this medication on June 18. This decision made Rusty Yates doubt the doctor's grasp on and approach to his wife's illness. Dr. Saeed suggested that she be supervised at all times when at home. Although Rusty Yates' mother, Dora Yates, looked after her while he worked, there was one hour between 9 am and 10 am, after he left and before his mother would arrive, in which Yates was alone with the children.

On the morning of June 20, Andrea Yates made tragic use of this time. Following a breakfast of cereal, she filled the bath tub three inches from the top and began methodically drowning her children one by one. She first placed two year old Luke in the tub face down and held his face under water until he stopped struggling. She then moved him to the master bed and put a sheet over his small, soaked, lifeless body. Then she did the same to Paul, age three, then John, age five. Her youngest child, six month old Mary, was in the bathroom crying throughout the first three murders. She was next. The oldest, Noah, age seven, entered the bathroom to find Mary's tiny body floating in the tub. Terrified, he ran from his mother's grasp, but she eventually overpowered him, drowning him in the same feces, vomit, and urine infested water in which his dead baby sister still floated. Later, Andrea Yates confessed that he put up the largest struggle, getting up for air on at least two occasions. She left Noah in the tub and put Mary on the bed with her other brothers. She positioned one of the boy's arms around Mary. At 9:50 am it was over. She called the police and her husband, and both arrived shortly after.

The officers who arrived that day to find the gruesome scene reported that Andrea Yates met them without emotion. She was taken to the police station where a tape recorded interview was conducted. She confessed to the murders as she did on the phone and at her home. She said that she believed she was guilty and should be punished for her failure as a mother. She claims she killed her children in order to ultimately save them from Satan.

Lawyers in this case

The lead prosecuting attorney, Kaylynn Williford, was aided by her partner Joseph Owmby. This was going to be an important trial for both Williford, as her first capital murder case, and Owmby, who stated that it was the most horrific case he had ever encountered. They charged Andrea Yates with the capital murders of Noah and of Luke and of Mary. In case they did not succeed in their prosecution, they would have the murders of two more children to fall back on. They decided to seek the death penalty.

After they won the competency hearing, Williford and Owmby prepared their strategy, which was to assert that Yates' mental illness was irrelevant, by focusing the jurors on the evidence that could prove she knew the difference between right and wrong at the time of the offense. The prosecutors presented Yates as a calculating killer who had knowingly killed her children for the selfish reason of escaping stress and punishing her husband whom she blamed for helping to create the life she loathed. Williford and Owmby cited the 911 call, her prison confession, and the methodical and preplanned nature of the killings in order to prove their case. Waiting until her husband left her alone with the children was evidence of planning, and calling the police and her husband directly after the killings showed an element of guilt for what she had done.

The prosecution also used the dramatic tactic of evoking the emotions of the jurors. For instance, they presented autopsy reports from medical examiners, which showed how the children fiercely struggled for their lives. They also entered the children's pajamas into evidence under the pretext of displaying how much smaller they were then their mother, but more importantly to further inflame the jury. They also showed photographs and family videos to the court, bringing the children to life in the eyes of the jurors. In Williford's closing statement, she asked the courtroom to be silent for a period of three minutes, so they could experience how long each child was held under water as they were murdered.

At first, Judge Belinda Hill appointed Robert Scott as Andrea's public defender. Scott's first and only act of importance was the request of a gag order. Soon after, Rusty Yates approached a family friend, George Parnham, to help out. He became Andrea Yates' new lawyer. Wendell Odom also joined the defense team. Their first order of business was to prove that Yates was not competent to stand trial, presenting hundreds of pages documenting her medical history and the opinions of the defense's psychological experts who interviewed her. In addition, they subpoenaed several jail employees, along with her mother and siblings, to provide first hand accounts of her illness. After the jury found her competent on September 24, the defense filed dozens of pretrial motions. The most important of the motions was a request that the Texas Criminal Code procedure prohibiting jurors from knowing the consequences of a not guilty by reason of insanity verdict be reconsidered. In other words, Parnham and Odom wanted the jurors to be aware that a not guilty by reason of insanity verdict involved mandatory hospitalization and treatment, and did not mean an outright acquittal as in a simple not guilty verdict. The defense attorneys also filed a motion to declare the M'Naghten test of insanity as written under Texas law unconstitutional due to its incompatibility with psychological definitions of mental illness. Unfortunately for Andrea Yates, these most crucial motions were not granted.

Parnham and Odom then went about the difficult task of proving that a mental disease or defect prevented Andrea Yates from differentiating between right and wrong. Since she had claimed on multiple occasions that she knew and believed her actions were not only illegal but also a mortal sin, they would have to show that her thought process leading to such declarations was a product of her disease, rooted in her psychotic state at the time. Their defense strategy relied almost entirely on a team of psychological experts who would attempt to explain to the jury how right and wrong needed to be interpreted more abstractly in the case. The experts testified that Yates' mental state prohibited her from understanding that what she was doing was wrong. In her delusional mind, killing her children was not only right but the only choice she had to save their eternal souls.

Psychoforensic professionals in this case

From the beginning it was obvious that the defense would plead insanity. Psychological experts became involved with the Yates case very early due to her longstanding mental instability. Professionals began meeting with Yates almost immediately after her arrest. Preliminary psychological evaluations conducted by court appointed psychiatrist Dr. Steve Rubenzer found Yates competent to stand trial, but her lawyers protested the ruling on the grounds that their psychologists had arrived at the opposite conclusion from their interviews with the defendant. The defense team got the competency hearing they requested, which began on September 18. At that time, Yates had been receiving treatment and antipsychotic medication for about two months. Her condition had significantly improved since her arrest in that she no longer experienced hallucinations and was able to converse to a reasonable degree. Her thought process, however, was still deeply rooted in Satanical delusions, and she had difficulty remembering. The defense's psychological experts testified that she was not yet ready for trial, while the prosecution's experts indicated that she met the competency requirements. Although the testifying psychological experts disagreed if and when she was or would be competent, all acknowledged that she was suffering from some form of mental illness.

Dr. Gerald Harris, a clinical psychologist, testified for the defense at the competency hearing. He conducted four interviews with Yates that began only a few days after her arrest. He argued that she was incompetent to stand trial because her delusional state left her unable to rationally assist her attorneys in the case against her. Harris insisted that she was unable to rationally answer most of the questions he posed and at times did not even realize he had asked a question. Dr. Harris recognized severe psychotic elements in her, including visual and auditory hallucinations, delusions, and impaired cognitive skills. During his interviews with her, she claimed that 666 was inscribed on her forehead, her hair was shaped like a crown, and that Satan spoke to her in her cell. He concluded that, due to her delusional state, she vehemently opposed a not guilty plea and stated that she desired the death penalty.

Dr. Lauren Marangell, a depression expert for the defense, testified that Yates would most likely be competent to stand trial after she had been on a consistent medication regiment. She concluded that, although Yates had made significant improvement while on Haldol since her arrest, more time on continuous medication was necessary at this time before she would be able to fully comprehend the court proceeding and be able to aid her attorneys in a rational manner.

Dr. Steve Rubenzer was appointed by the court without the knowledge of the defense attorneys to provide a psychological report indicating Yates' level of competence. At first, Judge Hill ruled in favor of Parnham's request to suppress Rubenzer's testimony, but toward the end of the hearing he was permitted to take the stand. Rubenzer had met with Yates on several occasions in order to administer the state's test of competency, on which he reported improved comprehension on successive tests and that she generally met the state's standards for competence. However, he also reported that her psychosis was not yet in full remission.

On September 24, Yates was found to be competent to stand trial. The criminal trial officially commenced in February 2002, and quickly became a battleground among the high profile psychological experts. For the defense, psychiatrists Dr. Melissa Ferguson, Dr. Phillip Resnick, Dr. Steve Rosenblatt, and Dr. Lucy Puryear testified that Andrea Yates could not comprehend that what she was doing was wrong due to her psychosis at the time of the offense and was therefore legally insane.

Dr. Ferguson, the prison psychiatrist, was the first expert called upon by the defense in order to paint of picture of Yates' mental state directly after arrest. She testified to the delusional thoughts that Yates had discussed with her while in prison. For example, Yates had stated Satan kept telling her that she was a bad mother and had raised her children incorrectly. The only way to save them from Hell was to kill them, and the only way to get rid of Satan was for her to be put to death.

Dr. Lucy Puryear attempted to educate the jury on the differences between postpartum depression and postpartum psychosis. She explained the rarity of the psychotic elements observed in Yates, occurring in only one in five hundred births. She also indicated the Yates' condition was not permanent and with treatment she could be rehabilitated. Yates had refused treatment in the past because she had been suspicious that Satan was controlling her doctors. Dr. Puryear also indicated that Yates' condition prevented her from rationally contemplating her options, because in her psychotic mind, killing her children was the only option for the only alternative would doom her children to an eternity in Hell.

Dr. Resnick, a psychiatrist from Case Western University, specialized in parents who killed their children. After meeting with Yates on two occasions, he concluded that her crime was an example of altruism. He tried to explain to the jurors that she believed her decision to kill her children was right even though she knew it was illegal. Resnick diagnosed her with severe depression and schizophrenia.

Dr. Rosenblatt testified that in his interview with Yates just five days after her arrest, she was in a state of deep psychosis. He therefore concluded that she must have been psychotic at the time of the offense because it would have taken weeks for her to get to the state in which he observed her. Dr. Rosenblatt contradicted Dr. Muhammud Saeed, who testified for the prosecution that he did not recognize any psychotic features in Yates just two days prior to the killings even though he had diagnosed her with depression accompanied by psychotic elements initially. On cross examination, Parnham accused Dr. Saeed of reworking his notes, which at the later time indicated a lack of psychotic elements in smaller handwriting, in order to protect his career.

Dr. Park Elliot Dietz was the prosecution's rebuttal witness. He testified after the defense's psychological expert witnesses. Dietz was a psychiatrist who had testified on the side of the prosecution in many prominent cases involving the insanity defense. He was good at simplifying psychological issues for juries to understand. His testimony was based on an interview with Yates conducted in November. He admitted that Yates was mentally ill but also presented the numerous ways that suggested that she knew right from wrong and that she knew her actions were wrong, both in the eyes of the law and of God. First, there were her own words, claiming that she was guilty of committing a mortal sin and deserved the harshest punishment of death under law. The true motive for the murders, according to Dietz, was a chance to escape a stressful and unbearable situation that she lacked the necessary control to improve. Dietz also mentioned that her keeping a secret, premeditated, and calculated plan, covering the bodies with sheets, and calling the police were all actions that pointed toward guilt. Further, he claimed that while she lacked proper and necessary supervision given her mental state and had never received good continuous care, she often made her own decision to forgo helpful medication.

Although Dietz was correct that Yates waited until no one was home to prevent her from killing her children, he also presented false evidence of premeditation. He claimed that she had watched a *Law and Order* television episode in which a mother killed her children by drowning them, and that this had planted the idea in her head. He recounted this statement and the prosecutor had used it in his summation to the jury. It was later discovered that the particular episode never aired, but Yates had already been found guilty. It was because of this error that the Texas appellate court later overturned her conviction.

Test of insanity

The case was tried in Texas, which followed the stringent standards of insanity set forth by the M'Naghten test. After the insanity plea was offered, the burden of proof shifted to the defense. In order to be found not guilty by reason of insanity under this test, the defense had to prove that the defendant was unaware or what she was doing or that what she was doing was wrong.

Case process

The majority of the crucial rulings made by Judge Belinda Hill favored the prosecution's case against Andrea Yates. Before the competency hearing began, Judge Hill ruled in favor of the defense by agreeing to throw out the competency report conducted by the state appointed psychiatrist, Dr. Rubenzer, without the knowledge of the defense attorneys. However, by the trial's conclusion, Dr. Rubenzer was allowed to testify that his evaluation deemed her competent. When the actual trial began, only a few minor motions made by the defense were granted. The defense's attempt to fight the capital murder charge also failed. Upon discovering a major flaw in the prosecution's key psychological expert, the defense asked for a mistrial. This request, like the others, was denied.

Although Andrea Yates' family members, jail attendees, and the police officers were introduced as witnesses by both the prosecution and defense, the majority of the testimony involved psychological experts. Ultimately the role of psychology was huge in this case, as the clashing opinions of high profile experts were presented one by one.

The trial jury included four men and eight women, all of whom were death qualified and therefore able to impose the death penalty if warranted. Seven of the jurors were parents themselves and two had college degrees in psychology. The jury only deliberated for a brief three hours before deciding on a guilty verdict. In forty minutes, they sentenced her to life in prison, forgoing the death penalty.

Media involvement

The media vigorously followed and recorded every detail of the Yates case with reporters arriving on the scene the same day that the fatal incident to took place. The nation watched with horror, intrigue and sadness as reporters described the shocking scene that the police had found inside the Yates home and presented footage of a distraught father's reaction to his wife's killing of all five of their children. While Andrea Yates was inside the house, Rusty Yates was outside screaming and pleading to know how she could do such a thing. As she was brought out in handcuffs by the police, he curled up in the fetal position on the front lawn and pounded the ground with anguish. Days later, *Time* reporter, Michelle McCalope attended the funeral for the Yates children, publishing an account of the tear inducing event and Rusty Yates' heartfelt eulogy.

This crime touched a nerve with the American public, eliciting strong emotional reactions and fiercely polarized opinions. The media wanted the scoop, and the nation wanted answers. How could a mother commit such an unthinkable crime against her own children? At the beginning, the public judged her harshly, finding her guilty and worthy of the most severe penalty of death, with the belief that only an evil person would commit such a crime. The local radio talk shows began to buzz with callers expressing their outrage and confusion over her behavior.

After Rusty Yates overcame his initial grief, he quickly began meeting with the demanding media in order to publicly campaign in support of his wife, claiming that the illness, not the person, was culpable for this tragic event. The nation learned that Andrea Yates had been suffering from depression for at least the past two years since the birth of their fourth child and had attempted suicide on two occasions. His ability to forgive her, coupled with new information concerning her mental illness, began to soften public opinion against her, and led many to rush to her defense.

A few unsuccessful efforts were made to stifle the media's involvement. On June 27, Judge Hill issued a gag order requested by the defense. However, items continued to leak to the press. The prosecutorial team, Williford and Ownby, told the press that they did not intend to make public their decision whether to seek the death penalty. And although no one was allowed to comment on that very decision made on September 5, both district attorney Chuck Rosenthal and Rusty Yates violated the order by meeting with *60 Minutes*. Rusty Yates also met with reporters from *Time* magazine, handing over family photos and talking about his wife. He hired an attorney, Edward Mallet, to fight the gag order. A prosecutor was appointed to probe the gag order violations when the trial was complete, but by then the issue was moot, and no one was dealt consequences for their violations.

The public began to follow the abundant information presented by the media, forming their own opinions about the controversial issues involved in the case. Although many felt that Andrea Yates was legally insane and ought to receive treatment for her disease, the majority of Americans did not seem to comprehend how a person who confessed could be unable to decipher between right and wrong. For the most part, the public's perception did not go beyond the literal interpretation of right and wrong, finding it very difficult to accept the more abstract definitions that were central to the defense's argument. The public was also relatively uneducated in the ideas and theories of mental illness, subscribing to many stereotypes and misconceptions of the mentally ill. After the guilty verdict on March 12, 2002, the nation then began to debate whether or not she deserved death. Some predicted death due to the lack of compassion that the jurors demonstrated with a quick return of a guilty verdict. Others, believing the guilty verdict was unfair, hoped for a sentence of life imprisonment. The public was upset to learn that the jurors were never informed of the consequences of a not guilty by reason of insanity verdict, which would in her case have ensured hospitalization and treatment for Yates.

In the aftermath of the trial, public opinion began to shift the blame elsewhere. After he had danced with the media for so long, public opinion turned on Rusty Yates. Many felt that he should share some of the culpability for his children's deaths because he neglected to heed the doctor's warning by leaving his wife unsupervised with the children. District Attorney Chuck Rosenthal received numerous emails insisting that Rusty Yates be investigated for disregarding the doctor's instructions. Rusty Yates and his attorney denied any wrongdoing, reiterating his claim that he had assumed one hour alone was not a cause for alarm. As it turned out, of course, he had been mistaken. Instead, Rusty Yates pointed his finger at the mental health system for mishandling his wife. Others agreed with his claim that the psychiatrists in charge of her care provided improper treatment and failed to adequately warn him about the dangers associated with her disease. In the end, Rusty Yates was never investigated. He set up a public website with family photos and information on post partum depression and psychosis, in an attempt to educate the public about the disease.

The Yates case generated a great deal of literature and a number of documentaries even after the trial's conclusion. Susan Spencer wrote a nonfiction book about the Yates case from beginning to end, titled *Breaking Point,* and Court TV aired a documentary in its *Mugshots* program, which included interviews with those involved in the case. Much of the nation was unsatisfied with how Yates was handled by the court system, pressuring for reform.

When the Texas appellate court in early 2005 overturned Andrea Yates' conviction, the media again became active immediately presenting special programs covering the decision and commenting on it. Reawakened to the issues already presented by the crimes, the trial, the verdict, and the sentencing, the appellate decision raised new issues, and the media once more turned its spotlight on Andrea Yates, the legal system, and the provision of care to the mentally ill.

Commentators

Timothy Roche, a reporter with *Time* magazine, closely followed the Yates case and trial from beginning to end, forming his own opinions of the case. He delved deeply into the Yates family history, reporting that a troubled family situation had an insidious outside influence on her mental illness. He also conducted post trial interviews with some of the principal characters involved. Roche provided his own opinion regarding the relationship between the psychological and legal aspects that led to the trial's outcome. He disagreed with Texas' wording of the insanity plea, specifically the troubles with the M'Naghten test. He complained that under M'Naghten rule it was impossible for the court system to handle sick people differently from the average killer.

A reporter with *CNN*, David Williams, provided commentary addressing the issue of postpartum depression and psychosis, and how people afflicted by this disease were handled improperly in the United States. He educated the public on the details of the disease, explaining why it could make insanity a difficult defense to prove. Because postpartum depression was a temporary and treatable depression, jurors had a hard time understanding how a defendant could appear completely normal at the time of the trial. Andrea Yates had undergone months of treatment and had been given antipsychotic medication between the incident and her trial, restoring her mental health to a much improved state. To the jurors she did not appear to be suffering from any mental illness, let alone psychosis. Williams also suggested the need for reform, pointing out that twenty nine countries recognized postpartum depression as a legal defense, including Britain, Canada, and Australia. By contrast, American law focused strongly on free will and personal responsibility and feared the exploitation of a postpartum defense. In addition, he said that the public felt little compassion towards those suffering from postpartum depression because society viewed the birth of a child as a reason to rejoice, and motherhood as a sacred gift not to be forsaken. These facts made it difficult for him to foresee changes regarding this issue in the near future.

Forensic psychologist Michael Welner also commented on the lack of support and help provided for women suffering from postpartum depression. Although twenty percent of births have resulted in postpartum depression, the American health system has failed to watch over new mothers for signs of mood swings as other countries have done for months after birth. In addition, Americans also have had difficulty understanding hormonal shifts that can lead to rare psychotic manifestations, such as incoherent, paranoid, and delusional thoughts, that occur in one of every five hundred births. Mothers suffering from postpartum psychosis have been much more likely to harm themselves than their children. Such violent acts have usually been committed with the belief that they are for the good of the child. Welner recommended that the American mental health system follow the lead of those countries that recognize the severity of postpartum diseases, by creating programs and advising immediate hospitalization for afflicted mothers.

Gamet Coleman, a Texas state representative and mental health advocate, offered his own commentary in an interview that appeared in *Mental Health Weekly*. Coleman told the reporter that he intended to introduce new legislation aimed at revising and redefining the Texas law regarding the insanity defense. He talked of the possibility of returning to the less severe pre-Hinckley standard of insanity, which also acknowledged defendants' inability to conform their behavior to what they knew to be right or wrong.

The insanity defense itself

This case provided an account of how the insanity defense failed due to the incompatibility of psychological and legal terminology. The psychological definition of mental illness was very different from Texas' definition of insanity. Although the psychological experts greatly differed in their opinions of whether or not Andrea Yates was insane, they all concurred that she was suffering from severe mental illness. The M'Naghten test of insanity was the toughest standard to meet. If Andrea Yates were not considered insane by that standards then the question was raised of who would be. Her case lent support for many to the argument that changes must be made to the law's standard of insanity. One recommendation was that the term insane should be eliminated because it is not used in psychology. Because scientists of the mind cannot agree on a uniform method of defining insanity, psychological testimony in insanity defense cases has widely been considered a complete mess. One of the defense team's pretrial motions stated that Texas' insanity plea was not in touch with the true nature of mental illness, and should therefore be declared unconstitutional. Although this motion was denied, its point was well documented and should be examined further.

Another important issue that came up in this trial concerned the provision in the Texas Criminal Code that prohibited jurors from knowing how a not guilty by reason of insanity verdict differed significantly from a not guilty verdict. Many jurors believed that finding a defendant not guilty by reason of insanity was the same as an outright acquittal, resulting in the defendant's immediate return to society. They were unaware that one found not guilty by reason of insanity was then evaluated and in serious cases such as Andrea Yates' would enter a mental institution for treatment, and would remain there until deemed both no longer dangerous and well enough to be released. In many cases, defendants found not guilty by reason of insanity spent more time in a mental hospital than they would have in prison had they been found guilty and sentenced there. It was possible that if the jurors had been aware of this information in the Yates' case, it might have swayed their opinion or even altered the ultimate verdict.

The jurors' decision may also have been affected by Andrea Yates' much improved mental state during the trial. She had been on consistent anti-psychotic medication, Haldol, for three months by the time the trial commenced. At the time of the murders, she was a very different person from the one observed by the jurors.

The case of Andrea Yates was misleading in one important way and correct in another. It was misleading because its high profile nature and the resultant intense media attention caused the public perception of the frequency with which the insanity defense is used to be tremendously inflated. In fact, the insanity defense is employed in a very small percentage of criminal trials. It was correct, however, because the guilty verdict was extremely representative of the outcome of most cases involving a plea of insanity. In fact, the great percentage fail.

Brief summary and significance of this case

The case study of Andrea Yates provides the quintessential example of how the insanity defense has failed to meet its purpose in the legal system. That purpose is to protect the accused afflicted by mental illnesses from experiencing the same fate as the ordinary criminal. When the standard of insanity is so severe, as it are under the M'Naghten test, it becomes extremely difficult to prove that anyone is insane because even the most psychologically disturbed defendants have a basic understanding of the difference between right and wrong. The real issue is that their mental state often clouds their judgment in issues concerning morality and legality, and the difference between right and wrong is no longer the difference between black and white. Depending on one's opinion, mental illness has been called either the reason for or an excuse for a defendant's inability to chose right over wrong. Some have argued that no matter the mental illness, one always has the power of choice to break or abide by the law. Others have concluded that some forms of severe mental illness eliminate this choice.

In my opinion, there needs to be a consensus on a more uniform and fair test of insanity in courts throughout the country, one that successfully reflects what is now known about the psychological nature of mental illness. This test should incorporate the ways in which mental illness can skew the afflicted individuals' understanding of accepted behavior under the law and their ability to control their behavior in accordance with the law.

Note about sources

The primary sources for information about Andrea Yates included Ramsland's "Andrea Yates: Ill or evil?", Roche's "Andrea Yates: More to the story", Spenser's *Breaking Point,* and Williams' "Postpartum depression: A difficult defense." Additional sources included McCalope's "Rusty Yates bids farewell to his five children" and Wrightsman et al's *Psychology and the legal system.* Various news sources contributed information concerning the Texas appellate court's overturning Andrea Yates' conviction.

Bibliography

Ackman, D. (1999). Goldstein lawyers put mental healthcare system on trial. *The Graduate School of Journalism Columbia University.* http://dackman.homestead.com/files/GoldsteinTrial.htm.

Alexander, S. (1983). *Very much a lady.* New York: Dell.

American Bar Association. www.abanet.org.

American Medical Association. www.ama-assn.org.

American Psychiatric Association (1982). The insanity defense: position statement. www.psych.org/edu/other_res/lib_archives/archives/820002.pdf.

American Psychiatric Association (1994). Diagnostic and statistical manual of mental disorders (4th Ed.). DSM-IV. Washington, D.C.: American Psychiatric Association

American Psychological Association. www.apa.org.

Arena, K. and Frieden, T. (2003). Hinckley wins unsupervised visits. www.cnn.com/2003/LAW/12/17/hinckley.decision.

Associated Press (2003a), November 22. Jury convicts man—again—of kidnapping therapist. *The Sun Link.* www.thesunlink.com/redesign/2003-11-22/local/325391.shtml.

Associated Press (2003b), November 21. Man convicted of kidnapping therapist. *The Columbian.* www.highbeam.com.

Bardsley, M. Most notorious serial killers: Jeffrey Dahmer. http://www.crimelibrary.com/serial_killers/notorious/dahmer/trial_5.html.

Barnes, M. (Director and producer). (1984). Frontline: The mind of a murderer. Boston: WGBH Educational Foundation.

Bartol, C. and Bartol, A. (2004). *Psychology and law: Theory, research, and application* (3d Ed.). Belmont, CA: Wadsworth.

Bikel, O. (Senior producer). (2002). Frontline: A crime of insanity. Boston: WGBH Educational Foundation.

Blashfield, J. (1990). *Why they killed*. New York: Popular Library.

Bonnie, R. (1983). The moral basis of the insanity defense. *American Bar Association Journal*, 69, 194.

Brownmiller, S. (1989). *Waverly Place: A novel*. New York: Signet.

Butler, A. (1998). Defining the neurobiology of insanity: Law, science, and the I-function reconciled. http://serendip.brynmawr.edu/bb/neuro/neuro98/202s98-paper3/Butler3.html.

Cahill, T. (1986). *Buried dreams: Inside the mind of a serial killer*. New York: Bantam.

Caplan, L. (1987). *The insanity defense and the trial of John W. Hinckley, Jr*. New York: Dell.

Caplan, L. (1992). Not so nutty: The post-Dahmer insanity defense. *New Republic*, 206, 18-20.

Chase, A. (2003). *Harvard and the Unabomber: The education of an American terrorist*. New York: Norton. [Reissued as: Chase, A. (2004). *A mind for murder: The education of the Unabomber and the origins of modern terrorism*. New York: Norton.]

Cliff, P. (2000), January/February. Another Andrew Goldstein trial. *New York City Voices*. http://newyorkcityvoices.org/jan00k.html.

CourtTV Online (1999). www.courttv.com/archive/people/1999/1015/hinckley_ctv.html.

Crego, M. (2000). One crime, many convicted: Dissociative identity disorder and the exclusion of expert testimony in State v. Greene. *Washington Law Review*, 75, 911-939.

Dahmer dilemma (1992), February 24. *The National Law Journal*, 16.

Davis, D. (1991). The *Milwaukee murders: Nightmare in apartment 213: The true story*. New York: St. Martin's.

D.C. Code § 24-301(j) 1981.

Dershowitz, A. (1994). *The abuse excuse: And other cop-outs, sob stories, and evasions of responsibility*. Boston: Little, Brown.

Dershowitz, A. (2004). The trial of Richard Herrin. *America on trial: Inside the legal battles that transformed our nation*. New York: Time Warner, 428-433.

Donaldson, K. (1976). *Insanity inside out*. NY: Crown.

Douglas, J. and Olshaker, M. (1995). *Mind hunter: Inside the FBI's elite serial crime unit*. New York: Pocket Books.

Dovre, L. (1984). *Jones v. United States*: automatic commitment of individuals found not guilty by reason of insanity. *Minnesota Law Review*, 68, 822-845.

Drukteinis, A. (1992). Serial murder: The heart of darkness. *Psychiatric Annals*, 22, 532-538.

Dvorchak, R. and Holewa, L. (1991). *Milwaukee massacre: Jeffrey Dahmer and the Milwaukee murders*. New York: Dell.

Ellis, J. (1986). The consequences of the insanity defense: proposals to reform post-acquittal commitment laws. *Catholic University Law Review*, 35, 961-1020.

Ephron, G. (2002). *Delusion: A mystery*. New York: St. Martin's.

Eth, S. (2000). The "insanity defense". *Morningside-Westside Bulletin*, 6, 2. http://www.mwcac.com.

False Memory Syndrome Foundation (2004). Washington jury rejects multiple personality defense of William Greene. *FMS Foundation Newsletter*, 13, 1. http://www.fmsfonline.org/fmsf04.101.html.

Fersch, E. (1974). Court clinic treatment in Massachusetts: Mental health care v. civil rights. *International Journal of Offender Therapy and Comparative Criminology*, 18, 275-282.

Fersch, E. (1975). When to punish, when to rehabilitate. *American Bar Association Journal*, 61, 1235-1237.

Fersch, E. (1976). The approach of a Massachusetts court clinic in the probate court. *International Journal of Offender Therapy and Comparative Criminology*, 20, 178-182.

Fersch, E. (1979). *Law, psychology, and the courts*. Springfield, IL: Charles C Thomas.

Fersch, E. (1980). Ethical issues for psychologists in court settings. In J. Monahan (Ed.), *Who is the Client?* (pp. 43-62). Washington, D.C.: American Psychological Association.

Fersch, E. (1980). *Psychology and psychiatry in courts and corrections*. New York: John Wiley & Sons.

Fersch, E. (1982), November 22. Guilty but mentally ill? *The Harvard Crimson*. http://www.thecrimson.com/article.aspx?ref=174430.

Fersch, E. (1982). Law and psychiatry. *International Journal of Offender Therapy and Comparative Criminology*, 26, 157-175.

Fersch, E., Goldfine, P., and Vrabel, J. (1978). The need for sanctuary from the community. *International Journal of Offender Therapy and Comparative Criminology*, 22, 68-79.

Fingarette, H. (1972). *The meaning of criminal insanity*. Berkeley, CA: University of California Press.

Flora, C. (2003), December 9. The brainwashing defense. *Psychology Today*. http://cms.psychologytoday.com/articles/pto-20031209-000001.html.

Flynn, L. (2000), March/April. The Andrew Goldstein verdict. *New York City Voices*. http://www.newyorkcityvoices.org/mar00g.html.

Freedman, D. (2001). False prediction of future dangerousness: Error rates and psychopathy checklist—revised. *Journal of the American Academy of Psychiatry & the Law*, 29, 89-95.

Frontline (2002). A crime of insanity. http://www.pbs.org/wgbh/pages/frontline/shows/crime/.

Gado, M. (2002). The killing of Lisa Steinberg. http://www.crimelibrary.com/notorious_murders/family/lisa_steinberg/1.html.

Gardner, M. (2003). Viewing the criminal sanction through Latter-day Saint thought. *Brigham Young University Law Review*, 3, 2003, 861-890.

Gaylin, W. (1982). *The killing of Bonnie Garland: A question of justice: A devastating examination of psychiatry, justice, and the insanity defense.* New York: Penguin.

Gaylin, W. (1995). *The killing of Bonnie Garland: A question of justice: A devastating examination of crime and accountability.* New York: Penguin.

George, K. (1999). Sex offender loses 'other personality' appeal, Supreme Court rules against Everett man. *Seattle Post-Intelligencer*, October 4. http://www.highbeam.com.

Gilman, R. (2000). Blame the victim?. *Morningside-Westside Bulletin*, 6, 2. http://www.mwcac.com.

Goldstein, A. (1967). *The insanity defense.* New Haven, CT: Yale University Press.

Gray, P. (1999). *Psychology (3d ed.).* New York: Worth.

Greene v. Lambert (2002). 288 F.3d 1081.

Greene v. Washington (2000). 529 U.S. 1090.

Gresham, A. C. (1993). The insanity plea: A futile defense for serial killers. *Law & Psychology Review*, 17, 193-208.

Gutheil, T. G. (1999). A confusion of tongues: Competence, insanity, psychiatry, and the law. *Psychiatric Services*, 6, 767-773.

Hagen, M. (1997). *Whores of the court: The fraud of psychiatric testimony and the rape of American justice.* New York: Regan Books.

Haley, J. (2003). Expert rules out identity disorder. *The Daily Herald.* http://64.233.161.104/search?q=cache:1K9k3ldNk9oJ:www.wsse.ca/nucleus2.

0/reason.php%3Fcatid%3D24%26blogid%3D2+reason+files+%22william+bergen+greene%22&hl=en.

Hans, V. and Slater, D. (1983). John Hinckley, Jr. and the insanity defense: The public's verdict. *The Public Opinion Quarterly*, 47, 2, 202-212.

Harris, R. and Resnick, P. (2003). Suspected malingering: Guidelines for clinicians. *Psychiatric Times*, 20, 68-71.

Hearst, P. (1988). *Patty Hearst: Her own story*. New York: Avon.

Holman, V. (2003). *Rescuing Patty Hearst: Memories from a decade gone mad*. New York: Simon & Schuster.

http://usgovinfo.about.com/library/weekly/aadcsniper.htm.

http://www.mental-health-matters.com.

http://www.pearsonassessments.com/clinical/malingering.htm

Humes, E. (1991). *Buried secrets: A true story of serial murder*. New York: Signet.

Johnson, J. (1990). *What Lisa knew: the truth and lies of the Steinberg case*. New York: G.P. Putnam's Sons.

Jones v. United States (1978). 396 A.2d 183.

Jones v. United States (1980). 411 A.2d 624.

Jones v. United States (1981). 432 A.2d 364.

Jones v. United States (1983). 463 U.S. 354.

Kaplan, L. (1984). *The insanity defense and the trial of John W. Hinckley, Jr.* Boston: David R. Godine.

Kenrick, D., Neuberg, S., and Cialdini, R. (2002). *Social psychology: Unraveling the mystery* (2d Ed.). Boston: Allyn and Bacon.

Kiesel, D. (1984). Spotting fake insanity: Prof questions the way courts use psychiatry. *American Bar Association Journal*, 70, 33.

Kornbluth, J. (1978), May 7. A fatal romance at Yale. *The New York Times*, p. SM 12.

Krakauer, J. (2004). *Under the banner of heaven: A story of violent faith*. New York: Anchor.

Langston, J. (2002), August 29. Greene's trial date set in '94 assault of therapist. *Seattle Post-Intelligencer*. http://highbeam.com.

Launders, M. and Spiegel, P. (1990). *I wish you didn't know my name: the story of Michele Launders and her daughter Lisa*. New York: Warner Books, Inc.

Lehr, D. and Zuckoff, M. (2003). *Judgment Ridge: The true story behind the Dartmouth murders*. New York: Harper Collins.

Lewis, D. (1998). *Guilty by reason of insanity*. New York: Ivy.

Linder, D. (2002). The trial of John Hinckley. *Jurist*. http://jurist.law.pitt.edu/famoustrials/hinckley.php.

Linedecker, C. (1994). *The man who killed boys*. New York: St. Martin's.

Low, P., Jeffries, J. and Bonnie, R. (1986). *Trial of John W. Hinckley, Jr.: A case study in the insanity defense*. New York: Foundation Press.

MacKay, R. (1996). *Mental condition defenses in the criminal law (Oxford Monographs on Criminal Law and Justice)*. Oxford, England: Oxford University Press.

Maeder, T. (1985). *Crime and madness: The origins and evolution of the insanity defense*. New York: Harper Collins.

McCalope, M. (2001). Rusty Yates bides farewell to his five children. http://archives.cnn.com/2001/06/27/funeral.time/.

McEnroe, P. (1992), March 2. Colleagues aided Dahmer prosecutor. *The National Law Journal*, 3.

Merrill, R., and Salazar, R. (2002). Relationship between church attendance and mental health among Mormons and non-Mormons in Utah. *Mental Health, Religion & Culture*, 5, 1, 17–33.

Meyer, P. (1982). *The Yale murder: The fatal romance of Bonnie Garland and Richard Herrin.* New York: Berkley Books.

Michaud, S. and Aynesworth, H. (1983). *The only living witness: A true account of homicidal insanity.* New York: Linden Press.

Montaldo, C. Profile of Andrea Yates. www.crime.about.com/od/current/p/andreayates.

Moore, M. (1999). A taxonomy of purposes of punishment. *Foundations of Criminal Law,* 60, 62-63.

Moran, R. (1981). *Knowing right from wrong: The insanity defense of Daniel McNaughtan.* New York: Simon & Schuster.

Moran, R. (1985). *Insanity defense (Annals of the American Academy of Political and Social Science, Vol 477).* Thousand Oaks, CA: Sage.

Nelson, P. (1994). *Defending the devil: My story as Ted Bundy's last lawyer.* New York: William Morrow.

Nemo, C. (1997). Johnny, we hardly knew ye! http://members.aol.com/karol666/page4/gacy.htm.

Nissman, D. (1980). *Beating the insanity defense: Denying the license to kill.* Lanham, MD: Lexington Books.

Noe, D. The John Hinckley case: Life at St. Elizabeths. www.crimelibrary.com/terrorists_spies/assassins/john_hinckley/12.html?sect=14.

Ottley, T. Ted Kaczynski: The Unabomber. www.crimelibrary.com/terrorists_spies/terrorists/kaczynski/1.html

Patty Hearst profile: Radically different. (2001). CNN. http://www-cgi.cnn.com/CNN/Programs/people/shows/hearst/profile.html.

Peck, M. and Scheffler, R. (2002). An analysis of the definitions of mental illness used in state parity laws. *Psychiatric Services,* 53, 1089-1095.

Pennsylvania v. DuPont, appeal from the judgment of sentence of May 13, 1997, In the Court of Common Pleas, Delaware County, Criminal Division, at No. 26-96. http://www.superior.court.state.pa.us/opinions/a11005.pdf.

Perlin, M. (1993). *The jurisprudence of the insanity defense.* Durham, NC: Carolina Academic Press.

Perlin, M. (2000). "For the misdemeanor outlaw": the impact of the ADA on the institutionalization of criminal defendants with mental disabilities. *Alabama Law Review,* 52, 193-239.

Pope, K. (2004). Malingering research update. http://kspope.com/assess/malinger.php.

Ramsland, K. Andrea Yates: Ill or evil? www.crimelibrary.com/notorious_murders/women/andrea_yates/.

Ramsland, K. Hearst, Soliah and the S.L.A. http://www.crimelibrary.com/terrorists_spies/terrorists/hearst/.

Redding, R., Floyd, M., and Hawk, G. (2001). What judges and lawyers think about the testimony of mental health experts: A survey of the courts and bar. *Behavioral Sciences and the Law,* 19, 583-594.

Roberts, E. (2000). Judicial system 'guilty' in Goldstein verdict?. http://naminycmetro.org/director_goldstein.htm.

Robinson, D. (1996). *Wild beasts and idle humours: The insanity defense from antiquity to the present.* Cambridge, MA: Harvard University Press.

Robinson, P. (1982), June 9. Criminals and victims. *New Republic,* 37-38.

Robinson, T. (1977), December 2. Lack of 'flair' kept Dr. Peele from top job at St. Elizabeths. *The Washington Post,* p. B7.

Roche, T. (2002), March 18. Andrea Yates: More to the story. *Time.* http://www.time.com/time/nation/article/0,8599,218445,00.html.

Rogers, R. and Shuman, D. (2000). *Conducting insanity evaluations* (2d Ed). New York: Guilford.

Rohde, D. (1999a), October 22. Defense rests murder case with a video confession. *The New York Times.* http://www.texas-justice.com/nytimes/confession991022.htm.

Rohde, D. (1999b), October 31. Family's absence at trial underscores mental illness. *The New York Times.* http://www.shanj.org/news/family.htm.

Rohde, D. (1999c), November 7. Juror and court system assailed in mistrial. *The New York Times.* http://www.juryproject.org/Reports/News/assailed.html.

Rolde, E., Fersch, E., Kelly, F., Frank, S., and Guberman, M. (1975). A law enforcement training program in a mental health catchment area. In J. Monahan (Ed.), *Community mental health and the criminal justice system.* New York: Pergamon, 82-86.

Schrader, P. (Director). (1988). *Patty Hearst.* Atlantic Entertainment Group/Zenith Productions.

Sherbell, G. (1997). Battered Nussbaum not too late with suit against Steinberg. *The Forensic Echo*, 1, 6. http://echo.forensicpanel.com/1997/5/1/batterednussbaum.html

Silver, E., Cirincione, C., and Steadman, H. (1994). Demythologizing inaccurate perceptions of the insanity defense. *Law and Human Behavior*, 18, 63–70.

Simon, R. (1999). *The jury & the defense of insanity.* Piscataway, NJ: Transaction Publishers.

Simon, R. and Aaronson, D. (1988). *The insanity defense.* New York: Praeger.

Slovenko, R. (1995). *Psychiatry and criminal culpability.* New York: Wiley.

Spenser, S. (2002). *Breaking point.* New York: St. Martin's.

Steadman, H., McGreevy, M., Morrisey, J., Callahan, L., Robbins, P, and Circincione, C. (1993). *Before and after Hinckley: Evaluating insanity defense reform.* New York: Guilford.

Stephens, M. (1988), December 20. It's news, but is Steinberg's case really significant? *Newsday*, p. 63.

Stern, J. (2003). *Terror in the name of God: Why religious militants kill.* New York: Ecco.

Stevens, S. (1979). *By reason of insanity.* New York: Carroll and Graf.

Sullivan, J. (2003a), November 21. Insanity defense fails for attacker. *The Seattle Times.* http://archives.seattletimes.nwsource.com/cgi-bin/texis.cgi/web/vortex/display?slug=greene21m&date=20031121&query=william+bergen+greene.

Sullivan, J. (2003b), August 27. Retrial may hinge on insanity plea; multiple personalities could have played a role in a man's attack on his therapist. *The Seattle Times.* http://archives.seattletimes.nwsource.com/cgi-bin/texis.cgi/web/vortex/display?slug=greene27n&date=20030827&query=william+bergen+greene.

Szasz, T. (1960). The myth of mental illness. *American Psychologist,* 15 (February), 113-118.

Szasz, T. (1984). *The therapeutic state: Psychiatry in the mirror of current events.* Buffalo, NY: Prometheus Books.

Szasz, T. (1987). *Insanity: The idea and its consequences.* New York: Wiley.

Thaler, P. (1994). *The watchful eye: American justice in the age of the television trial.* Westport: Praeger.

Trowbridge, B. and Williams, C. (2000). Arguing future dangerousness: New techniques for assessing the risk of violence. *Washington Criminal Defense,* 14.

Turkington, C. (1996). *No holds barred: The strange life of John E. duPont.* Atlanta: Turner.

Ullman, J. (1992). 'I carried it too far, that's for sure.' *Psychology Today,* 25, 28-32.

Virginia State Crime Commission. (2002). SJR 381: not guilty by reason of insanity: a bill referral study. http://leg2.state.va.us/dls/h&sdocs.nsf/By+Year/RD312004/$file/RD31.PDF.

Wallace, S. (2002), May 22. From behind bars: One of NY's most infamous criminals. http://abclocal.go.com/wabc/news/investigators/WABC_investigators_052202steinberg.html.

Washington v. Greene (1998). Court of Appeals of Washington, Division One. 92 Wn. App. 80.

Washington v. Greene (1999). Supreme Court of Washington. 139 Wn.2d 64.

Weiner, A. (1982), November 15. An insane verdict. *The Harvard Crimson.* http://www.thecrimson.com/article.aspx?ref=169462.

Williams, D. (2002). Postpartum depression: A difficult defense. http://archives.cnn.com/2001/LAW/06/28/postpartum.defense/.

Williams, D. (2003). Punishing the faithful: Freud, religion, and the law. *Cardozo Law Review*, 24, 2181-2218.

Winslade, W. and Ross, J. (1983). *The insanity plea: The uses and abuses of the insanity defense.* New York: Charles Scribner's Sons.

Worth, R. and Sarat, A. (2001). *The insanity defense (Crime Series).* New York: Chelsea House Publications.

Wrightsman, L., Green, E., Nietzel, M., and Fortune, W. (2002). *Psychology and the legal system* (5th Ed.). Belmont, CA: Wadsworth.

0-595-34412-7